MANAGING DIVERSITY

M. Christopher Brown II
GENERAL EDITOR

Vol. 5

PETER LANG
New York • Washington, D.C./Baltimore • Bern
Frankfurt • Berlin • Brussels • Vienna • Oxford

MANAGING DIVERSITY

(Re)Visioning Equity on College Campuses

EDITED BY T. Elon Dancy II
FOREWORD BY Jerlando F. L. Jackson
AFTERWORD BY Lemuel Watson

PETER LANG
New York • Washington, D.C./Baltimore • Bern
Frankfurt • Berlin • Brussels • Vienna • Oxford

Library of Congress Cataloging-in-Publication Data

Managing diversity: (re)visioning equity on college campuses /
edited by T. Elon Dancy II.
p. cm.
(Education management: contexts, constituents, and communities; vol. 5)
Includes bibliographical references.
1. Minority college students—United States. 2. Education, Higher—
Social aspects—United States. 3. Universities and colleges—United States—
Administration. 4. Educational equalization—United States.
I. Dancy, T. Elon.
LC3727.M36 378.1'982900973—dc22 2010001567
ISBN 978-1-4331-0758-0 (hardcover)
ISBN 978-1-4331-0757-3 (paperback)

Bibliographic information published by **Die Deutsche Nationalbibliothek**.
Die Deutsche Nationalbibliothek lists this publication in the "Deutsche
Nationalbibliografie"; detailed bibliographic data is available
on the Internet at http://dnb.d-nb.de/.

The paper in this book meets the guidelines for permanence and durability
of the Committee on Production Guidelines for Book Longevity
of the Council of Library Resources.

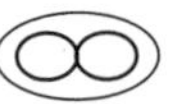

29 Broadway, 18th floor, New York, NY 10006
www.peterlang.com

Printed in the United States of America

To the "family"—the village griots,
research leaders, scholars, academic midwives,
frientors, peers, and role molders who have supported me
in my efforts to be whole; And
To the memory of Dr. Len Foster,
a griot in this village and a master manager of diversity
whom I was privileged to know.

TABLE OF CONTENTS

FOREWORD

What Music Can Teach Us about Managing Diversity in Higher Education

Jerlando F.L. Jackson

An interesting fact about me that most of my colleagues do not know is that I was a musician prior to my journey in the field of higher education. For approximately 15 years, my role as a musician guided my decision making. Unlike many of my high school classmates, I selected my undergraduate institution purely based on my major. I needed an institution that was a university and not a music conservatory, with both a strong performing arts school and percussion program in the southeastern part of the United States. Among the handful of institutions that met these criteria (interestingly all were non-flagship universities) was the University of Southern Mississippi, which was ultimately my choice.

Being a percussionist demanded the development of organization and time-management skills. Unlike other instrumentalists, percussionists have to master a family of instruments instead of just one. One has to be equally proficient on the marimba and jazz vibes as well as the snare drum or drum set. Without organization and time-management, it would be very difficult to maintain a practice schedule that cultivated such proficiency. Likewise, the time commitments were extremely demanding if one planned to graduate in a reasonable timeframe. In reviewing my undergraduate transcript after all of these years, it was interesting to observe that I completed 176 hours as an undergraduate. With the average undergraduate degree requiring between 124–129 hours, one could easily see why both organization and time-management skills were necessary.

A closer examination of my transcript shows that, in addition to regular coursework, I organized band practice, private lessons, and individual practice. In addition to the regular course load, I would have multiple organized band rehearsals daily that would require at least 2 hours each (e.g., Wind Ensemble, Marching Band, Orchestra, Drum Line, Steel Band, and Carillon) and at least 4 hours of individual practice time to prepare for my musical responsibilities. Accordingly, each day I generally had to commit approximately 8 hours to music. There were two courses that stood out in my walk down memory lane: Conducting I and II. These courses stood out because conducting requires the difficult task of getting people (as few as 4 and/or as many as a hundred or more) to function as one focused entity.

Conducting is the use of hand gestures to provide direction to a group of performers during a performance (music in this case). The chief function of the conductor is to provide musical expression to the performers; namely, tempo, dynamics, and articulation. How fast or slow the performers are to play is based on the tempo set by the conductor. A conductor is tasked with selecting the proper tempo based on the music's origin and the skill set of the performers. The dynamics of the music is expressed by the conductor with the size of hand movement and gestures. Conductors guide the articulation of musical phrasing with the style by which they fashion their movements or gestures. For example, conductors may elect for a passage to be more expressive by employing smooth movements.

To be truly effective, a conductor must be extremely familiar with the music score. The score is the musical map that arranges how each performer contributes to the performance. While each performer only has a sheet of music with just his or her part, the conductor has a score with everyone's part. Therefore, he or she is the only one with information to put all the pieces together. In turn, prior to any rehearsal of a score, the conductor must have knowledge of the score in its entirety and each performer's part. He or she must be able to know if a performer is playing their part incorrectly or out of key. Likewise, a good conductor will provide cues to help performers know when they should be playing. Naturally, this becomes more difficult as the size of the musical ensemble increases. Generally, the tool of choice that conductors use to get their ensemble on the same page is the baton. The baton makes it easier to follow the movements and gestures of the conductor.

Those charged with managing diversity in higher education struggle to find expressive gestures to get their campuses to follow tempo, dynamics, and articulations. These individuals would benefit greatly from skills employed by music conductors. There is a parallel between getting performers to play together and getting a campus to work together toward diversity goals. The kind of preparation that conductors must do is equally beneficial. Developing and studying the equivalent of a score is an analogous sort of work for higher education in crafting campus other diversity plans. Using these plans, one could develop a strategy on how to obtain the institution's diversity goals.

In *Managing Diversity,* T. Elon Dancy II has assembled a group of scholars who have done an excellent job of problematizing the challenges of addressing equity on college campuses. The scholars examine critical topics that advance new perspectives on diversity, challenge identity politics, and highlight inequities in higher education. Dancy should be applauded for including often-ignored areas related to the diversity challenge on campus—namely, language, intersectionality of the academy, and displaced students. These areas represent an evolution in understanding that diversity and difference touches every aspect of higher education.

No doubt, there is a need to adopt comprehensive and systematic thinking about managing diversity in higher education. Dancy and his associates do an excellent job of exploring in-depth topics that support this notion. Without appropriate plans of action, institutions cannot fully benefit from diverse talents on their campuses. Higher education is at a crossroads where questions are abounding about who, how, and in what ways should individuals, groups, and peoples be fully integrated in a culture and ethos. *Managing Diversity* ushers in a new era of thoughtful planning that pushes higher education institutions to evolve into "America's Institutions."

ACKNOWLEDGMENTS

This book would not have been possible without the help of many. I am particularly thankful to M. Christopher Brown II, whose support of this project was important in seeing it completed. I am also grateful to Christopher Myers and the production staff of Peter Lang Publishing, who invested necessary time, efforts, and resources in producing this book. Additionally, I thank the authors whose work comprises this volume. It was a pleasure working with each of you.

I also thank James Earl Davis for his feedback on this book. James, I will never forget your selfless nature during some of my most selfish times. At the University of Oklahoma, I am particularly thankful to my colleagues in the Jeannine Rainbolt College of Education and the Department of Educational Leadership and Policy Studies. My colleagues at OU have supported me in various ways that have made the completion of this work possible. I also thank the Center for Educational Development and Research (CEDAR) at OU, particularly Christiaan Mitchell, and my graduate assistant, Jessie Gregory, whose efforts helped this manuscript advance in the publication process. Finally, I thank my parents, Gwendolyn and Theodis Dancy, my brother, Theron, supportive friends, peers, and colleagues for their support of me in my quest to achieve my goals and realize my dreams.

CHAPTER ONE

An Introduction to Managing Diversity: A Mandate or an Oxymoron?

T. Elon Dancy II

My teaching experience in higher education and student affairs leadership is situated within two large doctoral-granting universities in the southeast and southwest regions of the United States of America. Many students enrolled in my graduate courses make clear that they are hungry to learn from conversations that are willing to "go there." My students perceive these kinds of conversations to be honest and courageous in disrupting silences around student differences, campus diversity, social provocation and controversy. Some of these students confess an ignorance about perspectives other than their own and suggest that this ignorance is easily maintained in areas like the "bible belt"—an informal term referring to a concentration of socially conservative Evangelical Protestants across the southern United States. Many of my students are natives of the southeast and southwest regions of America. Notwithstanding, they insist that class participation may be their first and perhaps only time to engage in conversations about the realities of diversity on campus. These students must become more conscious about the world in which they inhabit given that all of their professional goals involve serving college students. By the time they reach the end of the course, students argue that colleges and universities have more work to do in aligning missions they espouse and missions they practice as these missions involve diversity and evolving student realities.

The mission of an institution of higher education conveys that institution's assumptions, values, and purposes to its personnel, students, and the broader society. Educational policies, programs, and day-to-day practices emerge from the mission of the institution (Kuh, Schuh, Whitt, and Associates, 1991). Yet, institutional mission statements reflect social trends and social transformations. As the country becomes increasingly diverse, colleges and universities must continue to reconsider what it means to graduate individuals who are competent, active, and productive in society. Increasingly, across America colleges and universities affirm the role that diversity plays in enhancing teaching and learning in higher education (Bauman, Bustillos, Bensimon, Brown, & Bartee, 2005). Many students enrolled in my graduate courses assert they are ambitious for expanded conversations about diversity. In addition, they attempt to make meaning of what collegiate personnel can do and should do given the challenges and considerations campus diversity presents to collegiate leadership, management and practice. This book brings together scholars whose chapters inform these conversations.

Managing Diversity: (Re)Visioning Equity on College Campuses is a much-needed contribution to the literature. The book offers empirical, scholarly, and personal space to interrogate the seemingly elusive but undeniable challenges postsecondary institutions face in managing diversity. Book chapters are offered in a variety of voices—those which detail theoretical, conceptual, sociohistorical, and globalized meanings of diversity, those which highlight college personnel narratives around social justice and equity, and those which illustrate identity politics and provocative topics among students, faculty, and staff that continue to present formidable challenges to collegiate equity agendas. The book is multidisciplinary in its analysis of literature, drawing from education, feminist studies, health policy, critical race studies and theory, psychology, sociology, anthropology, organizational behavior, and law. The intent is to add to what we know in diversifying and making more inclusive collegiate contexts; to present new frameworks for thinking about diversity, equity, and inclusion; and to identify and detail policy and practice implications. Tangentially, the book title reflects commitment to accountability-based action as higher education is compelled by courts and legal opinion to maintain a diverse and inclusive campus.

Writer and management consultant Peter Drucker offered the familiar adage—"Leadership is doing the right thing, and management is doing things right." "Doing things right" evokes skill development. This book is titled *Managing Diversity* to intentionally encourage college and student affairs leaders to think about engaging the work of diversity as a skill that must be performed well to benefit all students academically and socially. The book acknowledges that while we may lead for diversity, we must also develop skills for competent management of diversity. Competent management is a necessity to meet accountability demands. In this vein, the book argues that managing diversity rests squarely on existing norms for management including organizational conflict, program planning, campus crisis, media management, budgeting and fiscal management and other forms of management. As the adage suggests, leadership and management are connected and one should not be forsaken for the other. While leadership may be more or less innate, this book also recognizes that good leaders may also be good managers. I believe that effectively managing diversity brings colleges and universities closer to shaping better outcomes among students in a world full of global and social unrest.

The legal notion of diversity as a compelling interest of an institution of higher education was defined by Justice Lewis Powell's decision in the 1978 Supreme Court case, *Regents of the University of California v. Bakke*. We are also called to act in the wake of substantial research highlighting the benefits of diversity to students' education outcomes (antonio, 2001; Bowen & Bok, 1998; Chang, 1996, 2001; Gurin, Dey, Gurin, & Hurtado, 2003; Hurtado, Milem, Clayton-Pedersen, & Allen, 1999). I am convinced that a variety of court decisions, widespread perplexity regarding affirmative action, and a rapidly changing American societal mosaic mandate colleges and universities to pay close attention to issues of diversity on their campuses. We must all become more proactive in assessing campus climate as the changing social landscape only promises to make issues of diversity and equity more nuanced and complex. In various ways, both student affairs professionals and faculty have responsibilities to shape campus environments that work to insure equity of access as well as social and academic success. To that end, chapters in this volume consider, highlight, and describe those responsibilities.

This collection of chapters is organized into three parts. Part One presents new perspectives on the diversity concept, expanding ways of thinking about campus diversity. The second part of the book considers identity politics on college campuses. Chapters include voices, testimonials, and narratives describing the ways in which various participants in higher education navigate identity politics in the field. Part Three considers contexts within higher education that demand attention to issues of identity and equity as well as the interplay between the two.

Two chapters in Part One explore the relationship between diversity and equity in academe. One chapter, by Rebecca Ropers-Huilman and Kathryn A. E. Enke, describes the inherent ways in which the concepts of diversity and interdisciplinarity (i.e., work across academic disciplines) are related and shape how interdisciplinary academic programs focused on oppressed groups (i.e., ethnic studies, women and gender studies, sexuality studies) are valued on college campuses. After describing complexities associated with interdisciplinary scholarship, Ropers-Huilman and Enke offer important questions and ideas about interdisciplinarity aimed toward enhancing collegiate diversity agendas. Subsequently, they provide policy and practice recommendations for academic institutions and programs seeking to foster equity through diversity and inclusion.

In another chapter, Roland Mitchell and Kirsten Edwards engage the intersections of white privilege and teacher privilege to construct a compelling argument about how scholars of color in majority-white institutions are granted "honorary whiteness", a term that describes the cognitive dissonance faculty of color experience in predominantly white collegiate contexts. More specifically, the authors draw upon the narratives of Black and White professors to illustrate the ways in which faculty race impacts the teaching and learning process in collegiate classrooms. Samuel D. Museus and Frank Harris describe elements of institutional culture as these shape minority college students' experiences. The authors engage the concept of institutional culture vis-à-vis the concept of institutional climate—important distinctions as they delineate campus responsibilities for ensuring success among students of color.

Part One ends with T. Elon Dancy's chapter which argues the case for effective management of diversity on college campuses. He situates this argument in a review of historical literature around collegiate diversity movements and legal opinion that creates compelling interest in successful diversity management on campus. In addition, he reviews extant empirical research that considers the benefits of diversity for organization and college student outcomes. The chapter ends with practical strategies for colleges interested in effectively managing diversity.

In Part Two, *Identity Politics on College Campuses,* Penny Pasque analyzes the diaries of eleven diverse women who held elected positions in national higher education associations and worked in various capacities within higher education. The diaries, written over a nine-year period, offer valuable insight to the field about how the work of colleges and universities might develop in ways that are inclusive of women. Fred A. Bonner II, Dave Louis, and Chance W. Lewis engage identity intersections in their chapter, exploring the experiences of African American men in college who are both poor and high-achieving. The authors describe both challenges and supports for this group of students, highlighting the ways in which intersectionality is linked to student perceptions as oppressed in collegiate contexts. They offer transferable ideas to colleges, focusing largely on the importance of mentoring in ensuring successful futures among this group.

In the following chapter, Terrell L. Strayhorn argues for racial and sexual identity considerations in diversity work in colleges. His arguments rest on data analysis of African American and LGBT student narratives. The chapter describes the ways in which student groups coalesce among each other to attain equitable treatment on campus. Part Two ends with T. Elon Dancy's chapter which considers the identity politics of gender among men in colleges. He offers men's gender constructions, manhood, and masculinities as additional dimensions that push the diversity concept in colleges and universities. He highlights men's issues in higher education among college students, faculty, and administrators as sites to explore disparate trends in higher education. Dancy calls for more empirical study in this area, conceptualizing this research as partner to feminist work. He also offers the term, effemophobia, as a novel way to envision men's intolerance of vulnerability in men.

In Part Three, *(In)Equities in Collegiate Contexts,* a chapter written by Sharon Fries-Britt, Toyia Younger, and Wendell Hall explores the experiences of minority students who are majoring in physics in college. The authors investigate students' academic experiences, paying attention to student/faculty interactions. Fries-Britt, Younger, and Hall report analytical findings from a larger, five-year study of academic, social, and racial experiences of minority students who were succeeding in physics. Recommendations for campuses include establishing meaningful connections beyond the classroom for minorities in physics. This study also encourages faculty to become expansive in their pedagogy by creatively structuring activities that account for the various ways that all college students learn.

In Chapter 11, Robert T. Palmer considers the sociocultural contexts of Asian, African American, and Latino students. He highlights critical issues, considerations, and caveats for collegiate personnel who provide counseling services or otherwise advise these student groups. In Chapter 12, Lorenzo DuBois Baber investigates the issues involved for predominantly White collegiate contexts in developing diverse "spaces" into culturally inclusive "places." He argues that creating opportunities for inclusion in these contexts involves challenging traditional notions of exclusion. Baber's study investigated the experiences of fifteen African American students in their efforts to identify a supportive place within the predominantly white institution they attended. His findings add clarity for the field in understanding the factors African American students may consider in identifying places of belonging.

Part Three closes with Marybeth Gasman's chapter in which she describes how faculty members' roles enable them to fight for equity in higher education. She draws upon a personal account, paying attention to how she made meaning of her identities and how her background shapes her research agenda in higher education. She illustrates compelling examples of the ways in which faculty may manage issues of difference across their teaching, research, and service.

This volume offers practical nourishment to student and academic affairs administrators and faculty who are called to engage ever-evolving work connected to growing pluralism on college campuses. Faculty might use this volume in developing curricula related to topics of diversity and social justice in higher education. Perhaps most importantly, this volume might serve as a resource for college or graduate students hungry for conversations about campus diversity, inclusion, and equity. While experiences of many groups in colleges and universities are discussed, some student groups (e.g., American Indians) and collegiate contexts (e.g., community colleges) are hardly discussed. Largely, this reflects the submissions from authors when a call was issued. There is ample space and place in the literature for many to engage in dialogue about the critical topic of diversity in higher education. While recognizing the limitations of this project, I yet consider it productive to highlight extensions of the diversity concept and to join the impassioned debate around diversity and equity in higher education.

References

antonio, A. 1. (2001). Diversity and the influence of friendship groups in college. *The Review of Higher Education, 25*(1), 63–89.

Bauman, G. L., Bustillos, L. T., Bensimon, E. M., Brown, M. C., & Bartee, R. D. (2005). *Achieving equitable outcomes with all students: The institution's roles and responsibilities*. Washington, D.C.: Association of American Colleges and Universities.

Bowen, W., & Bok, D. (1998). *The shape of the river: Long-term consequences of considering race in college and university admissions*. Princeton, NJ: Princeton University Press.

Chang, M. (1996). Racial diversity in higher education: Does a racially mixed student population affect educational outcomes? Unpublished doctoral dissertation. University of California, Los Angeles.

Chang, M. (2001). The positive educational effects of racial diversity on campus. In G. Orfield (Ed.), *Diversity challenged: Evidence on the impact of affirmative action* (pp. 175–186). Cambridge, MA: Harvard Education Publishing Group.

Hurtado, S., Milem, J. F., Clayton-Pedersen, A. R., & Allen, W. (1999). *Enacting diverse learning environments: Improving the climate for racial/ethnic diversity in higher education*. ASHE-ERIC Higher Education Report. Washington, DC: George Washington University.

Kuh, G. D., Schuh, J. H., Whitt, E. J., Andreas, R. E., Lyons, J. W., Strange, C. C., et al. (1991). *Involving colleges: Successful approaches to fostering student learning personal development outside the classroom*. San Francisco: Jossey-Bass.

PART ONE

New Perspectives on the Diversity Concept

CHAPTER TWO

Diversity and Interdisciplinarity: Exploring Complexities at the Intersections of Academy

Rebecca Ropers-Huilman
Kathryn A. E. Enke

Interdisciplinarity, or work across disciplines, is well established in academic settings. For example, area studies, ethnic studies and gender/women's studies are programs that have been active on many campuses for several decades. Yet, interdisciplinary efforts are taking shape in new ways to respond to emerging problems and opportunities in society. Recently, interdisciplinary research has been buoyed by a new sense of energy and legitimacy, largely because scholars, administrators and students see a broader need for those with multiple perspectives to work together to address the complex problems facing society today (as in bioethics or ethnic studies, for example; National Academy of Sciences, 2005). Interdisciplinary programs are now established at the intersections of many academic disciplines, including those in science, mathematics, humanities, arts, and the social sciences. The resulting interdisciplinary fields can readily argue that their efforts are related to the core engagement missions of their institutions, ever present in institutions of all types in the United States today. Such missions articulate institutions' commitment to serve as dynamic and comprehensive community partners in efforts to better our world (Bringle, Gamers, & Malloy, 1999). These partnerships require having multiple methods, paradigms, perspectives, and questions represented at the problem-solving table.

Diversity and interdisciplinarity are inherently related in several ways. The complex problems of our world require a diverse set of solutions, both locally and globally. Interdisciplinary solutions, therefore, must be informed by a variety of diverse perspectives, not only from across academic departments, but also from and across cultural groups inside and outside of the academy. This diversity of perspectives is what truly drives discovery. Additionally, a number of interdisciplinary programs (such as disability studies, gender studies, ethnic studies) explicitly focus on furthering research, teaching, and service with and about diverse groups. These interdisciplinary programs have great potential to transform the ways in which equity and diversity are constructed and experienced within the academy and, moreover, in the broader society.

Different disciplines vary in their informal and formal agreements about what constitutes "good" research and teaching within their fields of study. Some units are in high agreement (such as chemistry and mathematics), while others support a more diffuse set of expectations and definitions of valuable scholarly interactions (such as education and political science) (Braxton & Hargens, 1996; Del Favero, 2005). These disciplinary expectations (and their rigidity or flexibility) shape multiple dimensions of academic work, to include faculty work, administrative decision-making, and student interactions.

Interdisciplinary efforts, then, often must bridge gaps not only between subject areas, but also in expectations around how students, faculty members, and administrators interact with each other and contribute to the program and university. As they attempt to bridge these gaps, though, interdisciplinary initiatives risk perpetuating academic structures that have themselves not always valued diverse perspectives and those from diverse backgrounds. Certain disciplines (and the paradigms and practices that inform them) attract more diverse participation than others. For example, in 2005, 21.3% of all doctoral degree recipients in education were scholars of color, while in the physical sciences, only 13.0% were scholars of color. In that same year, 66.7% of all doctoral recipients in education were women, whereas in the physical sciences, only 26.4% were women (*The Chronicle of Higher Education Almanac,* 2008). Academic cultures are shaped both by disciplinary expectations as well as by the cultures and expectations of their participants. In most institutions, they are also embedded in institutional climates that developed around the idea of relatively structured (and separate) disciplines. These realities serve to create environments that may subtly (with behavioral norms related to collaboration and data-sharing) or not so subtly (with differential funding availability for departments and programs) support the status quo in academic practices. And, as is exemplified in many of the chapters in this volume, maintaining the status quo will not lead to diversity outcomes that are just and fair for all members of our society.

To provide a resource for those interested in supporting interdisciplinary efforts that firmly embrace an institutional mission that incorporates diversity and equity, we focus in this chapter on complexities associated within and between academic programs on college and university campuses. While we believe that these complexities are likely true for many interdisciplinary programs, we focus in this chapter on those programs explicitly concerned with furthering research, teaching, and service associated with diverse groups whose perspectives have not been fully incorporated into traditional academic settings (ethnic studies, gender/women's studies, disability studies, sexuality studies, etc.). Further, we provide recommendations for academic institutions and programs to consider as they seek to envision interdisciplinarity as an opportunity to foster equity through diversity on their campuses.

Current Complexities of Interdisciplinary Scholarship

The current complexities facing those interested in interdisciplinary scholarship are many. We acknowledge at the outset that different types of institutions will likely have different experiences with interdisciplinary research, teaching, and service. Those differences will often be associated with institutions' missions. It is thus reasonable to expect that some of the complexities we note will take on varying shapes and will be more or less urgent in different contexts. Additionally, although we argue that interdisciplinary programs have both an explicit and implicit potential to enhance equity and diversity across institutions and fields, we expect that the complexities we note below may vary depending on the direction and field of one's interdisciplinary efforts.

1. Colleges and universities often centrally invest in new interdisciplinary programs, or fund the potential for new ideas, rather than

providing necessary support to allow established interdisciplinary efforts to innovate and flourish. Since programs such as ethnic studies and women's studies have been in existence for some time on many campuses, these programs often are not seen as being prime for new growth and investment. Additionally, as there are interdisciplinary fields with greater funding potential (often in science-related or technology-related fields), institutions often determine that they want to seed programs that may bring substantial future dollars to the institution. This lack of growth in institutional investment in diversity-oriented established programs leads to the symbolic and material devaluing of research and scholars associated with equity efforts among diverse peoples. It is useful to ask: What systemic structures ensure the valuing of programs that bring together diverse scholars from multiple disciplinary perspectives?

2. Directors and faculty within interdisciplinary programs that are explicitly focused on diversity-related research, teaching, and service are often asked to validate their existence in the university. For example, women's studies programs at many institutions have a small number of students deciding to major in women's studies, even as they teach high numbers of students in lower-level courses. Women's studies classes contribute to the education of a large number of students, but women's studies faculty and administrators are asked to justify their place in the academy given the low numbers of majors. Institutions often do not recognize that the existence of scholars who are grounded in knowledge about equity and gender constructions is valuable to institutions in many other ways (Slagter & Forbes, in press). For example, these scholars can be instrumental in informing institutional policies related to equity, diversity, and fair treatment. However, when institutional accountability measures determine productivity (and associated resources) primarily by majors, the value of interdisciplinary programs focused on diversity to those students who take one or two courses is overlooked. It is important to ask in these interchanges: Where and how is value assigned to diversity-oriented interdisciplinary programs? By whom? Who puts forth the effort to justify interdisciplinary efforts focused on diver-

sity? Is that effort both recognized and valued? Do central administrators explicitly articulate the value of interdisciplinary efforts focused on diversity?

3. A tension exists between balancing the scholarly growth of an academic field with allowing new ideas from those who are not necessarily fully conversant with the terms of that field. In many cases, potential new contributors to the field are excluded because they do not use the field's established terms to express their contributions. Students, faculty, and community members all have the potential to enhance understandings in diversity-related interdisciplinary fields. How do we take seriously that ability to contribute? How are potential new contributors to the field introduced to the key terms and concepts of the field such that they can contribute to its future shaping? How do potential contributors learn to speak each other's language such that they can engage in authentic and culturally responsive dialog about common problems and interests? How can interdisciplinary fields move from parallel play to interactive play in which each contribution both informs the field and remains inclusive of new perspectives?
4. Interdisciplinary scholars who have their academic homes in disciplinary units are often torn between the need to meet the demands of their home department and the desire to contribute to interdisciplinary units. When junior scholars are recruited to institutions, those who are interested and engaged in interdisciplinary thinking may be attracted to interdisciplinary centers or programs that exist on their campuses. However, if they are primarily housed in an academic discipline, they need to meet the criteria of that department if they are to achieve promotion and tenure. In some cases, there is a synergy between the disciplinary and interdisciplinary homes that creates a vibrant and dynamic environment for the new scholar. However, in other cases, scholars are told implicitly (in hallway conversations) or explicitly (by the department chairperson or senior faculty members) that they need to curtail their contributions to interdisciplinary units until they have received tenure under the guidelines of their disciplinary unit. Alternatively, while some departments espouse interdisciplinarity, some faculty members are more comfortable in situating

their work as an "academic specialization" within their own field, rather than as an interdisciplinary effort that clearly contributes to a different unit on campus. For those interested in facilitating involvement of interdisciplinary scholars in diversity-related interdisciplinary efforts: What are the formal agreements between interdisciplinary faculty members' multiple units of affiliation that ensure interdisciplinary work will be valued? What processes ensure that new interdisciplinary faculty members have the interdisciplinary mentoring they need to develop within the field? Are explicit expectations for productivity inclusive of interdisciplinary efforts?

5. Staffing courses in interdisciplinary programs often relies on partnerships and the good will of more established units, since many interdisciplinary programs are primarily staffed by faculty members who have their academic homes in other disciplinary units. Curricular coherence is inherently difficult in interdisciplinary fields unless sustained conversations explicitly address curricular matters. The need to regularly find instructors who want to teach, and who are supported by their chairpersons and/or deans in doing so, both detracts from the unit's capacity to engage in other programmatic and scholarly efforts as well as thwarts the potential for an interdisciplinary unit to provide a coherent educational experience for students. It is important to consider: What arrangements exist to ensure that diverse faculty members can dedicate the time needed to develop coherent offerings for students that introduce them to the multiple paradigms and terms that ground the (emerging) field? How can faculty members' teaching contributions to interdisciplinary programs be regularized so that students, faculty, and administrators can concentrate on enhancing curricular experiences?
6. The advising of students in interdisciplinary programs is often piecemeal. For students who are interested in doing interdisciplinary scholarship, there is not always a clear path to quality informal and formal advising that incorporates the breadth of their interdisciplinary thinking. For example, if a student is interested in using sociological perspectives to study American Indian history, she might not find the advice of her student cohort and fac-

ulty advisors as useful for her scholarly interests as a student with a more solidly disciplinary interest. It is useful in diversity-related interdisciplinary fields to ask: Since social and academic integration are so important to students' experiences (Pascarella & Terenzini, 2005), who constitutes students' cohorts and informal academic groups? How is students' scholarly work understood and evaluated? By whom? What institutional and/or professional organizations are students encouraged to belong to? What journals are they encouraged to read or publish in? While these questions pertain to both undergraduate and graduate students, they are perhaps most poignant for doctoral students in the early stages of fashioning their academic careers.

7. Programmatic structures are highly varied in their faculty composition. For example, some diversity-related interdisciplinary programs consist entirely of affiliated faculty from other units. Others have a core faculty with some affiliates from other units on campus or, less often, outside campus. Decision-making structures for those units vary as well. Diversity-related interdisciplinary programs attempting to be inclusive of diverse perspectives and people need to develop these structures inclusively while also doing so in ways that preserve the program's intentions and integrity. It is important to ask: Who is informed about or asked to join the unit? Who is asked to (or allowed to) participate in decision-making? What is the rationale behind that structure? What ends does that rationale serve? What do those practices limit?
8. Interdisciplinary programs may require new facilities and technological capacities to foster collaborative interchange among those connected to the program (students, faculty, staff, community, etc.). If all those involved are located in separate spaces, the dynamic synergy that is a hallmark of interdisciplinary efforts will be much more difficult to establish. For those who are seeking to bridge geographical distances (whether local, national or international) to facilitate interdisciplinary dialogue, technology needs (involving storage, security, and communication, for example) may require substantial attention. To support interdisciplinary efforts, programs must ask: Where do students, faculty, and others interested in our program come together? Where are the points of

synergy for members of the interdisciplinary unit? Is the program well served by current technological communication options? Are there other options that should be considered?

9. Cluster hiring has been seen as an effective way to recruit, hire, and retain faculty of color or faculty who are involved in cutting-edge inquiry that may not be well established or well understood by others in academic settings. As such, that strategy is particularly useful in supporting interdisciplinary efforts. Cluster hiring, however, is a strategy that requires long-term investment to fund several faculty members and their research needs over time. Institutions should ask: Is there sufficient investment in a particular interdisciplinary program to allow for cluster hiring of diverse faculty who would lead and/or contribute substantially to that program? If so, how can we support those hired as part of a cluster to maximize their contributions to the institution and field?

The complexities identified above are relevant not only to programs that are specifically focused on diversity and equity (such as gender studies, comparative race studies, etc.). Instead, all interdisciplinary programs (and all academic units) have the capacity to foster diversity if they are intentionally structured to do so. The complexities above indicate some barriers to stable structures that, if removed, would allow a more central focus on diversity and equity within the programs and the institutions in which they are located.

Recommendations for Academic Institutions and Programs

Given the number of complexities listed above, it is evident that academic institutions and programs face substantial challenges as they consider the intersections of diversity and interdisciplinarity. We offer the following recommendations to academic institutions and programs that are committed to thinking about interdisciplinarity as an opportunity to foster equity—and high-quality scholarship—through diversity on their campuses. Some of these recommendations are in direct response to the challenges listed above. Others come from our personal involvement with interdisciplinary efforts within institutions and nationally in the field of women's studies, and from our own familiarity with interdisciplinary issues at several research institutions across the United States. We believe that these recommendations are feasible—and would be beneficial—at multiple types of institutions that value both diversity and interdisciplinarity.

Acknowledge and explore the inherent connections between diversity and interdisciplinarity

Connections between diversity and interdisciplinarity may not be immediately evident to all audiences, but we hope that this chapter helps make the case for inherent connections between these two values that enrich scholarly interaction. Interdisciplinarity relies on a diversity of perspectives as a catalyst for discovery. Those perspectives become available as we work across academic departments and with diverse cultural groups inside and outside of the academy. Powerful lessons for this scholarship can be taken from existing interdisciplinary programs that are explicitly diversity oriented. Yet, we want to emphasize that if diversity and equity are to be core values of the institution, they cannot remain integrated into only certain programs. Instead, values of equity and diversity must be incorporated into every interdisciplinary program that is developed. Recommendations include the following:

- Consider how diversity and interdisciplinarity are both marginalized at different types of institutions, and consider the ways in which they can be integrated within existing programs as well as new initiatives.
- Review how resources are allocated to diversity and interdisciplinarity efforts, and consider opportunities to partner rather than compete for limited funding.
- Consider systematic options for how various individuals and groups interested in diversity and interdisciplinary efforts could join forces to generate support for their common goals.
- Ensure that high-level administrative leaders who have a vested interested in diversity and interdisciplinarity are communicating with each other to strengthen and inform each other's efforts.

Consider the benefits to students and faculty of interdisciplinary engagement, and articulate those benefits as they relate to the institutional mission

Interdisciplinary efforts have arisen in academic situations for many reasons. One reason that should not be overlooked is that interdisciplinary engagement is generative for many faculty and students alike. For those scholars who are more invested in addressing problems than in particular disciplinary structures or who appreciate teaching with and learning from those in other disciplines, interdisciplinary engagement may energize them in both their research and teaching. In many cases, faculty members' interdisciplinary engagement will enrich their interactions with students and create positive teaching and learning relationships. Recommendations to maximize this potential include:

- Ensure that there are opportunities for teaching that is both interdisciplinary and team based as well as explicitly collaborative and interdisciplinary.
- Determine how interdisciplinary engagement is explicitly connected with the more traditional measures of productivity in academic settings, such as research productivity or enhanced student learning. Ensure that those connections are clearly articulated.

Conduct a diversity audit to evaluate how diversity is currently constructed, utilized, and embraced within existing interdisciplinary units

It is important to understand and evaluate how diversity is currently understood within existing interdisciplinary units. All interdisciplinary programs (and all academic units) have the capacity to foster diversity if they are intentionally structured for this goal. Yet we know that many interdisciplinary programs have not deliberately considered diversity when constructing and articulating their goals and plans for the future. Existing interdisciplinary programs that are explicitly diversity focused may serve as models for other units during the audit process. In conducting a diversity audit, interdisciplinary units can be enhanced by doing the following:

- Consider how diversity is defined, valued, measured, and incorporated into planning and evaluation processes. Ensure that diversity is a key measure of success for our interdisciplinary efforts and that excellence is defined as including equity.
- Review how diversity is manifest in typical unit functions, including admissions, unit decision-making, assessment, course/curricular development, and review and hiring.

- Find out how people from diverse backgrounds and with diverse perspectives view their interactions (scholarly and otherwise) within the unit.
- Consider how each unit balances time and emphasis between global education and research and research and education on domestic diversity issues, and ensure that is in line with the unit's and institution's priorities.

Celebrate wins and successes in diversity in visible and public ways

Public celebration of progress toward diversity and interdisciplinary goals demonstrates the value of such goals to multiple audiences, including the campus community, the local community, and, possibly, national and international audiences. Visible acknowledgement of success also provides validation for those involved in diversity and interdisciplinary efforts. We believe it is important to recognize those who are actively working toward diversity and to publicly bring attention to the work yet to be done. Public celebration of diversity efforts as they take shape in interdisciplinary education and scholarship may inspire others to consider involvement. Our recommendations include the following:

- Consider how the successes of interdisciplinarity and diversity are framed in public celebrations and outlets. Ensure that public interactions frame them as mutually enhancing, and that those interactions both celebrate successes and acknowledge the work yet to be done.
- View public celebrations as potential catalysts to involve new individuals and groups in fostering equity and diversity.

Ensure that diversity and interdisciplinarity are seen as necessary elements of institutional excellence

As institutions mindfully plan for the future, they must ensure that interdisciplinarity and diversity are expressed as core values of institutional environments. The influence of interdisciplinarity and diversity on every academic unit should be explicitly understood and incorporated. Diversity and interdisciplinarity cannot be seen simply as add-ons to institutions' missions, to be dealt with only when surplus time or resources are available.

Institutions should recognize that there is value in scholarly work even if connected to those programs with low numbers of majors. We should avoid unit value assessments based on the numbers of degrees conferred and focus instead on units' contribution to a "scholarship of engagement," which includes research, teaching, integration, and application (Boyer, 1990). Many interdisciplinary programs with low numbers of majors are still contributing significant knowledge in their field, teaching large numbers of non-majors in survey courses, building intellectual bridges between different areas of thought within the academy, and finding application for their work within the community outside of the academy. Interdisciplinary programs such as ethnic studies and women's studies are working especially hard to bring voices of individuals from groups underrepresented in higher education into the academy.

As various institutions consider how diversity and interdisciplinarity are viewed in relation to institutional excellence, we suggest the following recommendations:

- Review mission statements, planning documents, assessment procedures, and budgets to ensure that interdisciplinarity and diversity are constructed as genuinely central to academic excellence. Ensure that institutional structures and cultures fully legitimize diversity and interdisciplinarity.
- Ensure that there are systematized opportunities for diverse people and perspectives to come together to ignite innovation and drive discovery in the space between the disciplines.

Conclusion

We urge that institutions use the new and established energy around interdisciplinarity to ensure that the values associated with equity and diversity take firm root on their campuses. Both diversity efforts and interdisciplinarity have the potential to challenge traditions within higher education and transform institutions. Scholarship related to both diversity and interdisciplinarity challenges traditional epistemologies, pedagogies, structures, and purposes of higher education. That scholarship provides new ways of knowing and new sources of knowledge and interrupts traditional curricular structures and discipline-based models of education. It has the potential to broaden the base of "experts" whom we can rely on to help solve our world's complex problems. In these ways, diversity and interdisciplinarity have the ability to fundamentally alter the values and culture of the academy. We hope that these recommendations for discussion and action will help academic institutions and programs address the complexities associated with interdisciplinary work in ways that explicitly value the connection between diversity and interdisciplinarity. We believe that the new and established energy around interdisciplinarity can provide impetus and opportunity for action toward equity and diversity on our campuses.

References

Boyer, E. L. (1990). *Scholarship reconsidered: Priorities of the professoriate.* Princeton, NJ: Carnegie Foundation for the Advancement of Teaching.

Braxton, J. M., & Hargens, L. L. (1996). Variations among academic disciplines: Analytical frameworks and research. *Higher Education: Handbook of Theory and Research, 11,* 1–45.

Bringle, R. G., Gamers, R., Malloy, E. A. (1999). *Colleges and universities as citizens.* Boston: Allyn and Bacon.

Chronicle of Higher Education Almanac. (2008). The Chronicle of Higher Education. Retrieved from http://chronicle.com.floyd.lib.umn.edu/ on February 6, 2009.

Del Favero, M. (2005). The social dimension of academic discipline as a discriminator of academic deans' administrative behaviors. *The Review of Higher Education, 29*(1), 69–96.

National Academy of Sciences, National Academy of Engineering, & Institute of Medicine. (2005). *Facilitating interdisciplinary research.* Washington, DC: National Academies Press.

Pascarella, E., & Terenzini, P. (2005). *How college affects students: A third decade of research.* San Francisco: Jossey-Bass.

Slagter, J. T., & Forbes, K. (in press). Sexual harassment policy, bureaucratic audit culture, and women's studies. *National Women's Studies Association Journal.*

CHAPTER THREE

Success Among College Students of Color: How Institutional Culture Matters

Samuel D. Museus
Frank Harris

The promotion of racial and ethnic equity has long been recognized as an important function of higher education. The value of equity is evident in higher education discourse, and the leaders of America's colleges and universities often tout their commitment to ensuring access to success for increasingly diverse student populations (see, for example, Kellogg Commission on the Future of State and Land-Grant Universities, 1998). Yet, despite higher education's role as the equalizer of opportunity, substantial racial and ethnic inequities persist (Berkner, He, & Cataldi, 2002; Bensimon, 2007; Harris III & Bensimon, 2007). While many factors may be responsible for the inequities within postsecondary education, researchers consistently find and report that the unwelcoming environments that college students of color encounter is one of those influences (e.g., Allen, 1992; Ancis, Sedlacek, & Mohr, 2000; Feagin, Vera, & Imani, 1996; Harper & Hurtado, 2007; Harper & Quaye, 2007; Kiang, 2002; Lewis, Chesler, & Forman, 2000). The vast majority of this research, however, focuses on campus racial climates (see Harper & Hurtado, 2007). Similarly, when institutional leaders discuss creating welcoming environments for students of color, the discourse often focuses on fostering positive racial climates on college and university campuses.

While higher education researchers and practitioners hoping to promote racial and ethnic equity should understand how campus racial climates affect the experiences and outcomes of students of color, it is equally important for them to understand the role that institutional cultures play in shaping the experiences of their undergraduates of color. Institutional culture is an especially critical consideration because it influences just about everything that happens on a college campus, albeit to varying degrees (Kuh, 2001/2002). Yet, little attention is typically given to understanding the ways in which institutional culture influences the experiences and outcomes of racial and ethnic minority college students (Museus, 2008a). In this chapter, we discuss the importance of culture in promoting racial equity in institutions of higher education and success among college students of color. In doing so, we adopt the stance that positive racial climates are a necessary, but not sufficient, condition for cultivating environments that are equitable and conducive to minority student success.

In the next section, we define and distinguish between the concepts of institutional climate and culture. Then, we offer an overview of the small body of literature that is focused on understanding how institutional culture shapes the experiences and outcomes of students of color. We conclude with some important considerations in efforts to promote institutional cultures conducive to racial and ethnic equity and minority student success on college campuses.

Separating the Concepts of Institutional Climate and Culture

The difference between institutional climate and culture is an important distinction (Bauer, 1998). These two concepts are often used interchangeably, but they are not the same. While campus climate has been defined as the "*current* perceptions, attitudes, and expectations that define the institution and its members" (Bauer, 1998, p. 2), campus culture refers to the *deeply embedded* patterns of values, beliefs, and assumptions that shape behavior within an institution (Kuh & Whitt, 1988). More specifically, in one of the most comprehensive reviews of literature on institutional culture in the context of higher education, Kuh and Whitt (1988) defined culture as the "collective, mutually shaping patterns of norms, values, practices, beliefs, and assumptions that guide the behavior of individuals and groups in higher education and provide a frame of reference within which to interpret the meaning of events and actions" (pp. 12–13). This definition underscores the intricacy of institutional culture. Indeed, the concept of culture is complex and the various aforementioned elements of institutional culture interact in complex ways to create an invisible tapestry that exhibits a powerful influence on the behavior of people and communities on college and university campuses.

Because institutional culture is so complex and deeply embedded in organizations, it is less malleable than institutional climate. This means that institutional culture is likely to prove more difficult for institutional leaders to understand and change as part of efforts to create more welcoming learning environments for college students of color. Indeed, it is much easier to initiate small-scale efforts, such as offering campus climate forums or creating a cultural center, to provide a safe space for racial and ethnic minority students. Such efforts can cultivate environments where students feel a brief sense of belonging because they can share their struggles with peers who have also encountered difficulty in adjusting to unwelcoming environments. This also means, however, that the impact of many campus climate initiatives can quickly fade if they are isolated initiatives. If, for example, a Black student who has encountered racism on campus attends an administrator-organized climate forum and is able to discuss her experiences in a safe space but hears derogatory comments within days after the forum, the administrative efforts to foster a positive environment might have minimal impact. This example underscores the importance of fostering an institutional culture that perpetuates values, beliefs, and assumptions that reinforce the message that students of color are welcome on campus.

It is important to recognize the complexity of institutional culture and avoid oversimplifying that intricacy, but parsing the various elements of culture is also important for purposes of discussion. While culture consists of many different elements, we underscore five of those cultural characteristics for the purposes of this chapter: cultural values, assumptions, beliefs, orientations, and integrity (Schein, 1992). Espoused *values* are shared beliefs about what is important (Whitt, 1996), whereas enacted values are beliefs upon which actions are taken by members of the group (Museus, 2007). Cultural *assumptions* constitute an implicit system of *beliefs* "that influences what people in the culture think about, how they behave, and what they value" (Whitt, 1996, p. 191). In addition, an *orientation* refers to an inclination in thought and interest (e.g., sexual orientation), and cultural orientation exists when a culture promotes a certain direction in thought or interest. Finally, researchers have discussed the notion of cultural *integrity* and defined it as aspects of an institution that engage the cultural backgrounds of individuals from different heritages (Tierney, 1992, 1999). In the following sections, we discuss the slowly emerging understanding of how some of these elements of institutional culture can shape minority students' experiences.

Some might question whether efforts to change existing institutional cultures are worthwhile or futile. In fact, there are some who believe that cultures develop only organically and that structural changes in institutional policies or practices do little to change campus culture in meaningful or observable ways. While we acknowledge that transforming campus cultures in ways that are conducive to the success of racial and ethnic minority students is a long and challenging process, we oppose the assumption that this is an unattainable goal or one that is not worth pursuing. Rather, we agree with Hurtado, Milem, Clayton-Pedersen, and Allen (1998) that "the success of efforts to achieve institutional change will rely on leadership, firm commitment, adequate resources, collaboration, monitoring, and long-range planning" (p. 296), and we further assert that such investments can only facilitate long-lasting change if they are able to become deeply embedded into the culture of postsecondary institutions.

Institutional Cultures in Higher Education

Institutional culture is one of the most salient forces operating within colleges and universities. Historically, however, most of the discourse on campus culture has been aimed at understanding whether and to what extent students of color experience difficulties finding a sense of belonging in the cultures of predominantly White institutions (PWIs) (e.g., Feagin, Vera, & Imani, 1996; Hurtado & Carter, 1997; Hurtado, Carter, & Spuler, 1996; Turner, 1994). Only recently have scholars begun to move beyond understanding the difficulty of minority students in finding membership in the cultures of PWIs to using cultural frameworks to understand the experiences of college students of color (Gonzalez, 2003; Guiffrida, 2006; Kuh & Love, 2000; Museus, 2007, 2008a; Rendón, 1994; Rendón, Jalomo & Nora, 2000; Steele, 1999; Tierney, 1992, 1999). This literature is sparse, leaving much to learn about the relationship between institutional culture and the experiences and outcomes of minority students. Nevertheless, this research does offer some insights into how culture may be a critical consideration in educators' efforts to effectively serve students of color.

Recall that college students of color often report experiencing isolation from the cultures that exist at PWIs (Davis, 1994; Fries-Britt, 1998; Fries-Britt & Turner, 2002). One reason is that predominantly White campuses perpetuate cultures grounded in predominantly White, middle-class thinking about the business of higher education. If educators hope to maximize the success of minority students, they need to understand how various elements of their institutional cultures are affecting the racial and ethnic minority students whom they serve. In this section, we outline five of these cultural elements that should be considered by educators concerned with equity and minority student success. We do not make the claim that these cultural elements will make a difference for all of the students of color at a given institution, nor do we claim that all colleges or universities are ready to effectively incorporate these elements into their cultural fabric. However, we believe that institutions that are serious about racial and ethnic equity and want to maximize the success of their college students of color should consider these cultural factors in efforts to increase minority student success at their respective institutions.

Espoused vs. Enacted Diversity Values

One example of an element of institutional culture that shapes the experiences of individuals and groups on college campuses is a college or university's mission. Specifically, missions often include the identification of values that serve as indicators of the vision that guide the institution. While an espoused mission is the one that is endorsed by the institution, enacted missions are those that manifest in the behavior of people within that organization. Evidence suggests that congruence between the espoused and enacted missions might be an important factor in fostering success among college students (Kuh, Kinzie, Schuh, Whitt, & Associates, 2005). Many institutions have long-standing missions and corresponding values that are based on those of traditional (e.g., White, middle-class) college students. Postsecondary institutions that are serious about racial and ethnic equity and minority student success must decide whether missions and values are culturally biased and favor those in the majority. Especially relevant for students of color is whether institutions espouse values of diversity. Moreover, racial and ethnic minority students can be conscious of the incongruence between espoused diversity values and the extent to which diversity is an enacted value of their institution (Museus, 2007). Students may perceive educators who tout diversity values as insincere if those values do not manifest in programs and practices across their campuses. Institutions seeking to create welcoming environments for students of color should not only incorporate values of diversity into their institutional, departmental, and programmatic missions, but they should also take measures to ensure that institutional and programmatic policies and practices across the institution are congruent with espoused diversity values.

The Salience of Collective Cultural Orientations

Another important aspect of institutional cultures that may be critical in cultivating environments conducive to the success of racial and ethnic minority college students is the value of collective orientation (Guiffrida, 2006; Museus, 2008b). Individualist cultural orientations have historically dominated perspectives of college students' success (Astin, 1993, Tinto, 1987, 1993), but many college students of color might come from cultures of origin with collective orientations. Kuh and Love (2000) observe that the level of incongruence between students' home and campus cultures is associated with adjustment difficulty and decreased likelihood of success. This line of thinking suggests that racial and ethnic minority students who come from collectively oriented cultures may experience fewer adjustment difficulties and a greater likelihood of success if they encounter institutional cultures that are collective in orientation themselves.

Empirical evidence suggests that collectivist orientations might contribute to success among racial and ethnic minority college students (Museus, 2008b). Specifically, colleges and universities with relatively high and equitable success rates among students of color have been associated with institutional values of networking and collaboration. Networking and collaboration can aid in the cultivation of campus environments that maximize minority undergraduates' linkages to various institutional agents on campus. For example, collectivist cultures can engender increased collaboration across and integration among programs and services on campus, and these strong connections across the institution can lead to minority students' increased access to campus resources and support. Students of color may more easily access a wide range of programs and services indirectly when there is greater integration among various units across college campuses.

Institutional Practice: How Cultural Integrity Matters

The third cultural element associated with racial and ethnic minority students' success is cultural integrity, which refers to educational practices that engage students' cultural backgrounds (Tierney, 1999). Because many students of color must travel a longer cultural distance than their majority peers to make the transition from their home cultures to the cultures of PWIs, they must make greater adjustments and are pressured to relinquish traditional cultural values and beliefs in order to integrate into the cultures of their college campus (Kuh & Love, 2000; Tierney, 1992, 1999; Tinto, 1987, 1993). Over the past two decades, several scholars note the importance of educational practices in validating minority students' cultural backgrounds and alleviating pressure placed on these students to dissociate from their cultural heritages (Museus, 2008d; Rendón, 1994; Tierney, 1992, 1999; Torres, Howard-Hamilton, & Cooper, 2003). This scholarship suggests that colleges and universities that truly value the success of their minority students should be willing to diversify and adapt institutional cultures to the diverse communities from which the students entering their campuses come.

On campuses across the nation, minority students create their own spaces in which they can meet and interact with students from similar cultural backgrounds, express and advocate for their cultural communities, and feel that their cultures are validated (Harper & Quaye, 2007; Museus, 2008d; Rendon, 1994; Tierney, 1992, 1999). While ethnic minority student organizations are an incredibly valuable aspect of the institutional environment and serve many purposes for students of color (Guiffrida, 2003; Harper & Quaye, 2007; Museus, 2008d), they are not enough to create equitable and supportive campus environments. In fact, many racial and ethnic minority students do not seek involvement and peer support outside of those ethnic organizations because they find that their presence and perspectives are not welcomed or valued in mainstream student activities. Indeed, those who choose to participate in mainstream student organizations must often suppress their cultural identities in order to assimilate into these environments (Harper & Quaye, 2007; Taylor & Howard-Hamilton, 1995). Universities seeking to foster success among college students of color must make efforts to shape institutional cultures that envision diversity among students as valuable.

Believing Minority College Students Are Assets

Beliefs and assumptions about racial and ethnic minority undergraduates are also important aspects of institutions' cultures that can have a profound impact on the experiences of those students. Historically, higher education research and social discourse includes assumptions that students of color come to college with deficits and subsequently deserve blame for their low rates of success (Valencia, 1997). Assumed deficits are manifested in stereotypes of racial and ethnic minority students as academically inferior or, in the case of Asian American students, academically superior (Fries-Britt & Turner, 2001; Lewis et al., 2000; Museus, 2008c). These assumptions may adversely affect the anxiety experienced by, as well as the performance and success of, students of color (Steele, 1999). Assumptions that students of color are academically inferior or superior can also impede minority students' desire and willingness to engage in learning processes (Museus, 2008c). Moreover, these assumptions correspond with the notion that many racial and ethnic minority students are a burden, rather than a valuable asset. Assuming that students of color are academically inferior also fuels cultural beliefs that those students consume educational opportunities and resources that are deserved by other more qualified college students (Lewis et al., 2000; Museus, 2008c).

If postsecondary educators are to eradicate stereotypes about the deficits of college students of color, they must adopt frameworks that diverge from deficit perspectives and take the position that racial and ethnic minority students as assets that can inform learning processes and contribute to feelings of inclusion within institutional environments. This is not only important in fostering success among racial and ethnic minority undergraduates, but it is critical to enhancing the educational experience for all students (see Dancy, Chapter 5, this volume). A large body of empirical work confirms that exposure to diversity and interactions across race facilitate the development and success of students from all racial backgrounds (Chang, 1999; Chang, Witt, Jones, & Hakuta, 2003; Gurin, 1999; Jayakumar, 2008). Exposure to college students' diverse cultural heritages, perspectives, and knowledge can contribute to academically challenging and educationally rich learning environments for all students, regardless of their racial or ethnic background. Thus, cultivating an institutional culture in which racial and ethnic minority college students are viewed as assets not only can help students of color learn and adjust but is also critical if postsecondary educators are to maximize the benefits of diversity for all students.

Institutional Responsibility for Minority Student Success

Perspectives of college student success that dominate higher education discourse primarily emphasize the role of self-determination (e.g., Astin, 1993; Tinto, 1987, 1993). Consequently, these views perpetuate common assumptions that students are solely responsible for their own success rather than recognizing how others, too, are accountable in shaping student success (Bensimon, 2007; Rendón, Jalomo, & Nora, 2000). However, these traditional perspectives are changed as the higher education field diversifies its thinking about the institutional role in shaping success among students of color. Specifically, scholars in higher education underscore the need to forgo perspectives that students must detach from their cultural heritages, must integrate into the cultures of their respective campuses, and must adopt new points of view about collegiate responsibility for student student success (Bensimon, 2006, 2007; Kuh & Love, 2000; Rendón et al., 2000; Tierney, 1992, 1999). Traditional perspectives on college student success are especially problematic for students of color, many of whom originate from communities in which seeking help is possibly deemed culturally abnormal. Moreover, empirical studies of high-performing institutions have highlighted the role of institutional responsibility in the success of college students in general (Kuh et al., 2005), and students of color in particular (Museus, 2008b). This work highlights institutional opportunities to shape in college educators strategies and behaviors that effectively serve students of color. Strategies include emphasizing college educator responsibility rather than expecting racial and ethnic minority students to seek out services themselves.

Conclusion: Promoting Equity through Transforming Institutional Cultures

In this section, we conclude by offering recommendations to stimulate dialogue and help institutions think about how to embark upon work of cultural transformation. We recognize that cultural change is not simple and does not usually happen in a short span of time. Moreover, such transformation might be easier in one institutional context than another. One college, for example, may hold a large grant to pursue institutional change to better serve students of color, while another college's culture is pessimistic about re-shaping structural barriers and thus reacts viscerally to ideas of change. In the former case, the following recommendations may inform institutional transformation endeavors while, in the latter, recommendations may be implausible until the contextual constraints shift, becoming more amenable to change. Our intent is not to provide a recipe for cultural transformation at either type of campus; rather, our objective is to present what we believe are important considerations for institutions that hope to intentionally shape environments conducive to racial and ethnic minority student success.

Search and Hiring Processes

Our first recommendation is focused on enacting espoused institutional values of diversity. Faculty play a central role in shaping the cultures of colleges and universities. Not only do they influence institutional decision-making processes, but they are also key institutional agents in the experiences of college students of color (Guiffrida, 2005; Museus & Neville, 2008). Across colleges and universities, faculty members are largely liaisons between racial and ethnic minority college students and campus culture. If institutions seek to transform their cultures to truly respect diverse student bodies, they must be serious about hiring faculty who evince commitment to engaging and learning from students' cultural heritages, perspectives, and knowledge. This will likely involve seeking faculty of color but also entails recruiting and hiring majority faculty members who are knowledgeable about diverse communities from which the undergraduates on a particular campus come. We do not suggest simply *espousing* the importance of hiring faculty of color but rather *enacting* the value of diversity by structurally infusing it into search and hiring processes.

To enact the value of diversity in search and hiring processes, decision-makers must go beyond incorporating a question about diversity into an interview protocol or keeping diversity in their minds as the hiring process unfolds. Such actions represent tokenized treatments of the notion of diversity, rather than serious commitments to the diversification of faculty ranks. Instead, decision-makers should intentionally recruit candidates from diverse backgrounds and infuse discussion about how and in what ways candidates contribute to the diversity of their programs, departments, colleges, and surrounding communities. At some institutions, provosts and academic deans scrutinize recommendations for faculty hires and engage in conversations about diversity with search committees themselves. Administrators are potentially positioned to offer incentives to hiring committees that seriously consider processes.

Integrating Cultural, Academic, and Social Aspects of Experience

The second recommendation deals with viewing minority students as assets and engaging their cultural backgrounds in practice. Colleges and universities must integrate cultural, academic, and social aspects of diverse students' identities into institutional work. This accomplishes a two-fold goal of re-envisioning students of color as assets and maintaining institutional integrity around issues of diversity. More specifically, faculty, administrators, and staff must search for teachable moments among students' cultural heritages, academic curricula, and extracurricular activities. Such intersections can positively impact minority students' senses of belonging as students gain culturally relevant knowledge, sharpen academic and professional skills, and foster social connections across their respective campuses.

Consider for example the Asian American Studies Program at the University of Massachusetts, Boston in which students engage in educationally enriching activity, express their cultural identities and find a sense of empowerment. Undergraduates connected to this program take courses with Asian American faculty but also work with program faculty and staff members to administer an outreach program for youth in surrounding Asian American communities. In addition, student participants regularly organize co-curricular campus activities through which they may engage and establish cross-campus connections. In short, students access faculty and staff in non-traditional ways, which promotes enhanced learning experiences.

Creating Collective Cultures through the Integration of Programs and Services

The third suggestion is focused on building a collective orientation into the work of educators. College educators who wish to cultivate collective institutional cultural orientations must begin by breaking down structural barriers that isolate ethnic enclaves from vital programs and services on campus. Ethnic enclaves are defined in the literature as experiences that are largely important to college students of color including ethnic studies programs, targeted support programs, and cultural centers (Chang & Kiang, 2002; Museus, 2008d; Patton, Morelon, Whitehead, & Hossler, 2006). Institutions can foster strong connections and collaborations among groups, programs, and services if they can maximize the resources to which students of color experience easier access, integrating college students of color into the mainstream cultures of their campuses (Museus, 2008b).

Deconstructing structural barriers and incorporating enclaves into the mainstream cultures of the campus is not an easy task, but it is not an unrealistic one either. The Equal Opportunity Program (EOP) at the State University of New York at New Paltz that serves low-income students (many of whom are from underrepresented racial and ethnic minority backgrounds) is an example of an institution that does this work. The EOP offers its students first-year seminars in collaboration with an ethnic studies department on campus. Moreover, academic advisors in the EOP maintain open lines of communication with faculty and staff across their campus so they may direct students to support appropriate to the situation. In this program, academic advisors are in position to connect students to a wide array of resources and support across campus (e.g., faculty, other mentoring and support programs). Campus connectedness, as this program demonstrates, contributes to a collective orientation in which minority student inclusion is promoted and access to resources maximized.

Assuming Responsibility for Understanding and Addressing Inequities

Our final recommendation is that institutions should assume the responsibility of understanding and reflecting upon the inequities that exist within their institutions and how practice contributes to those inequalities. Institutions must intentionally incorporate the organizational learning process into their efforts to transform institutional cultures in ways that better serve students of color. Learning organizations are not only structured to facilitate and perpetuate organizational members' acquisition of knowledge but also to provide opportunities for collective sense making, critical dialogue, and the dissemination of knowledge across institutions (Garvin, 1993). Several scholars (e.g., Bensimon, 2005; Kezar, 2005; Smith & Parker, 2005) argue that organizational learning is very useful in institutional efforts to assess commitment to issues of equity and diversity.

One example of how institutions can assume responsibility for addressing inequities and promoting minority student success is by using the *Equity Scorecard,* an organizational learning process developed by Estela Bensimon and her colleagues to assist campuses in achieving equity in student outcomes. Institutions using the Equity Scorecard engage in the process of systemic problem-solving by bringing together campus-based teams of faculty and administrators who meet regularly to examine student outcomes data that are disaggregated by race and ethnicity. Those teams reflect upon the ways in which practices they employ in the classroom, in advising sessions, or on committees to establish institutional policies either reproduce or help eradicate inequitable outcomes. In addition, the teams lead campus-wide discussions about what constitutes timely progress towards quantitatively measured goals. Finally, team members disseminate acquired knowledge from the Equity Scorecard process in two ways. First, they generate comprehensive reports for institutional leaders that describe data analysis, highlight inequities, indicate established equity benchmarks, and recommend actions to meet defined goals for achieving equity outcomes. Second, team members lead town-hall meetings, workshops, retreats, and other dialogues focused on the team's findings. By generating and disseminating knowledge about existing inequities, institutions shape a culture of responsibility and accountability for achieving equitable outcomes.

References

Allen, W. R. (1992). The color of success: African-American college student outcomes at predominantly White and Historically Black public colleges and universities. *Harvard Educational Review, 62*(1), 26–44.

Ancis, J. R., Sedlacek, W. E., & Mohr, J. J. (2000). Student perceptions of campus cultural climate by race. *Journal of Counseling and Development, 78*(2), pp. 180–85.

Astin, A. W. (1993). *What matters in college? Four critical years revisited.* San Francisco: Jossey-Bass.

Bauer, K. W. (1998). Editor's notes. *New Directions for Institutional Research,* No. 98, pp. 1–5.

Bensimon, E. M. (2006). Learning equity-mindedness: Equality in educational outcomes. *The Academic Workplace, 17*(1), 2–21.

Bensimon, E. M. (2005). Closing the achievement gap in higher education: An organizational learning perspective. In A. Kezar (Ed.), *Organizational learning in higher education: New directions for higher education* (pp. 99–111). San Francisco: Jossey-Bass.

Bensimon, E.M. (2007). The underestimated significance of practitioner knowledge in the scholarship of student success. *The Review of Higher Education, 30*(4), 441–469.

Berkner, L., He, S., & Cataldi, E. F. (2002). *Descriptive summary of 1995–96 beginning postsecondary students: Six years later.* Washington, DC: U. S. Department of Education.

Chang, M. J. (1999). Does racial diversity matter?: The educational impact of a racially diverse undergraduate population. *Journal of College Student Development, 40,* 337–395.

Chang, M.J., & Kiang, P. (2002). New challenges of representing Asian American students in U.S. higher education. In W. A. Smith, P. G. Altbach & K. Lomotey (Eds.), *The racial crisis in American higher education: Continuing challenges for the twenty-first century* (pp. 137–158). Albany, NY: SUNY Press.

Chang, M. J., Witt, D., Jones, J., & Hakuta, K. (2003). *Compelling interest: Examining the evidence on racial dynamics in colleges and universities.* Stanford, CA: Stanford University Press.

Davis, J. E. (1994). College in Black and White: Campus environments and academic achievement of African American males. *Journal of Negro Education, 63*(4), 620–33.

Feagin, J. R., Vera, H., & Imani, N. (1996). *The agony of education: Black students at White colleges and universities.* New York: Routledge.

Fries-Britt, S. (1998). Moving beyond Black achiever isolation: Experiences of gifted Black collegians. *The Journal of Higher Education, 69*(5), 556–576.

Fries-Britt, S., & Turner, B. (2001). Facing stereotypes: A case study of Black students on a White campus. *Journal of College Student Development, 42*, 420–429.

Fries-Britt, S. L., & Turner, B. (2002). Uneven stories: Successful Black collegians at a Black and a White campus. *The Review of Higher Education, 25*(3), 315–30.

Garvin, D. A. (1993). Building a learning organization. *Harvard Business Review, 71*(4),78–91.

Gonzalez, K. P. (2003). Campus culture and the experiences of Chicano students in a predominantly White university. *Urban Education, 37*(2), 193–218.

Guiffrida, D. (2005). Othermothering as a framework for understanding African American students' definitions of student-centered faculty. *The Journal of Higher Education, 76*(6), 701–23.

Guiffrida, D. A. (2003). African American student organizations as agents of social integration. *Journal of College Student Development, 44*(3), 304–319.

Guiffrida, D. A. (2006). Toward a cultural advancement of Tinto's theory. *The Review of Higher Education, 29*(4), 451–472.

Gurin, P. (1999). Selections from "The Compelling Need for Diversity in Higher Education, Expert Reports in Defense of the University of Michigan." *Equity and Excellence in Education, 32*(2), 36–62.

Harper, S. R. (2005). Leading the way: Inside the experiences of high-achieving African American male students. *About Campus, 10*(1), pp. 8–15.

Harper, S. R., & Hurtado, S. (2007). Nine themes in campus racial climates. In S. R. Harper, & L. D. Patton, Responding to the realities of race on campus. *New Directions for Student Services.* San Francisco: Jossey-Bass.

Harper, S. R., & Nichols, A. H. Are they not all the same? Racial heterogeneity among Black male undergraduates. *Journal of College Student Development, 49*(3), 199–214.

Harper, S. R., & Quaye, S. J. (2007). Student organizations as venues for Black identity expression and development among African American male student leaders. *Journal of College Student Development,* 48(2), 127–144.

Harris III, F., & Bensimon, E. M. (2007). The Equity Scorecard: A collaborative approach to assess and respond to racial/ethnic disparities in student outcomes. In S.R. Harper & L.D. Patton (Eds.), *Responding to the realities of race on campus: New directions for student services,* (pp. 77–84). San Francisco: Jossey-Bass.

Hurtado, S., & Carter, D. (1997). Effects of college transition and perceptions of the campus racial climate on Latina/o college students' sense of belonging. *Sociology of Education, 70,* 324–345.

Hurtado, S., Carter, D., & Spuler, A. (1996). Latina/o student transition to college: Assessing difficulties and factors in successful college adjustment. *Research in Higher Education, 37,* 135–157.

Hurtado, S., Milem, J. F., Clayton-Pedersen, A. R., & Allen, W. R. (1998). Enhancing campus climates for racial/ethnic diversity: Educational policy and practice. *Review of Higher Education, 21*(3), pp. 279–302.

Jayakumar, U. M. (2008). Can higher education meet the demands of an increasingly diverse and global society?: Campus diversity and cross-cultural workforce competencies. *Harvard Educational Review, 78*(4), 1–28.

Kellogg Commission on the Future of State and Land-Grant Universities (1998). *Returning to our roots: Student access.* National Association of State Universities and Land-Grant Colleges.

Kezar, A. J. (2005). What campuses need to know about organizational learning and the learning organization. In A. J. Kezar (Ed.), *Organizational Learning in Higher Education: New Directions for Higher Education,* 7–22. San Francisco: Jossey-Bass.

Kiang, P (2002). Stories and structures of persistence: Ethnographic learning through research and practice in Asian American Studies. In Y. Zou and H. T. Trueba (Eds.), *Advances in ethnographic research: From our theoretical and methodological roots to post-modern critical ethnography*. Lanham, MD: Rowman & Littlefield.

Kuh, G. D. (2001/2002). Organizational culture and student persistence: Prospects and puzzles. *Journal of College Student Retention: Research, Theory & Practice, 3*(1), 23–39.

Kuh, G. D., Kinzie, J., Schuh, J. H., Whitt, E. J., & Associates (2005). *Student success in college: Creating conditions that matter.* San Francisco: Jossey-Bass.

Kuh, G. D., & Love, P. G. (2000). A cultural perspective on student departure. In J. M. Braxton (Ed.), *Reworking the student departure puzzle* (pp. 196–212). Nashville: Vanderbilt University Press.

Kuh, G. D., & Whitt, E. J. (1988). *The invisible tapestry: Culture in American colleges and universities*: ASHE-ERIC Higher Education Report Series, No.1. Washington, DC: Association for the Study of Higher Education.

Lewis, A. E., Chesler, M., & Forman, T. A. (2000). The impact of "colorblind" ideologies on students of color: Intergroup relations at a predominantly White university. *The Journal of Negro Education, 69*(1/2), 74–91.

Museus, S. D. (2007). Using qualitative methods to assess diverse campus cultures. In S. R. Harper & S. D. Museus (Eds.), *Using qualitative methods in institutional assessment: New directions for institutional research*, 29–40. San Francisco: Jossey-Bass.

Museus, S. D. (2008a). *Focusing on institutional fabric: Using campus culture assessments to enhance cross-cultural engagement.* In S.R. Harper (Ed.), Creating inclusive environments for cross-cultural learning and engagement in higher education. Washington, DC: National Association of Student Personnel Administrators.

Museus, S. D. (2008b). *Generating ethnic minority success: Campus cultures and minority student access to social networks.* Paper presented at the 2008 Annual Meeting of the Association for the Study of Higher Education, Jacksonville, FL.

Museus, S. D. (2008c). The model minority and the inferior minority myths: Inside stereotypes and their implications for student involvement. *About Campus, 13*(3), 2–8.

Museus, S. D. (2008d). The role of ethnic student organizations in fostering African American and Asian American students' cultural adjustment and membership at predominantly White institutions. *Journal of College Student Development* 49(6), 568–586.

Museus, S. D., & Neville, K. (2008). *The role of institutional agents in the socialization of minority students: Implications for research and practice.* Paper presented at the 2008 Annual Meeting of the Association for the Study of Higher Education, Jacksonville, FL.

Patton, L.D. (2006). The voice of reason: A qualitative examination of Black student perceptions of the Black culture center. *Journal of College Student Development, 47*(6), 628–646.

Patton, L. D., Morelon, C., Whitehead, D. M., & Hossler, D. (2006). Campus-based retention initiatives: Does the emperor have clothes? *New Directions for Institutional Research,* 9–24.

Rendón, L. I. (1994). *A systematic view of minority students in educational institutions.* Presentation to the Panel on Educational Opportunity and Postsecondary Desegregation, Southern Education Foundation, Austin, TX, Feb. 10, 1994.

Rendón, L. I., Jalomo, R. E., & Nora, A. (2000). Theoretical considerations in the study of minority student retention in higher education. In J. Braxton (Ed.), *Reworking the student departure puzzle* (pp. 127–156). Nashville: Vanderbilt University Press.

Schein, E. H. (1992). *Organizational Culture and Leadership.* (2nd ed.) San Francisco: Jossey-Bass.

Smith, D. G., & Parker, S. (2005). Organizational learning: A tool for diversity and institutional effectiveness. In A. J. Kezar (Ed.), *Organizational learning in higher education: New directions for higher education,* 113–125. San Francisco: Jossey-Bass.

Steele, C. (1999). A threat in the air: How stereotypes shape intellectual identity and performance. *American Psychologist, 52*(6), 613–629.

Taylor, C. M., & Howard-Hamilton, M. F. (1995). Student involvement and racial identity attitudes among African American males. *Journal of College Student Development, 36,* 330–336.

Tierney, W. G. (1992). An anthropological analysis of student participation in college. *The Journal of Higher Education, 63*(6), 603–618.

Tierney, W. G. (1999). Models of minority college-going and retention: Cultural integrity versus cultural suicide. *The Journal of Negro Education, 68*(1), 80–91.

Tinto, V. (1987). *Leaving college: Rethinking the causes and cures of student attrition*. Chicago: University of Chicago Press.

Tinto, V. (1993). *Leaving college: Rethinking the causes and cures of student attrition* (2 ed.). Chicago: University of Chicago Press.

Torres, V., Howard-Hamilton, M. F., & Cooper, D. L. (2003). Identity development of diverse populations: Implications for teaching and administration in higher education. *ASHE-ERIC Higher Education Report* (Vol. 29, No. 6). San Francisco: Jossey-Bass.

Turner, C.S.V. (1994). Guests in Someone Else's House: Students of Color. *Review of HigherEducation 17*(4), 355–370.

Valencia, R. R. (1997). Introduction. In *The evolution of deficit thinking: Educational thought and practice* (pp. ix–xvii). London: The Falmer Press.

Whitt, E. J. (1996). Assessing student cultures. In M. L. Upcraft and J. H. Schuh (Eds.), *Assessment in student affairs: A guide for practitioners.* San Francisco: Jossey-Bass.

CHAPTER FOUR

Power, Privilege, and Pedagogy: Collegiate Classrooms as Sites to Learn Racial Equality

Roland W. Mitchell
Kristen T. Edwards

Introduction

Peggy McIntosh's (1988) ground-breaking "White Privilege and Male Privilege: A Personal Account of Coming to See Correspondences through Work in Women's Studies" set the tone for numerous scholars and activists to start theorizing the wages of whiteness and the interlocking hierarchies of racism and sexism (Asher, 2007; Villalpando and Bernal, 2002; Ladson-Billings and Tate, 2006; Scheurich and Young, 1997; Tatum, 1992). McIntosh defines privilege as a type of entitlement that is unearned and steeped in inequitable power relations. Operationalizing White privilege, McIntosh posits:

> I think Whites are carefully taught not to recognize White privilege, as males are taught not to recognize male privilege. So I have begun in an untutored way to ask what it is like to have White privilege. I have come to see White privilege as an invisible package of unearned assets that I can count on cashing in each day, but about which I was "meant" to remain oblivious. White privilege is like an invisible weightless knapsack of special provisions, maps, passports, codebooks, visas, clothes, tools, and blank checks.

The timeliness of McIntosh's research on race and gender within the rapidly changing political/social landscape of the late 20th century sparked a plethora of studies that scrutinized other unearned privileges associated with sexual orientation, class, cultural and/or faith community membership. However, the ways in which privilege shapes teaching and learning between faculty and students are largely understudied in the literature.

College faculty participate in systemic inequities that masquerade as natural components of teaching and learning. First, faculty assume duly needed leadership positions within their classrooms. Second, faculty are charged with engaging aspects of the educative process that afford the creation and nurturing of knowledge between themselves and students. They are often privileged in classrooms based on an expertise or mastery of a subject matter that is laboriously earned, potentially positioning students as receivers, filers and keepers of education (Freire, 1970). Thus, teaching and learning in collegiate classrooms precipitate a type of privilege considered *teacher privilege*.

In the following sections, we discuss the ways that systems of oppression coalesce to privilege and disadvantage individuals and groups within society. Accordingly, we assume that teacher privilege is rooted in and shaped by white privilege in America. We then narrow our focus specifically to college classrooms to conduct inquiry into the ways in which the teaching profession, despite its explicit focus on challenging many societal ills, holds potential for sustaining and further disseminating oppression. To illustrate the complex nuances associated with privilege systems, we focus specifically on the experiences of educators teaching in majority-White American classrooms. We conduct an in-depth analysis of the ways in which issues associated with racial and ethnic identity intersect with systems of privilege. The discussion portion of our chapter consists of data-driven illustrations that compare and contrast the current state of equity on college campuses to our admittedly utopic vision of possibilities. Our concluding remarks provide recommendations for educational policy makers through a sober discussion of the steps needed for establishing more equitable learning environments.

Understanding Privilege through Linguistic Oppression

The power of words/language to shape meaning within human communities is immeasurable. Numerous scholars, linguists, philosophers and cultural workers in general attest to the ways that shared levels of understanding communicated through language is a social process and an essential building block for establishing a community

(Sheriff, 1989; Hall, 1996; Barthes, 1964; Derrida, 1980; de Sassure, 1983; Peirce 1992). Exercising control of language shapes the ways in which the material world is conceptualized. However, language like numerous other aspects of human communities is constantly in flux, malleable, negotiated, and ultimately highly contested in society. For instance, the power associated with controlling language cannot be overstated in contemporary debates concerning the legitimacy of standard English versus vernacular forms of English (i.e. Ebonics or Spanglish) (Fecho, 2003; Delpit & Dowdy, 2003; Gee, 1996; Freire, 1973). Subsequently, higher-status groups impose standards, including language, on others. Therefore, to understand the power relations within a community, look closely at that community's linguistic system.

Defining pedagogy is salient given how we interrogate the concept of teacher privilege through the power of words. According to *The American Heritage Dictionary* (1991) pedagogy is "the art or *profession of teaching;* preparatory training or instruction." This colloquial definition illustrates an everyday understanding of the term pedagogy, but closer examination locates a pedagogue as "a schoolteacher or educator; one who instructs in a pedantic or dogmatic manner." Pedagogue derives from the Latin *Paedagogus* which, loosely translated, refers to a boy (or male) leader. Further, the definition of pedantic is "characterized by a narrow, often ostentatious concern for book learning and formal rules." The definition of dogmatic is "characterized by an authoritative, *arrogant assertion* of unproved or unprovable principles, derived from the Latin *dogmaticus* or Greek *dogmatikos,* meaning belief. A scholar is defined as, "a specialist in a given branch of the humanities." And finally, the definition of professor is "a teacher of the *highest rank* in an institution of higher learning."

A well-developed caste system exists within these definitions beyond pedestrian discussions of training and instruction. The definition of pedagogue, for example, is replete with power relations illustrating aspects of an environment that has firmly decided, whether justly or unjustly, who is the holder of knowledge, who is the leader, whose knowledge is valued, where valued knowledge derives, and how that knowledge is disseminated. Subsequently, the language associated with teaching and learning has evolved with implicit hierarchal power arrangements that dramatically influence the ways that we think about schooling today.

The search for the lineage of the words defined above reveals Latin/Greco-Roman origins albeit Mesopotamia and Egypt provides the foundation on which the Greco-Roman ideas are founded (Diop, 1963; Asante, 1990; Hilliard 1993). Thus, the extent to which racial/cultural linguistic hegemony influences Western culture is apparent. Further, the setting of the origins of pedagogy summons patriarchal images of men like Plato and Aristotle as wise, omnipotent pedagogues. Even more, the fetishization of a particular type of knowledge (authoritative, *arrogant assertion* of unproved or unprovable principles, a narrow, often ostentatious concern for book learning and formal rules) is closely coupled with a schematic determining who should be the active producers and passive receivers of knowledge. As critical theorists meticulously document, roles of knowledge producer and receiver unsurprisingly evolved over history to reflect the norms of the dominant White supremacist patriarchal order in the United States (Giroux, 1983; Pinar, 2006; Pinar & Castenell, 1993; Apple 1995). According to this order, descriptors like "rational," "professor" (college-level educator), and "adult" are attributed to the masculine while "irrational," "teacher" (K-12 educator) and "adolescent" are attributed to the feminine. The existing educational order has cleverly situated these distinctions within the allusion of meritocracy. Those who acquire enough "knowledge" are valued. According to this line of thought, any privileges these individuals receive within the academy are rightly afforded. Subsequently, the academy has become a reflection of the larger society it functions within.

Denise Taliaferro-Baszile (2006) poignantly observes that it is easy for professors of color to "underestimate just how profoundly racism, sexism, capitalism, and hypocrisy penetrate the deep structure of U.S. higher education (p. 197)." Therefore, we replace "White" with "Scholar" or "Professor," but the rules remain the same. The more closely one's skin is associated with White or one's knowledge is "exhaustive," the more opportunity to dominate and oppress other groups within a community (e.g., the academy), regardless of how "unproved" or "unprovable" one's knowledge. We do not assume that all knowledge acquired in the academy is oppressive and erroneous but challenge assumptions that language, knowledge production, and societal norms are neutral. Whites are afforded privileges because of the color of their skin, and professors who hold Ph.D.s may have much to learn despite constructions as "authorities." Recall that Peggy McIntosh states, "Whites are carefully taught not to recognize White privilege." Professors may be carefully taught not to recognize teacher privilege. Scholars are taught that their academic credentials somehow endow them with the right to be right, regardless of scholarly discussions of reflexivity and reciprocity (Mazzei & Jackson 2009).

Engaging teacher privilege with the experiences of faculty of color adds a compelling caveat. One may reasonably assume that privileged groups may more comfortably move into another privileged situation that others (i.e., White men who become professors in majority-White institutions) (Goodman, 2001). Privileged groups often convince themselves that privilege does not exist and that every benefit received is linked to merit and abilities. However, oppressed groups not only recognize privilege but experience a certain sense of cognitive dissonance resulting from the willful indifference required to function within that system (Collins, 1990). In fact, the production and reproduction of privilege rely on the interdependence between dominant and subordinate groups in which a limited number of the subordinate group are afforded privilege (Fine, 1997). In the following section, we discuss this phenomenon among professors of color on majority White college campuses.

Honorary Whiteness

In discussions with students, professionals, and researchers of color on majority White college campuses, substantive evidence that Whiteness may be bestowed upon non-Whites emerged. We found that, when people of color were vested with institutional power historically reserved for Whites, they concurrently enabled interlocking systems of oppression—White privilege and teacher privilege. Consequently, one researcher of color referred to these instances as granting educators of color *honorary Whiteness*. The preliminary findings of the literature in this chapter suggest that this phenomenon is most observable when recipients of honorary Whiteness are in positions integral to the continuation and/or expansion of existing systems of race-based oppression. However, this process is often complicated by forces to resist oppression. People of color in academia are often cognizant of the ways in which entitlements are limited. Subsequently, they recognize that the *true* intent of honorary Whiteness is the strengthening of systems of race-based oppression.

Engaging these issues for professors of color on majority White campuses is wrought with contradictions. For example, Lavada Taylor-Brandon (2006) argues that, when separated, identities as Black, woman, and teacher are culturally disadvantaged in White supremacist patriarchal environments. Patricia Hill Collins (1990) further elaborates on this concept, describing her experiences moving from the protective enclave of her supportive Black community to the academy. According to Collins, the steps associated with becoming a "legitimate" scholar or "knower" weres filled with choices and sacrifices. She asked herself the following questions: Do I retain my voice and remain ignored in scholarly discourse or do I adopt the voice of the academy and be heard? And am I really heard? Is it *my* voice? So am I silenced even when being silenced? But is it worth it to be heard?

Charles R. Lawrence III (1995) further elaborates, observing the ways in which African American cultural voices are often compromised in the academy:

> I experience a strong sense of ambivalence as I help black law students to understand and work with legal doctrine. As they become fluent in this new language, I watch them internalize its assumptions and accept its descriptions and meanings. I see them lose fluency in first and second languages of understandings that they brought with them to law school. I also watch myself struggle to maintain some fluency in languages that are expressive of liberating themes. This is particularly difficult when one is submerged in an institutional and professional culture where neither these languages nor the themes they express are valued or rewarded (p. 343).

The academy provides a commodity, a benefit, a privilege associated with learning a new language. However, this privilege requires forfeiting the everyday language and subsequent cultural norms of indigenous communities. Thus, honorary whiteness is afforded to non-Whites as long as the rules of Whiteness are followed. Collins remembers that she was "privileged" with an elite education. Yet, this same elite education teaches scholars that they are the only individuals "qualified to produce theory (p. xii)" and are qualified to interpret their and everyone else's experiences. She notes conflict between her raced and gendered identities and the privilege of interpreting others' lives and experiences.

Scholars of color invest countless hours becoming indoctrinated with canonical knowledge often situated within oppressive traditions. Paraphrasing Paulo Freire (1970), scholars of color have spent the better part of their adult lives ingesting the poison of the oppressor, so even attempts at liberation are done in oppressed ways. As Whites are born into privilege in society, professors are "born" into privilege in the graduation hooding process. However, faculty of color, unlike Whites, are not afforded afforded the benefit of naiveté. As W.E.B Du Bois so poignantly stated in the *Souls of Black Folks* (1903/2007):

> The Negro is a sort of a seventh son…gifted with second sight in this American world….It is a peculiar sensation, this double consciousness, this sense of always looking at oneself through the eyes of others (p. 8).

So while privilege affords some White professors the right to reside in a space of taken-for-granted entitlements, this oppressive system demands that scholars of color engage in a type of willful ignorance. Taliaferro-Baszile (2006) terms this as "ontoepistemological in-between" space—the space where she does not quite belong. The term refers to a space within majority White colleges and universities where scholars of color are both privileged and disadvantaged, the space where they are honorary Whites and yet still something else.

Vital seeds of resistance to oppressive educational practices exist albeit professors of color experience numerous indignities teaching in collegiate contexts. Further, we believe that professors of color who are granted honorary whiteness represent an instance where the limits (or the sensitive underbelly) of privilege systems are exposed. Interlocking systems of white/male/academic privilege are fractured when historically marginalized groups participate in academic circles.

In these instances exists the space where real emancipatory potential can be nurtured.

Faculty Marshaling Teacher Privilege: Dialogues from the Academy

The Gaze of Conservative Frat Boys and Girls

We conducted an inquiry into the teaching of attorney Richard Mason for a compelling illustration of teacher privilege as a means for disrupting White privilege. Mason is a White law professor at a majority-White university in the southeastern region of the United States. This institution, like the majority of the schools in the region, has a sordid segregationist past that still significantly influences the campus environment today. However, despite Professor Mason's racial/ethnic membership in the majority culture on campus, he is constantly concerned with how his students' perception of his racial identity either enables or challenges the race-based privilege system at the university.

In our discussions, we interrogated possibilities for attacking what we consider to be the roots of these privilege systems. Professor Mason felt that White professors' cognizance of the ways their teaching either enables or challenges white supremacist academic structures is crucial. Consequently, Mason called for White professors' openness about privileges associated with being in the majority rather than avoiding topics about their own race-based entitlements or discussions of race/racism at large. Mason described the ways in which he uses his racial identity in helping students encounter subject matter about society and the institution where he is employed. Mason reflects:

> I think [racial identity] affects everybody's teaching; it's just a matter of how aware you are of it. For example, I see that by being a White professor at a law school I come in with certain credibility on racial issues that I wouldn't have if I were African American. I lose a little however, because I'm viewed as just a liberal and so that makes me sort of not quite neutral....There's no question that the position [as a White person] gives me credibility that I wouldn't have if I wasn't White, with those conservatives.

Professor Mason assumes that teachers' racial identity can affect their credibility with students when talking about certain issues. His comments suggest that beliefs associated with race influence teachers' and students' experiences in class. Mason did not merely remark on this in a general sense; he applied it specifically to the way that he, as a White professor in a majority-White classroom, was situated within a variety of student beliefs about race.

Mason stated that he felt pressure to earn credibility with conservative White American students whom he referred to as "frat boys and girls." Attaining credibility required assuming stances more closely aligned with White Anglo-Saxon Protestant (WASP) values. Mason assumed these positions, he noted, as a means of navigating various interpretations of his white skin and progressive left-leaning politics. Concurrently, Mason was concerned about losing credibility with his White students who may view him as a "race traitor" (Garvey & Ignatiev, 1996) or treasonous to a specific conception of Whiteness given Mason's beliefs. Mason strategically informs his teaching with his insights concerning racial discourses. Mason's aim is to establish both relationships and subsequent lines of communication with students whose abilities to fully engage the experiences of people of color were stunted by socializing in racist contexts. Mason is additionally aware that students of color experience the institution, and his classroom, differently than majority students. Accordingly, Mason used these differences as part of his pedagogical repertoire to provide expanded learning opportunities for all students.

Mason describes himself as a liberal teacher of law, supporting many programs and trends that have afforded marginalized groups more equitable standing in society. In class, Mason often addresses issues associated with African American history and the 20th century struggle for civil rights. Mason believes that students of color potentially view him as an ally or advocate since he includes these topics in class discussion. He observes that his continued relationships with some of his students of color prove how they appreciate inclusive teaching. In addition, he reflected on how students of color consider him an example of how to address White supremacy in class.

Mason's pedagogy required delicate balance. He was interested in signaling solidarity with his students of color, but he was also attentive to how "conservative frat boys/girls" respond to him when he offers liberal interpretations of the law. In his opinion, these interpretations paired with his explicit discussions of race may sometimes cost him credibility with his White students. As a consequence, Mason occasionally articulates legal arguments in more conservative ways to maintain credibility with this segment of this class. The gaze of the "conservative frat boys/girls" (students who tend to be White, politically conservative, middle to upper class, and make up the majority of the class) still influenced his thinking about his practice despite Mason's self-identified "left-leaning" political views.

We find Mason's tension essential for White professors who seek to challenge oppression through their teaching. A central part of this challenge is sensitivity about communicating across muted lines of understanding within classrooms resultant from histories of racism. Consequently, Mason adeptly teaches in a manner that engages White students in broader perspectives while simultaneously establishing an environment where students of color feel their experiences are central to the learning process. Occasionally, Mason assumed positions that de-emphasized concerns to which he is strongly committed. Mason recognizes the privilege in this environment associated with his white skin and scholarly standing and uses it to draw all students, Black and White, in the educative process. In short, he marshals the prevailing privilege system in a way that establishs a more equitable and engaging learning environment for all students.

Helping Students of Color Raise Their Voices

> Every time I teach this course there are some students that I know are coming from a similar location that I'm from. I understand the experiences of coming to view the world in similar ways… I understand they are protecting themselves; they are protecting their communities. It makes it difficult for me not to say you need to speak truth to power. And there have been times when after class I've said to them "I know what it's been like and what you want to say. You need to say it and consider me your back stop. I'm here; you're taken care of; so you need to say it." But I know that's a lot to demand from someone—to embrace their own ability in a place in which whatever I'm saying is a measurement of me and everyone that's considered to be like me.
>
> —Dr. Cameron Patrick

Cameron Patrick is an African American professor who teaches communication studies courses at the same university as Professor Mason. Patrick described the ways in which faculty and students of color are constantly reminded of the ways in which race matters. He further argues that White professors socialized in majority White contexts do not share this awareness. Patrick's comments demonstrate understanding of the complexity of the relationship that he shares with students of color who are also keenly sensitive/susceptible to race-based oppression. Patrick's dual positioning as professor and member of a historically marginalized community lends insight about implicit/explicit barriers to students of color within these environments (Collins, 1998; Jones, Castellanos & Cole 2002; DeSousa, & Kuh 1996; Talifero-Braszile, 2006). Therefore, when Patrick says to students of color, "You need to say it and consider me your backstop," he understands the vulnerability of students of color in these contexts and uses his title as a professor to support them in their efforts to be heard.

However, despite the commonalities that Patrick shares with students of color he is also a member of the academic community. At its best this membership means participation in the pursuit and dissemination of meaningful knowledge and at its worst this means the continued propagation of discourses that scaffold existing privilege systems. Consequently, Patrick resides on the margins of two often tumultuous communities. One, he consideres home and he characterized it as being in relation to that of his African American students. And the other is a more recently encountered scholarly community in which he (supposedly) enjoys all the entitlements associated with being a professor (Banks, 1998).

Patrick has endured the rigors of earning a terminal degree, the polemics of the tenure process as well as the supporting research activities as part of his indoctrination to academia. However, in subsequent conversations Patrick also discussed a recognition that each phase of this process was informed by the knowledge that institutions and in some cases the actual disciplinary discourses that he studied, were conceived with only the vaguest notion that Black people would ever be included. But now as a result of enduring all the material and symbolic trauma associated with a Black aspiring academic navigating a White institution (Paul, 2001) he has achieved membership in the community. Through this membership, he has been granted what we have to this point termed as Honorary Whiteness.

According to a historically racist (yet still ubiquitous) representation of people of color, the very nature of the socialization within academia is intended to "teach out" their innate inarticulate, unlearned, and irrational nature. One could even argue that just as was suggested during the heyday of the Trans-Atlantic Slave Trade, that the dehumanization that Africans experienced through the Middle Passage (or in our case socialization into academia) can be rationalized as worthwhile when one considers the leaps in knowledge, culture and morality they experienced through contact with Whites (Anderson, 1988; Watkins, 2001). Consequently, for the purposes of this study, the difference between Mason's or McIntosh's use of Teacher Privilege to open up a space for critical engagement in majority White settings and the experiences of professors of color like Patrick is undeniable. Because before professors of color can attempt to use entitlements associated with Teacher Privilege to challenge White supremacy they must first be *properly* seasoned or indoctrinated and subsequently earn Honorary Whiteness. Once proven worthy, having been socialized out of their genealogical inferiority, they then are worthy of the entitlements with which White academics are naturally endowed. This phenomenon can be observed in law, business, medicine, the humanities and fine arts as well. People of color may be grudgingly welcomed into the fold, but they must be certified and proven worthy by being stripped of their perceived *ethnicness* first.

Patrick and Mason shared similar beliefs that professors' critical reflections on issues associated with race/racism and privilege systems are both a necessary and constructive factor for challenging the linkages between education and systemic oppression. Further, both professors found this insight useful in the historically racially exclusive spaces in which they teach. However, the ways in which these faculty considered their race influenced the nature of the relationships between students and teachers, the delivery/reception of subject matter, and ultimately the pedagogical environment itself. Subsequently, it is necessary for understanding the connection we draw between honorary Whiteness and teacher privilege (Delpit, 1995; Delpit & Dowdy 2003; Dibble & Rosiek, 2002).

Discussion

The point that we want to highlight by comparing Mason's (White) and Patrick's (Black) use of Teacher privilege is to argue that regardless of race all educators must play a unique role in dismantling privilege systems. In fact, we believe that the distinctions between the ways that professors of color and White professors enact these challenges (as represented by the need for professors of color to be granted Honorary Whiteness) provide vital resources for strategic approaches to attacking oppression from varying positions. In our assessment, understanding discourses associated with race and academia and the intentional manipulation of them; regardless of a teacher's race, gender, sexual orientation, class, geographical location, etcetera is of utmost importance for dismantling systems of oppression. And subsequently, the personal recognition of where a professor fits into this matrix amounts to accepting the power/responsibility that they have in challenging the foundations of privilege systems.

We believe that being a man does not free one of the responsibility of working to dismantle patriarchal systems, nor should White people consider the work of challenging White supremacy solely people of color's responsibility. As a result of taking seriously this charge, both professors walked a thin line between being considered a credible member of the academy or being discredited and labeled treasonous to segments of their disciplinary communities and institutions. By challenging whiteness in his teaching Mason risked being framed in opposition to the dominant White power structure. And by challenging Whiteness as a professor of color, Patrick risked losing the entitlements that he was granted by academia. However, when asked about occupying a position on the margins of the academy as a result of his practice and beliefs, Professor Mason simply responded, "I know the risks but do you really want to be in-league with a bunch of racists?" We acknowledge the levity of Mason's remark while still recognizing that he hints that potential for resisting oppression already exists within the academy. Further, Mason's comments illustrate that the desire to participate in this resistance is not exclusively relegated to people of color, women or other traditionally marginalized communities.

Implications for Policy

In this chapter we set out to examine the ways that the entitlements associated with being a teacher can be marshaled to improve learning outcomes for all students. To do this we explored the ability of faculty to utilize Teacher Privilege for libratory outcomes with careful attention to the distinction between the use of Teacher Privilege by faculty of color and White professors. Our intent was to conceptualize possibilities for dismantling systems of oppression at predominantly White colleges and universities by both groups. The findings from this inquiry suggest that higher education institutions need to change so that they support more diverse forms of knowledge based on a broader set of cultural discourses and a less canonized set of epistemologies. We argue that recognizing structures within higher education that inherently support Teacher Privilege is an essential part of ending the legacy of oppression in these contexts. Further, our research only briefly discussed the reality that one of the most potent means of rectifying the resulting problems may already reside within college and university cultures.

Consequently, our suggestions for higher education policy are multi-layered. First there is a dire need for structures that support and require the kind of inquiry on culturally responsive practice that this chapter describes. Support for professors to improve their teaching is something needed in general. This study corroborates that the need exists, and a core part of this change consists of formally including the knowledge and wisdom associated with non-majority communities. By taking seriously non-majority perspectives and the subsequent disruption of systems of oppression that will result, this study began to make an epistemic argument for targeted hires in the academy. Rather than argue that affirmative action hires should be made to redress past wrongs, in essence benefiting only the person hired, this study indicates that such hires could be made based on the knowledge the professor has that will enable libratory practice.

Our study recognizes that a person who has experienced being the target of specific kinds of racial oppression possesses insights that can be helpful when providing service to students of color and improving teaching in general. However, we also want to point out (1) that such insights are not always possessed by those who bear the signifiers of a particular racial group, (2) where such insights are possessed they are not always used, (such use depends on the ideology and disciplinary training of the professor), and (3) such personal experiences are not the only source of insight that enable the type of culturally responsive educational practice we are advocating (Gay, 2000).

This observation has many complex implications for university hiring practices. One implication is that it challenges traditional targeted hiring practices and makes an epistemic argument suggesting that targeted hires possess valuable knowledge and understandings that provide the needed insights for challenging systemic oppression in their classrooms, campuses and their broader disciplinary communities. One must recognize that not all Black teachers have the type of insight and understanding or ideological and political beliefs needed to challenge privilege systems.

It follows, therefore, that this standard could be applied to all hires, White and Black, male and female, straight and gay. We might well ask what knowledge enables European American teachers to teach African American students or what knowledge enables an African American professor to teach Native American students as well, and how might we recognize such knowledge in a teaching candidate. We realize by raising such questions, we could be accused of initiating a dangerous conversation. This kind of argument could lead the reactionary to conclude that no targeted hires are needed at all. We have proceeded despite these concerns for two reasons. First, we believe the conversations we are currently having about higher education are already dangerous. There is little if any concern for students/faculty of color on major United States campuses beyond a concern for having more black bodies (but not too many) on our campuses. There is little evidence of the concern for the subjectivities of students/faculty of color on campuses or of institutional support for those with such concerns. In short, we do not see where there is that much to lose.

Second, we do not believe a thorough and critical examination of college teaching practices will ever yield a conclusion that erases the experience of difference many students and faculty of color have in contemporary majority White university settings. It may complicate our understandings of that difference. It may lead us in surprising directions. But we believe the experience of difference is empirically real. And we believe we need to approach that reality like scholars with, open, critical, and inquiring minds.

Conclusion

Through this chapter we broadly set out to conduct inquiry into the deep-rooted institutional norms that structure academia to appear accessible to some and contested territory to others. Specifically, in this chapter we examined the role of professors in setting the boundaries of these contested spaces within their classrooms. Our overarching goal was to bring to the surface the cleverly concealed legacy of race-based entitlement that permeates all aspects of academia. However, through this endeavor we also sought to acknowledge that within the white supremacist, sexist, hierarchal system that dominates higher education, there also resides the potential for the development of a profoundly powerful tradition of resistance to oppression. Therefore, we sought to mine the best parts of this tradition to establish educational environments that lead to more equitable college campuses.

At the heart of this project was a frank recognition that there is a documentable history of the roots of the white supremacist, patriarchal, heterosexist and ultimately interlocking privilege systems that led to the current state of our educational system. In response to these realities we argue that there is no neutral space outside the influence of privilege systems. Throughout the chapter we drew on literature, personal conjecture and data-driven examples, of libratory responses by academics (White and Black) to that oppression. We recognize that we may be critiqued that advocating participation in an unjust system, even if it is framed as strategic and in an emancipatory manner, is naïve, reactionary, and may even risk exacerbating an already dire situation. However despite the gravity of these critiques, we are unwilling to concede the immeasurable good that can be achieved by participation in teaching, service and research to the defenders of the status quo—potential racist, sexist, homophobes and ultimately those who wish to support systems that are morally bankrupt. Therefore we are willing to let go of the aspiration for virgin ground before we take action. We are willing to meet colleges and universities, academia and ultimately the U.S. where they are and start the work of challenging these systems. Further, we consider it a dangerous proposition to stand outside the walls of academia and lob critiques because to stand outside higher education in the U.S. means standing outside of society.

Audre Lorde (1983) posited, "The master's tools will never dismantle the master's house." We would never be so bold as to disregard the opinion of such an eminent scholar. However, through this chapter we ask, if the master's tools *built* the master's house, how would they not at least be used as part of the process of its destruction? We realize we may have overly pragmatic views. Yet as aspiring academics and developing scholars, we are a part of the system. As such, we have come to realize that it is necessary to change the system from the inside. In our current place in history, the voice of the Outsider is disregarded in the academy, and even the voices of certain superstar scholars like bell hooks or Cornel West for example, are often fetishized in such ways that they take on an a *carnival attraction* in the academy as opposed to being deeply engaged. Subsequently, even the "Outsider-within" is silenced. As suggested by Collins (1990), the outsider that lies dormant within academics of color can grow increasingly smaller while navigating the halls of the academy. Therefore in the tradition of Thurgood Marshall and the Legal Defense Fund when they used the principles and doctrines of the United States Constitution to argue for the integration of public schools (Samuels, 2004), we believe that the principles of the academy and the privilege afforded the professoriate can be used to accomplish the greater good. However, we are also cognizant of the short-comings of Marshall's efforts, how in many ways his arguments delegitimized the position of the pre-*Brown* historically Black educational enterprise. The tools, when used by the professor, must be done so with caution and thoughtfulness. In our recognition of the current system, professors of color must guard against what Freire characterized as the "ingestion of the oppressor." We cannot be limited to oppressive methods of liberation. So while we acknowledge our privileged positions, our functioning within those positions must be deliberately emancipatory.

With that being said, the thoughtful professor of color is in an incredible position within the academy. He/She has the opportunity to continue dominant academic discourse and reap the benefits of "Highest Ranking Knower" or he/she can use his/her privilege to acknowledge "other" sources of knowledge and write the experiences of marginalized communities into pedagogy. Lawrence (1995) describes this teacher privilege for social justice as acceptance of people of color's "positioned perspective" and giving that positioned perspective authority. Or not removing the privilege from our positioned perspective. We believe people of color (and specifically scholars) have a responsibility to write our stories and the stories of our ancestors. Lawrence states:

> Practitioners...must learn to *privilege* their own perspectives and those of other outsiders, understanding that the dominant legal discourse is premised upon the claim to knowledge of objective truths and the existence of neutral principles. We must free ourselves from the mystification produced by this ideology. We must learn to trust our own senses, feelings, and experiences, and to give them authority (or privilege), even...in the face of dominant accounts of social reality that claim universality (p. 338).

So as McIntosh takes her White privilege and engages others in the issue of social justice, we argue that faculty of color should use their Teacher Privilege or positioned perspective to add primacy to their own cultural epistemologies. Instead of functioning as catalysts for the academy, exclusively serving to speed up or continue the process of cultural assimilation and White patriarchal dominance, professors purposefully using Teacher Privilege must become inhibitors or anti-catalysts, slowing down and ultimately retarding this social process. However, oftentimes in the academy we find faculty of color using their position to further privilege Eurocentric patriarchal scholarship. Much of the research concerning the experiences of faculty of color at predominantly White institutions focuses on the trials and struggles they face while navigating a White space. While we definitely do not want to minimize the importance of this line of research, we believe it is necessary for faculty of color to also recognize the privilege associated with their position. And in so doing, they will be more cognizant of the use of Teacher Privilege for just ends as opposed to its use for perpetuating dominant discourses. This latter use is tempting in that it affords the possibility of reaping the benefits from privileged positions and in so doing continuing the system of disenfranchisement. When we focus solely on the struggle of minority faculty, it becomes easier to ignore our "sell-out" practices. Because of our own hardships, we may feel justified in disengaging with our responsibility to the continued struggle towards liberating pedagogy.

Scholars interested in liberation must take specific and conscious measures in their classrooms and scholarship to provide liberatory spaces. For Lawrence (1995) working towards social justice in his classroom means leaving space for "feeling and experience." He recognizes that the story and experiences of people of color have been systematically excluded from the dominant discourse and that this "academic" discourse is accepted as "universal." To deconstruct this universality and generalizability he allows his students to tell their stories, and he infuses the stories and experiences of other minorities into his courses. In so doing he takes the stories of people of color (scholarly and everyday) and places them alongside dominant discourse, which in turn produces the necessary "dissonance" for emancipatory pedagogy and scholarship. Lawrence's classroom allows students (minority and non-minority) the space to acknowledge that voices of color are not heard in the canonized literature. It is this acknowledgment that begins the work of social justice. It is also this experience of duality that produces empathy, which in turn provides liberation. As he goes on to explain, this liberation is not only experienced by students of color but by other marginalized groups within the academy. Our acknowledgment of belonging and not belonging or in-between-ness creates a space to more fully recognize and appreciate different and sometimes conflicting experiences of oppression. The unique understanding of people of color of oppression provides increased sensitivity to other groups' experiences of oppression. Therefore liberatory pedagogy for the faculty of color should be concerned with attacking or "inhibiting" oppression in all its forms, not just liberating people of color. Drawing on this vision of challenging oppression in all of its varying forms, we believe institutions can work towards the central vision of this book—the establishment of a more inclusive learning environment for the rapidly evolving diversity on college campuses.

References

Adair, V., Dahlberg, S. (Eds.) (2003). *Reclaiming Class: Women, Poverty, and the Promise of Higher Education in America.* Philadelphia, PA: Temple University Press.

American Heritage Dictionary. (1991). Boston, MA: Houghton Mifflin Company.

Anderson, J. (1988*). The Education of Blacks in the South 1860–1935.* Chapel Hill and London: University of North Carolina Press.

Apple, M. (1995). *Education and Power*. New York: Routledge.

Asante, M. (1988). *Afrocentricity* (rev. ed.). Trenton, N.: Africa World Press.

Asante, M. (1990). *Kemet, Afrocentricity, and Knowledge*. Trenton, NJ: Africa World Press.

Asher, N. (2007). Made in the (multicultural) U.S.A.: Unpacking tensions of race, culture, gender, and sexuality in education. *Educational Researcher, 36*(2), 65-73.

Baker, D. (1983) *Race, Ethnicity and Power*. London: Routledge.

Banks, J. (1998). The lives and values of researchers: Implications for educating citizens in a multicultural society. *Educational Researcher*, 27 (7), 4–17.

Barthes, R. (1985) Rhetoric of the image. In *The responsibility of forms: Critical essays on music, art and representation.* Transl. Richard Howard. Berkeley: U of California P.

Collins, P. H. (1986). Learning from the outsiders within: The sociological significance of black feminist thought. *Social Problems,* 33(6), 14–32.

Collins, P. H. (1990). *Black feminist thought: Knowledge, consciousness, and the politics of empowerment*. New York: Routledge.

Collins, P. H. (1998). *Fighting words: Black women & the search for justice.* Minneapolis, MN: University of Minnesota Press.

Crenshaw, K., Neil G., Gary, P. and Thomas, K. (Eds.) (1995). *Critical race theory: The key writings that formed the movement*. New York: New York University Press.

Delpit, L. (1995). *Other people's children: Cultural conflict in the classroom*. New York: The New Press.

Delpit, L., Dowdy, J. (2003). *The skin that we speak: Thoughts on language and culture in the classroom.* New York: The New Press.

Derrida, J. (1980). *Of grammatology.* Baltimore: Johns Hopkins University Press,1998, corrected edition.

de Saussure, F. (1983). *Course in general linguistics.* trans. Roy Harris, La Salle, Il: Open Court.

DeSousa, D. J. & Kuh, G. (1996). Does institutional racial composition make a difference in what Black students gain from college? *Journal of College Student Development, 37(3)*,257–267.

Dibble, N. & Rosiek, J. (2002). White-out: A connection between a teacher's white identity and her science teaching. *International Journal of Educational and the Arts,* 5(3). Available at http://ijea.asu.edu/index.html.

Diop. C. (1963). *The cultural unity of Black Africa: The domains of patriarchy and of matriarchy in classical antiquity*. London: Karnak House.

Du Bois, W. E. B. (2007). *The souls of black folk.* New York, NY: Oxford University Press.

Fecho, B. (2003). *Is this English?: Race, language, and culture in the classroom.* New York: Teachers College Press.

Fine, M. (1997). Witnessing Whiteness. In M. Fine, L. Weis, L. Powell, & L. Mun Wong (Eds.), *Off White: Readings on race, power, and society* (pp. 57–65). New York: Routledge.

Friere, P. (1970). *The pedagogy of the oppressed*. New York, NY: Continuum Publishing.

Freire, P. (1973). *Education for critical consciousness*. New York: Seabury.

Freire, P. (1994). *Pedagogy of hope: Reliving pedagogy of the oppressed.* New York: Continuum.

Garvey, J., & Ignatiev, I. (Eds.) (1996). *Race traitor*. New York: Routledge.

Gay, G. (2000). *Culturally responsive teaching: Theory, research and practice*. New York: Teachers College Press.

Giroux, H. (1983). *Theory and resistance in education*. New York: Bergin and Harvey.

Gee, J. (1996). *Social linguistics and literacies: Ideologies in discourses* (2nd ed.). London: Taylor & Francis.

Goodman, D. J. (2001). *Promoting diversity and social justice: Educating people from privileged groups*. Thousand Oaks, CA: Sage Publications.

Gordon, D. (2003). *Black identity: Rhetoric, ideology, and nineteenth-century black nationalism.* Carbondale and Edwardsville, IL: Southern Illinois University Press.

Gregory, S. (2000). Strategies for improving the racial climate for students of color in predominately White institutions. *Equity and Excellence in Education, 33*(3), 9.

Hall, S. (1996). *Race: The floating signifier*. Northhampton, MA: Media Education Foundation.

Harvey, D. (1990). *The condition of postmodernity: An enquiry into the origins of cultural change*. Cambridge, MA: Blackwell.

Hilliard, A. (1991) Do we have the will to educate all children? In *Educational Leadership, 49* (1), 31–36.

Hilliard, A. (1993). *50 plus: Essential references on the history of African people.* Baltimore, MD: Black Classic Press.

hooks, B. (1994). *Teaching to transgress*. New York: Routledge.

Jones, L., Castellanos, J., & Cole, D. (2002). Examining the ethnic minority student experience at predominantly White institutions: A case study. *Journal of Hispanic Higher Education, 1(1),* 19-39.

Kuh, G. D., Kinzie, J., Schuh, J. H., & Whitt, E. J. (2005). *Student Success in College: Creating Conditions that Matter.* San Francisco, CA: John Wiley & Sons, Inc.

Ladson-Billings, G. (1994). *The dreamkeepers successful teachers of African American children*. San Francisco: Jossey Bass.

Ladson-Billings, G., Tate, W. D. (2006) *Education research in the public interest: Social justice, action, and policy.* New York, NY: Teachers College Press.

Lawrence, C. (1995). The word and the river: Pedagogy as scholarship as struggle. In K. Crenshaw, N. Gotanda, G. Peller, & K. Thomas (Ed.) *Critical race theory: The key writings that formed the movement*. New York: The New Press.

Lorde, A. (1983). There is no hierarchy of oppression. *Interracial Books for Children Bulletin,* 14, Council on Interracial Books for Children.

MacLeod, J. (1987) *Ain't no makin' it*. Boulder, CO: Westview Press.

Marable, M., Mullings, L., (Eds.) (2000). *Let nobody turn us around: Voices of resistance, reform, and renewal.* Boston, MA: Rowman & Littlefield Publishers, Inc.

Mazzei, L., & Jackson, A. (2009). *Voice in qualitative inquiry: Challenging conventional, interpretive, and critical conceptions in qualitative research.* New York: Routledge.

McIntosh, P. (1988). White privilege and male privilege: A personal account of coming to see correspondences through work in women's Studies. Working Paper #189, published in *Peace and Freedom,* July/August 1989; reprinted in *Independent School,* Winter 1990.

Meeks, K. (2000). *Driving while black: What to do if you are a victim of racial profiling*. New York: Broadway.

Mitchell, R., & Rosiek J. (2006). Professors as embodied racial signifier: A case study of the significance of race in a university classroom. *The Review of Education,Pedagogy, and Cultural Studies, 28*(3-4). 395–379.

Mitchell, R. & Lee, T. (2006). Ain't I a woman?: An inquiry into the experiential dimensions of teacher's practical knowledge through the experiences of African-American female academics. *The International Journal of Learning. 13*(7), 97–104.

Nieto, S. (2002). *Language, culture and teaching: Critical perspectives for a new century*. Mahwaha, NJ: Lawrence Erlbaum Associates.

Ogbu, J. (1987). Opportunity structure, cultural boundaries, and literacy. In *Language, literacy and culture: Issues of society and schooling,* edited by J. Langer. Norwood, NJ: Ablex Press.

Ogbu, J. (1990). Literacy and schooling in subordinate cultures: The case of black Americans. In *Going to School* edited by K. Lomotey. Albany, NY: SUNY Press.

Paul, D. (2001). *Life, culture and education on the academic plantation: Womanist thought and perspective.* New York: Peter Lang Publishing.

Peirce, C.S. (1992). *The essential Peirce: Selected philosophical writings, Vol. 1 (1867–1893),* Nathan Houser and Christian Kloesel (Eds). Bloomington and Indianapolis, IN: Indiana University Press.

Pinar, W. (2006). *Race, religion, and a curriculum of reparation: Teacher education for a multicultural society*. New York: Palgrave Macmillan.

Pinar, W., & Castenell, L. (1993). *Understanding curriculum as racial text.* Albany, NY: SUNY Press.

Samuels, A. (2004). *Is separate unequal?* Lawrence, KS: University Press of Kansas.

Scheurich, J. & Young, M. (1997) Coloring epistemologies: are our research epistemologies racially biased? *Educational Researcher,* 26(4), 4–16.

Sheriff, J. (1989). *The fate of meaning: Charles Peirce, structuralism and literature.* Princeton, NJ: Princeton University Press.

Solorzano, D. & Villalpando, O. (1998). Critical race theory: Marginality and the experiences of students of color in higher education. In C. Torres & T. Mitchell (Eds.), *Sociology of Education: Emerging Perspectives* (pp. 211–224). Albany, NY: SUNY Press.

Sowell, T. (1981). *Ethnic America*: A History. New York: Basic Books.

Taliaferro-Braszile, D. (2006). In this place where I don't quite belong: Claiming the onto-epistemological in-between. In T. Berry (Ed.) *From oppression to grace: Women of color dealing with issues in academia*. New, York: Stylus

Tatum, B. (1992). Talking about race, learning about racism: The application of racial identity development theory in the classroom. *Harvard Educational Review, 62*(1), 1-24.

Taylor-Brandon, L. (2006). Seen, not heard: A conversation on what it means to be black and female in the academy. In T. Berry (Ed.) *From oppression to grace: Women of color dealing with issues in academia*. New, York: Stylus.

Tillman, L.C. (2002). Culturally sensitive research approaches: An African American perspective. *Educational Researcher, 31*(9), 3–12.

Tillman, L.C. (Ed.). (2008). *Sage Handbook of African American education.* Thousand Oaks, CA: Sage Publications.

Tozer, S. E., P. Violas and G. Senese (2002). *School and society: Historical and contemporary perspectives,* 4th Edition. New York: McGraw-Hill.

Villalpando, O., and Bernal, D. D. (2002). A critical race theory analysis of barriers that impede the success of faculty of color. In W. A. Smith, P. G. Altbach, and K. Lomotey (eds.), *The Racial Crisis in American Higher Education: Continuing Challenges for the Twenty-First Century.* New York: State University of New York Press.

Walker, V. (2001). African-American teaching in the south: 1940–1960. *American Educational Research Journal*, Vol. *38*, No. 4, pp. 751–779.

Watkins, W. (2001). *The white architects of black education: Ideology and power in America 1865–1954*. New York: Teachers College Press.

West, C. (1990). *Race matters*. Boston, MA: Beacon Press.

West, C. (1993). *Prophetic thought in post-modern times.* Monroe, ME.: Common Courage Press.

CHAPTER FIVE

When and Where Interests Collide: Policy, Research, and the Case for Managing Campus Diversity

T. Elon Dancy II

America is changing at a rapid pace. America is increasingly pluralistic in race, gender, ethnicity, class as well as the ways in which people express behavior, faith, love, and creed. Social issues of the day are consistently levied against human rights doctrine. Pressure is increasing for individuals to develop competencies for a global citizenry. To meet social transformation and change, American colleges and universities are rethinking the characteristics that make them distinct and that contribute to higher education and society writ large (Kuh et al., 1991). Perhaps nowhere is this rethinking more readily located than in institutional mission statements. As more than 3,000 American institutions of higher education define and redefine their beliefs about student potential, teaching and learning, one certainty remains-American college graduates are charged to become culturally sensitive and culturally competent to meet the needs of the 21st century. In response, institutional mission statements affirm the role diversity plays in preparing students for social, civic, and professional futures.

Diversity in higher education is a topic about which scholars agree is troubling to collegiate work and policy (M. J. Chang & Kiang, 2002; Hurtado, 2007; Hurtado, Milem, Clayton-Pedersen, & Allen, 1999). College administrators are often in a quandary when personnel, students, or others argue that disparities exist between diversity-focused institutional programming and institutional core values and mission (Milem, 2003). Another way to envision diversity conflicts is that institutional priorities around diversity are often politically wedged between law and sociohistorical forces (Milem, Chang, & antonio, 2005). In addition, scholars have argued that this tension exists given that traditional institutional strategies fail to adequately centralize diversity and potentially assume the following: (1) diverse individuals must change, (2) diverse student, faculty, staff, and administrators are responsible for socializing each other, (3) individuals from underprivileged cultures must adapt to privileged culture, (4) only "identifiably" diverse students need aid, (5) equitable educational opportunities to all students or professional opportunities to personnel are not needed (6) educating the dominant culture about diverse colleagues is not needed (Mayhew, Grunwald, & Dey, 2006; Stage & Manning, 1992).

In developing this chapter, I conducted a multidisciplinary analysis of the scholarly and research literature toward understanding how effective management of diversity benefits the work of colleges and potentially works to relieve tensions that exist. A three-pronged framework is used in this effort. First, the sociohistorical and legal history is interrogated as it shapes colliding interests in diversity for higher education. Second, this chapter discusses how diversity benefits students and institutions. Student benefits are discussed in light of learning outcomes enhanced by the presence or work of diversity on campus, while institutional benefits refer to how diversity enhances organizational effectiveness nationally and internationally. Third, I propose methods for managing diversity, synthesizing discussion from empirical and scholarly literature.

Early Diversity Movements, Collegiate Desegregation, and Transdemography

Early Diversity Movements

Prior to the Civil War, higher education remained primarily the province of white men (Cohen, 1998; Thelin, 2004). Following the Civil War, the demise of slavery promoted other social revisions and reforms including educational exclusion. Women and formerly enslaved African Americans used this time to fight for educational access and equal rights. Responding to these new demands, higher education took action. Colleges and universities began to open admissions to both women and minorities during the mid-19th century albeit the process of equalization of educational opportunity occurred gradually.

Efforts to create a place for women and minorities generally derived from a need to protect the social, political, and economic dominance of White men. However, in 1837, Oberlin College became the first institution to admit women to (Cohen, 1998; Rudolph, 1962; Thelin, 2004). However, between 1861 and 1875, Matthew Vassar, Henry Wells, Sophia Smith, and Henry Durant created colleges exclusively for women (Geiger, 1999). These institutions allowed women to fully participate in higher education at institutions where they were the focus of both the curriculum and the administration. Yet, the purpose was to educate them to succeed at the tasks assigned to them in an industrializing society, which largely included rearing educated children to continue the progress of the nation (Geiger, 1999).

Systemic privilege emerged where predominantly White colleges and universities began to accept students who were not White Anglo-Saxon, Protestant (WASP) and men. When White women integrated predominantly White colleges, the conventions of then Victorian culture insisted upon separation of the sexes (Gordon, 1997). More specifically, men were viewed as natural leaders in public, political and economic venues while women were relegated to uneducated lives in which they tended to the household and children (Gordon, 1997). White women, particularly those who lived in the antebellum North, gained access to higher education given arguments that secondary education equipped women with tools needed to be better wives and mothers. Unmarried women largely used higher education to prepare themselves for teaching professions (Gordon, 1997). Southern women were expected to view higher education as preparation for roles as wives and mothers. During this period, restrictive admissions policies to maintain White Anglo-Saxon Protestant (WASP) tradition became strategic plan and policy.

In the early 1900s, colleges were still seeking to preserve higher education for the sons of WASP businessmen or professionals (Levine, 1997). In doing so, "elite" predominantly White colleges of the 1920s and 1930s were replete with ethnic and class prejudice. Critical numbers of liberal arts colleges chose to limit the size of their classes and seek national and upper-middle class students at the expense of local and more diverse students after WWI. With little accountability, restrictive admissions policies justified the exclusion of Jewish students, who were discriminated against when they applied to elite colleges in the Northeast. This "Jewish problem," as it is described in the literature, was further shaped by no formal admissions procedures, modest attempts to attract regionally diverse students, widespread anti-semitism, and an increase of Jewish applicants (Dancy & Brown, in press; Levine, 1997). Institutions adhering to quotas included Dartmouth, Harvard, and the New England colleges. Forthcoming litigation would work to dismantle such quotas and discrimination.

Collegiate Desegregation

Between the late 1930s and the early 1950s, colleges made minimal progress in racially desegregating. Legal challenges during this period resulted in decisions that sanctioned specific institutions for practicing race-based discrimination rather than addressing desegregation writ large. Defining cases of this period included *Sipuel v. Board of Regents of the University of Oklahoma* (1948), *McLaurin v. Oklahoma State Regents* (1950), and *Sweatt v. Painter* (1950). Although the Supreme Court stopped short of overturning the *Plessy* decision, they did make sufficient use and application of the Fourteenth Amendment in each of these cases (Brown & Lane, 2003). By aggressively applying the Equal Protection Clause of the Fourteenth Amendment in *Sipuel, McLaurin,* and *Sweatt,* the Supreme Court altered and limited the ability of states to discriminate in higher education. These rulings forced states to commit to segregation by providing equal facilities for different student groups or integrate. Although there was considerable impact on state policy in Texas and Oklahoma, change was not widespread nationally (Brown & Lane, 2003).

From the mid-1950s to the late 1970s, federal legislation and court cases impacted colleges and universities in all states. *Brown v. Board of Education* (1954) is largely regarded as a watershed case in impacting national policy on collegiate desegregation although the case primarily considered elementary and secondary schools (Bowen & Bok, 1998; Brown, 1999; Brown & Lane, 2003). In this case, parents of four black children sued the Board of Education in Topeka, Kansas for denying their children access to the school district's all-white public schools solely because of their race. Although the Board of Education provided schools specifically designated to educate African American children, these schools could not provide an equal education due to poor facilities, a lack of materials, weak curricula, and inadequately trained and compensated teachers. In the *Brown* decision, the Supreme Court finally reversed and overturned its earlier ruling in *Plessy v. Ferguson* (1896). Under *Plessy*, states had been given the legal right to operate race-based, dual educational systems. The U.S. Supreme Court now repealed its earlier ruling, forcing all states to provide the same education to all public school students. The Civil Rights Act of 1964 followed the *Brown* decision, shaping the arguments of this ruling into a legal reality. In addition, the *Brown* decision was also supported and specifically applied to higher education through *Florida ex rel. Hawkins v. Board of Control* (1954/1956), *Tureaud v. Louisiana State University* (1954), and *Adams v. Richardson* (1973).

Similar to the *Sipuel, McLaurin* and *Sweatt* cases, the case of *Florida ex rel. Hawkins v. Board of Control* involved a black student suing to gain access to a graduate/professional degree program. Scholars suggest that the Florida and U.S. Supreme Court's reluctance to apply the *Brown* decision to higher education contexts is reflected in this case (Brown & Lane, 2003). First, the court ordered that *Florida ex rel. Hawkins* be remanded for further review under the new legal standard (*Florida ex rel. Hawkins v. Board of Control of Florida,* 347 U.S. 971 [1954]). Oddly, the court did not issue a final decision in *Florida ex rel. Hawkins* until 1958. Eventually, the court ruled that the Board of Control could not deny admissions to University of Florida's graduate and professional schools on the basis of race but upheld Hawkins' denial from the University of Florida Law School (*Hawkins v. Board of Control,* 162 F. Supp. 851 [N. D. Fl. 1958]). Brown and Lane (2003) note a key difference between K-12 schools and collegiate contexts in the *Florida ex rel. Hawkins* decision. They observe that states are obligated by law to provide an equal elementary and secondary education to all students but not required to provide a college education to anyone. Brown and Lane further point out that, as demonstrated in the *Florida ex rel. Hawkins* case, the courts were reluctant to become involved in collegiate admissions decisions, making large-scale higher education desegregation difficult. Another case regarding higher education is also similar.

In the case, *Tureaud v. Louisiana State University* (1954), Black students wanted the State of Louisiana to allow them to enroll in a combined six-year arts and sciences and law program at Louisiana State University. The plaintiffs in the case argued that a similar state-sponsored program at Southern University was not equal to the program at Louisiana State University. The state attempted a failed compromise in light of precedents set forth in *Brown*. *Tureaud* extended the reach of *Brown* and *Florida ex rel. Hawkins* to all collegiate levels given that the six-year program involved in the case concerned both undergraduate and professional study (Brown & Lane, 2003). Notwithstanding, the win for collegiate desegregation in the *Tureaud* case still did not lead to desegregation policy across states.

In 1964, however, President Lyndon B. Johnson signed the Civil Rights Act of 1964, which led to many states' attempts to end segregation. Scholars argue that the Civil Rights Act of 1964 enhanced the implementation of *Brown v. Board of Education* (Brown and Lane, 2003; Williams, 1988). Specifically, Title VI of the Civil Rights Act provided previously nonexistent sanctions which punished institutions that failed to abide by anti-discrimination legislation. Title VI of the Civil Rights Act of 1964 prohibited segregated schools and colleges from receiving federal funds to ensure compliance.

The Civil Rights Act of 1964 also led to the development of diversity programs in addition to providing sanctions for noncompliance. Historically, diversity programs called for special consideration in employment, education, and contracting decisions for minorities and women. Title VI's premise was to end the practice of the "separate but equal" doctrine and to allow greater participation in higher education among American citizens. According to scholars, Title VI thus became the basis for diversity programs in higher education (Brown & Lane, 2003). In June of 1965, President Johnson issued Executive Order #11246 at the Historically Black Howard University in Washington D.C. Executive Order #11246 required equal opportunity employment. More specifically, federal contractors or federally assisted construction contractors were prohibited from discriminating based on race, color, religion, sex, or national origin. President Johnson observes,

> You do not wipe away the scars of centuries by saying: Now you are free to go where you want, and do as you desire, and choose the leaders you please. You do not take a person who, for years, had been hobbled by chains and liberate him, bring him up to the starting line of a race and then say, 'you are free to compete with all the others,' and still justly believe that you have been completely fair (Brunner, 2001, p. 4).

Brown and Lane (2003) argue that, in issuing Executive Order #11246, President Johnson effectively adopted one of the first diversity programs to be supported by the Civil Rights Act of 1964. The U.S. Department of Education also developed a variety of programs and initiatives designed to increase participation in higher education among women and students of color at previously segregated institutions. First, the department awarded fellowships to interested researchers from traditionally underrepresented groups. Second, the department gave priority in awarding grants for new facilities to institutions serving a significant number of economically disadvantaged students and students of color. Other federal agencies created set-aside programs for universities engaged in increasing participation among people of color. Colleges and universities followed this pattern.

Many colleges and universities also developed their own diversity programs, crafting goals, timetables, and incentives for recruiting persons of color. Notwithstanding, Office of Civil Rights (OCR) investigations found many Southern colleges and universities refused to comply with the Civil Rights Act of 1964. More specifically, nineteen southern and border states continued to operate dual higher education systems albeit that Title VI sanctioned this behavior.

Reversing this trend was the goal of *Adams v. Richardson* (1973). In this case, plaintiffs brought a lawsuit against Elliot Richardson, Secretary of Health, Education, and Welfare (HEW) who, the plaintiffs alleged, failed to enforce Title VI of the Civil Rights Act of 1964. The District of Columbia Circuit Court of Appeals ruled in favor of the plaintiffs. In addition, this court implemented mechanisms (i.e., less state control) to force HEW to uphold Title VI. Like cases before it, however, *Adams* did not define strategies for attaining desegregation or any related issues of applying and enforcing policy (Brown &

Lane, 2003). The following era, though, would be one in which desegregation efforts were heavily debated.

Post-1970s collegiate desegregation legislation continues to largely affect diversity programs today (Brown, 1999). Much dissension and debate have emerged in the wake of changing public priorities and divergent court decisions. Namely, *Regents of University of California v. Bakke* (1978) is one case which has complicated how colleges develop diversity programs and initiatives. In this case, Alan Bakke, a White male seeking admission to the University of California-Davis Medical School, charged the institution with practicing reverse discrimination after he was twice rejected. At the time, the UC-Davis Medical School operated a special admissions program in which disadvantaged members of underrepresented minority groups were chosen to fill 16 out of the 100 places allotted to each year's entering class. The Supreme Court upheld the California Supreme Court's earlier decision which found the admissions program to use a quota system and thus violating the Equal Protection Clause of the Fourteenth Amendment. However, the Supreme Court also reversed part of the California Supreme court's decision finding unacceptable considerations of race in the admissions process. Ambiguity emerged from the very justices who brought judgment. Justice Lewis Powell, who casted a swing-vote in the ruling, argued against race as a factor in the admissions process while simultaneously arguing an ethnically diverse student body carries educational benefits. (Brown, 1999; Justiz, Wilson, & Bjork, 1994). This ruling thus added little direction to higher education regarding the place and function of diversity programs. Subsequently, challenges to diversity programs and civil rights legislation emerged after judgment in *Bakke*.

In fact, a variety of legal challenges have sought more lucid judgment of collegiate diversity programs. Though neither considered collegiate contexts specifically, *Wygant v. Jackson Board of Education* (1986) and *Richmond v. Croson* (1989) impacted debate over diversity programs. In both cases, people of color received protections or differential treatments via quota systems which were later deemed violations of the Equal Protection Clause in the Fourteenth Amendment. Adding to the *Bakke* ruling, the Supreme Court argued that diversity programs must support a compelling interest of the state. The Court also established the "strict scrutiny" test to provide additional clarity regarding how diversity programs may be shaped. This ruling eliminated the general use of historical discrimination to justify the existence of diversity programs. The strict scrutiny test is referenced in significant legal disputes emergent in collegiate contexts. *Kirwan v. Podberesky* (1992), for example, led to the repeal of the Benjamin Banneker Scholarship Program at the University of Maryland (which served African American students) the Fourth Circuit Court eventually found that the university scholarship program did not satisfy the strict scrutiny test. The final resolution not only ended the Benjamin Banneker Scholarship but highlighted the difficulties institutions face in legally shaping diversity programs even within institutions with the worst histories of segregation (Brown, 1999).

Like *Podberesky*, *Hopwood v. State of Texas* (1994) also involved the *strict scrutiny* test. In this case, Cheryl Hopwood and three other White students filed suit against the State of Texas, the University of Texas Board of Regents, the University of Texas School of Law, and other affiliated defendants, Hopwood and her co-plaintiffs alleged that the defendants violated both the Equal Protection Clause of the Fourteenth Amendment and Title VI of the Civil Rights Act of 1964 by operating a quota system that gave preferential treatment to African American and Mexican American law school applicants. Eventually, the Fifth Circuit Court decided that University of Texas School of Law violated both the Fourteenth Amendment and the Civil Rights Act of 1964. In addition, the Fifth Circuit also ruled that the School of Law must eliminate race from its admissions decisions. Since the *Hopwood* decision, few states have successfully eliminated the use of diversity programs altogether and thus made the future of diversity programs and initiatives more uncertain (Brown, 1999).

Nationally, the use of diversity programs to achieve collegiate desegregation remains unresolved (Brown & Lane, 2003). State university systems in California and Texas, for example, have adopted various methods to maintain enrollments among students of color in certain universities. Given statewide elections, diversity programs and college systems were forced to think about attaining diversity in different ways. Subsequently, new priorities for college systems included reconsidering how qualifying exams are assessed or guaranteeing acceptances for students who graduate in the top 10 percent of their high school classes. However, attempts to enact legislation ending diversity programs in Michigan failed (Brown & Lane, 2003).

Diversity programs remain controversial in Michigan. In both *Gratz v. Bollinger* (2001) and *Grutter v. Bollinger* (2001), plaintiffs contended that University of Michigan admissions programs violated both the Equal Protection Clause of the Fourteenth Amendment and Title VI of the Civil Rights Act of 1964. Respectively, White undergraduates were rejected by the University of Michigan College of Literature, Science, and the Arts (LSA) and the University of Michigan Law School. In the *Gratz* ruling issued on February 26, 2001, the Southern Division of the Eastern District Court of Michigan found unconstitutional use of race in admissions by the University of Michigan College of LSA. This same court provided a similar decision a month later in the *Grutter* case, ruling that the University of Michigan Law School's admissions program violated both the Fourteenth Amendment and Title VI of the Civil Rights Act. In addition, the court also issued an injunction barring the Law School from considering race in its admissions process. Although the University is appealing the *Grutter* case, diversity programs at the University of Michigan appear likely to end (Brown & Lane, 2003). Today, transdemographic enrollments represent ways in which colleges may work to attain diverse enrollments.

Transdemography

Colleges, among other societal institutions, inherited the challenge of righting the effects of past wrongs. The perennial discourses on collegiate desegregation highlight this challenge. Notwithstanding, state coordinating boards and institutional boards of trustees are moving forward with implementing collegiate desegregation compliance initiatives (Brown, 1999; Brown, 2001; Brown & Freeman, 2004). The result is a collection of ad hoc policies and practices which promote changing the statistical composition of the student population within the corresponding institutions based solely on race—transdemography (Brown, 2002).

Transdemography offers colleges dominated by both Black and/or White enrollments an opportunity to enrich the student campus context and to encourage intercultural communication within the academic environment (Brown, 1999). However, transdemography simultaneously threatens to eradicate the rich campus culture for which colleges with population focus (i.e., HBCUs) are lauded, with scant implications for campuses populated primarily by White constituents (Brown & Freeman, 2004; Fleming, 1984; Garibaldi, 1984; Hytche, 1989; Roebuck & Murty, 1993). Current collegiate desegregation initiatives have as their primary aim attracting White students to Historically Black Colleges and Universities (HBCUs) (Brown, 1999; Brown & Freeman, 2004). As an interesting turn, existing compliance plans proffer limited resources or support for targeting significant increases in African American student attendance at Historically White Institutions (HWIs) within the respective states. Collegiate desegregation has morphed into a transdemographic enrollment initiative. It is important for scholars and administrators to attend to the unintended consequences that have and continue to emerge from these shifting enrollments, terrains, and possibly paradigms.

One way of attending to these consequences is through effectively managing diversity on college campuses. This requires thinking about diversity management differently from a diversity program as discussed above in the review of turbulently evolving legal policy. Thinking about diversity management as affirmative action programs likely leads to the debates which shaped the court cases in this section. Notwithstanding, colleges campuses benefit when personnel and policy pay close attention to inclusion of diverse individuals and work to manage diversity effectively. It is the research on these topics that the following section considers.

The Benefits of Diversity

Change is difficult in higher education, and if judged by past performance, change to enact diverse learning and professional environments is particularly hard. The values and organizational dynamics of higher education are unique and especially problematic for making foundational and cultural change. At their core, higher education institutions do function like corporations, hospitals, or any other type of for-profit or nonprofit organization. Irrational systems, nebulous and multiples goals structures, complex and differentiated campus functions, conflicts between espoused and enacted values, and loosely coupled systems of organization and governance are just some of the dynamics that make organizational change in higher education so hard. Such change requires frameworks and tools that are able to respond to these complex campus dynamics as well as to the external environment (Williams, Berger, & McClendon, 2005, p. 2).

In the above quote, Williams, Berger, and McClendon (2005) describe how diversity-focused change in higher education is complicated by the divergent interests of colleges to provide high-quality education while also holding true to national policy and core values shared across organizations. In this section, this chapter considers the ways in which diversity benefits colleges and universities in their capacities as organizations as well as spaces in which students are educated. First, research is explored that finds diversity as an educational benefit to students, demanding interventions that potentially conflict with organizational values and dynamics. Second, this chapter turns to the limited empirical work that considers how diversity influences colleges and universities organizationally. Research on how diversity influences organizational effectiveness in the private sector is more aptly located. Much of this work indicates that racial, cultural, and ethnic diversity advantages organizations and presents strategies for effectively managing diversity.

Educational Benefit for Students

Research describing the ways in which individuals benefit from diversity on campus undergirds sustained attention to diversity on college campuses and universities. Educational benefit refers to the ways in which educational experiences and outcomes of individual students are enhanced by the presence of diversity on campus (Milem, 2003). The research on the educational benefits of diversity for students clusters around three types: (1) structural diversity or the numerical representation of diverse groups on a campus; (2) informal interactional diversity or the actual experience students have with diverse peers; and (3) classroom diversity or the exposure to knowledge about race and ethnicity in formal classrooms (Gurin, Dey, Gurin, & Hurtado, 2003). In this framework, structural diversity represents a fundamental level of diverse interactions (Gurin et al., 2003). As benefits evokes diversity outcomes, three major types of outcomes are outlined in the literature.

First, learning outcomes describe students' active learning processes including campus engagement and academic learning as well as student motivation to engage and students' reflection on the value of the college experience after graduation (Gurin et al., 2003). Second, democracy outcomes refer to how higher education prepares students to become involved as active participants in an increasingly diverse society. In their work, Gurin and colleagues suggest three levels of democracy outcomes: citizenship-engagement, racial/cultural engagement, and compatibility of differences. Citizenship engagement describes students' interest and motivation in influencing society and the political structure, in participating in the community and volunteer service. Racial/cultural engagement refers to students' levels of cultural awareness and appreciation and their commitment to participate in activities that promote racial understanding. Compatibility of differences describes students' comprehension of common values across racial/ethnic groups and constructive ways in which to dissolve conflict. Milem (2003) expounds on Gurin et al.'s concepts with two types of diversity outcomes. Process outcomes reflect the ways in which students perceive diversity as shaping their college experiences. Material benefits describe students' material outcomes (i.e., higher salary) associated with attendance at diverse colleges. Much of the research on the relationship between diversity and student outcomes is conducted within these conceptual parameters.

Hurtado (2003) studied how colleges prepare students to live and work in a diverse democracy and the ways in which students learn from their interaction with diverse peers in college. Hurtado surveyed chief academic officers at four-year institutions, entering freshman classes at ten public universities, classroom-based studies, focus groups, document analysis and administrator interviews. Regarding the benefits of diversity on college campuses, Hurtado found that students who report frequent contact with diverse peers experience greater cognitive complexity, self-confidence in being culturally aware and see conflict as natural in the democractic process. More specifically, positive and meaningful interactions were found to predict cognitive, social and democratic outcomes. Additionally, diversity courses or diversity-related programming had a consistently positive effect on most educational outcomes. This research joins with other widely cited research findings which emphasize the significant impact diversity-focused courses have on cultural understanding and overall satisfaction in college (Astin, 1993). Additional studies have also sought to understand the link between diversity and learning on college campuses.

Chang (1996) studied racial diversity in higher education with the understanding that little consensus exists regarding the essentiality of racially diverse campus to college student educational gains. He found that White students largely benefit in developing cultural competency from engaging racially diverse others and, in particular, discussing topics of race. Findings also indicated institutions with greater institutional diversity among collegiate personnel tend to have greater faculty diversity emphasis, diverse student bodies, and enhanced opportunities to promote learning around diversity (i.e., attending cultural awareness workshops, enrolling in ethnic studies courses).

Studying informal interactions with diversity, antonio (1998) examines the development of leadership skills, cultural knowledge, and understanding among college students. According to the author, findings suggest that casual interracial interaction is particularly beneficial among students with more racially homogeneous friendship circles, especially in developing leadership skills. In addition, findings indicate that frequent interracial interaction among students may be more important in developing cultural knowledge than involvement in formal activities such as cultural awareness workshops. antonio argues that the positive effects of interracial interaction on leadership ability and cultural knowledge support claims that a diverse student body matters in preparing students for multicultural citizenship.

Later, antonio (2001) studied diversity in the context of friendship groups at the University of California, Los Angeles (UCLA). More specifically, he was interested in the influence of friendship groups on students' development of racial understanding, cultural awareness, and interracial interaction. antonio observes that structural diversity in the student body increases opportunity for students to develop friendships with people of different cultures and ethnicities. He found that students identified racial diversity to be the most positive of their interpersonal experiences on campus. In addition, he argues that developing interracial relationships shapes a sense of courage in students to socialize across races. This finding brings to mind widely cited research findings which showed that students who reported frequent interactions with diverse peers were more open to diverse perspectives and willing to challenge their own beliefs (Pascarella, Edison, Nora, Hagedorn, & Terenzini, 1996). Additional study explores factors that predict these and similar cross-racial interactions among college students.

Saenz, Ngai, and Hurtado (2007) explore factors that promoted positive interactions across race for African American, Asian American, Latino, and White college students. Drawing upon survey data from incoming students at nine public institutions, the authors found that exposure to a predominantly White pre-college environment significantly predicted for interracial interactions. More specifically, diverse neighborhood, school, and peer group environments helped students become more comfortable in interactions across race. For Latino students, high SAT scores and gender (being female) was a high predictor for cross-race interaction. In a similar vein as research presented in this review, White students became more comfortable with cross-racial interactions after interacting with diverse peers.

Based on the review of research above, overwhelming evidence shows important relationships between diversity and student gains. Specifically, cross-racial interactions as well as campus and classroom opportunities to engage issues of racial/ethnic/cultural difference positively impact student outcomes. Considerable evidence also shows that students develop confidence in engaging topics of difference and competence for assuming roles in a diversified, global citizenry. In the next section, research is considered on how organizations engage topics of diversity to enhance effectiveness.

Managing Diversity as Organizational Benefit

Taylor Cox (1994) defines managing diversity as planning and implementing organizational systems and practices to maximize the potential advantages of diversity while minimizing the potential disadvantages of diversity. He notes that three types of organizational goals are achieved by managing diversity. Largely, these goals involve moral, ethical, and social responsibility, legal obligations of organizations, and economic performance goals. In a review of arguments on how diversity creates competitive advantage in organizations, Cox and Blake (1991) surmise that effectively managing diversity leads to the following constructive outcomes for organizations: (1) social responsibility goals are met; (2) cost advantage is created; (3) resource acquisition is increased; (4) marketing efforts are improved; (5) creativity is increased (6) better problem solving and decision making is promoted; and (7) system flexibility to better react to environmental changes is created. In this, and additional work (Cox, 1994) argues that properly managing diversity leads to lower turnover rates, greater time-on-task flexibility, and greater organizational productivity.

It is important that the concept of diversity management not be confused with affirmative action. Organizations more readily perceive affirmative action with legal obligation to diversify a workforce (Cox, 1994). Research evidence in the private sector casts doubt on the simple assertion that a diverse workforce inevitably improves organizational performance (Jayne & Dipboye, 2004). Diversity management, rather, involves strategies that recognize connectedness between inclusiveness and overall organizational goals and does not attempt to advantage a specific group as affirmative action does (Gilbert, Stead, & Invancevich, 1999). Though research shows affirmative action programs have made organizations more equitable, little research connects affirmative action programs to an organization's achievement of its goals (Reskin, 1998). However, research does show that inclusion of minority perspectives stimulates alternative ways to achieve goals (Cox, 1994). In addition, these groups are found in the research literature to be more creative in ways that move organizations effectively toward their goals.

However, Cox (1994) also identifies problems associated with organizations that seek to diversify. First, he observes that heterogeneity in groups may lead to lower levels of cohesiveness. Cox argues that cohesiveness is more attainable in groups that are homogeneous. Yet communication among diverse groups may negatively impact cohesiveness. Cox writes that communication among heterogeneous groups is less effective. Communication difficulty, Cox argues, is linked with discomfort in participating in groups, increased anxieties among organization members, and increased conflict and potential for conflict. Cox's observations lend support to arguments that mere diversification of individuals is not always positive.

Notwithstanding, research among colleges and universities does find the simple inclusion of women or faculty of color as important factors in enriching the primary missions of universities (Milem, 2003). In a recent study of diverse faculty impact on university work, Milem found race and gender to serve as significant predictors of the use of active learning methods in the classroom. These, in turn, positively impacted the learning process for students. In his recent review of research, Milem (2003) cited a study conducted by Statham, Richardson, and Cook (1991) which found that assistant professors were more likely to adopt participatory teaching practices than full professors. In this same research review, he notes other studies he conducted in which he found strong correlations between faculty members race and gender and student-centered approaches which positively impact student learning. The majority of research that considers issues of hiring or inclusion of collegiate personnel largely implicates faculty (Milem et al., 2005). However, a study is located that identifies factors for creating a positive climate for diversity and factor predictability regarding positive campus climate for diversity.

In their work, Mayhew, Grunwald, and Dey (2006) studied factors that influenced staff perceptions of their campus community as positive climates for diversity. Based on their empirical evidence, the researchers argue that an institution's ability to achieve a positive climate for diversity reflects not only the personal characteristics of staff members but also their perceptions of the work environment. Additional empirical work is needed to investigate how diversity impacts collegiate personnel and how diversity is managed in collegiate contexts.

This chapter has reviewed a range of policy and research that shapes higher education's understanding of how diversity matters to the work of colleges and universities. The research reviewed provides evidence that diversity not only matters in colleges but must be effectively managed in order to sustain positive outcomes for student learning. Therefore, it is important that institutional structures and practices that present barriers to diversity are identified, examined, challenged, and removed. It is additionally important to understand practical strategies that enhance colleges' and universities' abilities to manage diversity. These ideas are presented in the following section.

Managing Diversity in Colleges and Universities

As the research evidence shows, structural diversity alone does not guarantee that students will benefit from positive learning outcomes. Along these lines, Liu (1998) writes, "often neglected in the debate about diversity is the fact that achieving a racially diverse study body by itself is not sufficient to bring about desired educational outcomes. How that diversity is managed matters greatly" (p. 438). The chapter joins with additional writing that warns colleges and universities against thinking about challenges of diversity as concerning only affirmative action or admissions (Liu, 1998; Milem, 2003). Liu argues,

To establish a "compelling interest" in educational diversity, a university must

> demonstrate clear, consistent internal policies and practices designed to facilitate interracial contact, dialogue, and understanding on campus (Liu, 1998, p. 439)

With this in mind, this chapter offers ideas and strategic questions to campuses to help them in their efforts to effectively manage diversity. Ability to implement these strategies may vary depending on a number of institutional factors.

1. *Colleges and universities should thread diversity-focused questions through all aspects of planning and implementation.* Questions include: What policies, practices, and ways of thinking within colleges and universities (and their divisions and units) have differential impact on different groups? What organizational changes should be made to meet the needs of a diverse workforce we employ as well as the one we plan to graduate? Do these changes maximize the potential of all workers, positioning colleges to meet the demands of a global citizenry? These questions may be posed within academic affairs, within student affairs, and in conversations about collaboration between the two divisions. Collegiate personnel and students must be encouraged to challenge institutional barriers that present cultural barriers without fear of retaliation. This notion should be expressed in policy and among the senior leadership of the institution.
2. *College offices, divisions, and units should make every attempt to diver-*

sify personnel on multiple dimensions. First, colleges must continue to evolve their understanding of diversity. Dimensions of diversity include but are not limited to: age, ethnicity, ancestry, gender, affect, endeavor, physical abilities/qualities, race, sexual orientation, educational background, geographic location, income, marital status, military experience, religious beliefs, parental status, and work experience. Second, colleges should remember that, in organizations, heterogeneity is found to promote creativity, to produce thoughtful solutions to problems, and a higher level of critical analysis. Third, when diversifying personnel hires, college units should do the following: (1) specify in job announcements that skills to work effectively in a diverse environment are required; (2) recognize that diverse efforts may be required to recruit a diverse applicant pool, particularly underutilized minorities and women. A key question emerges: On what e-mail list-servs and websites or in what publications that center diverse issues might we advertise? (3) consider transferable skills (i.e., communication, coordination) alongside other desired skills; (4) use a panel interview format comprised of committees in which individuals represent various dimensions of diversity to represent different perspectives and to eliminate bias from the selection process. Soliciting feedback may also eliminate potential bias; (5) ensure disabled applicants have appropriate accommodations.

3. *Colleges and universities should mine opportunities where collegiate personnel and students may openly discuss racial, ethnic, and cultural issues*. Cultural awareness workshops involving college and university faculty and staff should be mandated. Colleges are also encouraged to recognize connectedness to atypical individuals or groups (i.e., board of trustee members, parents, community organizations, professional associations) in building committees, panels, groups, and teams who participate in cultural awareness and intercultural communications. Individuals or groups who facilitate these efforts should attempt to introduce knowledge of diverse cultures and oppressed groups to provide all with a language of awareness, pushing against language of assumption and bias. Such can engage simple but important questions: What does respect look like across cultures? How is it shown across cul-

tures? What are the politics of greeting each other, holding conversation, and eye contact? How do we know what various cultures need?

4. *Individual and team assessment must be developed.* Colleges and universities must recognize the importance of assessment given the accountability to students as shaped by national policy and large-scale research. College personnel must assess their own values, skills, understanding of norms and truth. They must also be able to recognize that these may not be shared by others and to envision difference as potential learning opportunities. Assessment teams, staff, or staff members must continue to monitor personnel work climate and student learning and engagement climate. Technology-based assessments conveniently lend themselves to these efforts. However, more in-depth assessments are conducted in focus group contexts. All staff must recognize the ways in which assessment benefits their offices and the ways in which they can act as assessors.
5. *Faculty may manage diversity in class.* Faculty are in position to shape classroom environments that clarify, tease out, and eradicate the presence of cultural stereotypes where they reside in-class and out-of-class. In complement, faculty who seek to shape an equity pedagogy must develop knowledge about different cultures as well as embrace communication patterns, norms, teaching that are culturally sensitive. Additionally, faculty should be creative in shaping in-class and out-of-class group projects that may hold potential for students to develop cross-cultural competencies.
6. *College units must envision connectedness where it is not readily apparent.* Colleges units (i.e., academic affairs, student affairs, fiscal affairs) and sub-units of these must not balkanize themselves. Rather, they are challenged to re-think means that achieve ends and, where possible, establish connections across campus in the interests of student learning and success. Academic affairs and student affairs collaborations are perhaps the most cutting-edge examples. Establishing student-centered communities or practicum opportunities, for example, where student affairs staff and faculty may participate to engage topics of diversity, ethnicity, or multiculturalism show tremendous promise to enhance learning

for all students.

7. *Colleges and universities must be inclusive in their recruitment strategies.* Colleges and universities that actively recruit students are required to be inclusive when inviting area, regional, or national high schools to send their students for recruitment weekends or visits. Colleges and universities should make efforts to diversify pools of alumni who may also formally and informally recruit on their behalf.

Given extant policy and research, the ideas presented above represent effective ways in which colleges and universities may potentially manage diversity. Colleges and universities should recall that they are reflections of the broader society, often mimicking society's thinking and actions (Bowman & Smith, 2002). When students arrive on campus, they should discover open institutional climates where difference is envisioned as important for learning, collaboration, and conflict resolution.

Conclusion

Like other organizations, managing diversity on college campuses focuses on maximizing the ability of all employees to contribute to college and university goals. Colleges and universities must intentionally divorce the concept of managing diversity from affirmative action. As described in this chapter, affirmative action focuses on specific groups who have experienced historical discrimination (i.e., people of color, women). Managing diversity, conversely, pushes beyond merely rectifying underrepresentation to envision ways in which racial, ethnic, and cultural diversity enhances college and university missions of teaching, research, and service. In policy and practice, these differences can be clear. Institutional commitment and conditions are necessary to transform practical ideas to reality.

References

antonio, a. l. (1998). *Student interaction across race and outcomes in college.* Paper presented at the American Educational Research Association.

antonio, a. l. (2001). Diversity and the influence of friendship groups in college. *The Review of Higher Education, 25*(1), 63–89.

Astin, A. W. (1993). *What matters in college?: Four critical years revisited.* San Francisco, CA: Jossey-Bass.

Bowen, W., & Bok, D. (1998). *The shape of the river: Long-term consequences of considering race in college and university admissions.* Princeton, NJ: Princeton University Press.

Bowman, P., & Smith, W. A. (2002). Racial ideology in the campus community: Emerging cross-ethnic differences and challenges. In W. A. Smith, P. G. Altbach & K. Lomotey (Eds.), *The racial crisis in American higher education: Continuing challenges for the twenty-first century*. New York: SUNY Press.

Brown, M. C. (1999). *The quest to define collegiate desegregation: Black Colleges, Title VI compliance, and post-Adams litigation.* Westport, CT: Bergin & Garvey.

Brown, M. C. (2001). Collegiate desegregation and the public black college: A new policy mandate. *Journal of Higher Education, 72,* 46-62.

Brown, M. C. (2002). Good intentions: Collegiate desegregation and transdemographic enrollments. *The Review of Higher Education, 25,* 263–280.

Brown, M. C., & Lane, J. (2003). Studying diverse institutions: Contexts, challenges, and considerations, *New directions for institutional research*. San Francisco: Jossey-Bass.

Brown, M.C., & Freeman, K. (Eds.). (2004). *Black colleges: New perspectives on policy and practice.* Westport, CT: Praeger.

Brunner, B. (2001). *Timeline of affirmative action milestones.* Retrieved March 6, 2002, from http://www.factmonster.com/spot/affirmative timeline1.html#1965.

Chang, M. (1996). Racial diversity in higher education: Does a racially mixed student population affect educational outcomes? Unpublished doctoral dissertation. University of California, Los Angeles.

Chang, M. J., & Kiang, P. N. (2002). New challenges of representing Asian American students in U.S. higher education. In W. A. Smith, P. G. Altbach & K. Lomotey (Eds.), *The racial crisis in American higher education: Continuing challenges for the twenty-first century*. Albany: SUNY Press.

Cohn, A. M. (1998). *The shaping of American higher education: emergence and growth of the contemporary system.* San Francisco: Jossey Bass.

Cox, T. H. (1994). *Managing cultural diversity in organizations: Theory, research, and practice.* San Francisco: Berrett-Koehler.

Cox, T. H., & Blake, S. (1991). Managing cultural diversity: Implications for organizational competitiveness. *The Executive, 5*(3), 45–56.

Dancy, T. E., & Brown, M. C. (in press). Predominantly white colleges and universities. In K. Lomotey (Ed.), *The encyclopedia of African American education.* Thousand Oaks, CA: Sage.

Fleming, J. (1984). Blacks in college: A comparative study of students' success in black and in white institutions. San Francisco: Jossey-Bass.

Garibaldi, A. (Ed.). (1984). *Black colleges and universities: Challenges for the future.* New York: Praeger.

Geiger, R. (1999). The ten generations of American higher education. In P. Altbach, R. Berdahl & P. Gumport (Eds.), *American higher education in the twenty-first century: Social, political, and economic challenges.* Baltimore: Johns Hopkins University Press.

Gilbert, J., Stead, B., & Invancevich, J. (1999). Diversity management: A new organizational paradigm. *Journal of Business Ethics, 21*(1), 61–76.

Gordon, L. A. (1997). From seminary to university: An overview of women's higher education, 1870--1920. In L. F. Goodchild & H. S. Wechsler (Eds.), *The history of higher education.* Boston, MA: Pearson.

Gurin, P. Y., Dey, E. L., Gurin, G., & Hurtado, S. (2003). How does racial/ethnic diversity promote education? *The Western Journal of Black Studies, 27*(1), 20–29.

Hurtado, S. (2003). *Preparing college students for a diverse democracy: Final report to the U.S. Department of Education. OERI. Field Initiated Studies Program.* Ann Arbor, MI: Center for the Study of Higher and Postesecondary Education.

Hurtado, S. (2007). Linking diversity with the educational and civic missions of higher education. *The Review of Higher Education, 30*(2), 185–196.

Hurtado, S., Milem, J. F., Clayton-Pedersen, A. R., & Allen, W. (1999). *Enacting diverse learning environments: Improving the climate for racial/ethnic diversity in higher education*. ASHE-ERIC Higher Education Report. Washington, DC: George Washington University.

Hytche, W. P. (1989). *A national resource--A national challenge: The 1890 land-grant colleges and universities*. Washington, D.C.: United States Department of Agriculture.

Jayne, M., & Dipboye, R. (2004). Leveraging diversity to improve business performance: Research findings and recommendations for organizations. *Human Resource Management, 43*(4), 409–424.

Justiz, M. J., Wilson, R.,& Björk, L. G. (1994). *Minorities in higher education*. Phoenix, AZ: American Council on Education.

Kuh, G. D., Schuh, J. H., Whitt, E. J., Andreas, R. E., Lyons, J. W., Strange, C. C., et al. (1991). *Involving colleges: Successful approaches to fostering student learning and personal development outside the classroom*. San Francisco: Jossey-Bass.

Levine, D. O. (1997). Discrimination in college admissions. In L. F. Goodchild & H. S. Wechsler (Eds.), *The history of higher education*. Boston, MA: Pearson.

Liu, G. (1998). Affirmative action in higher education: The diversity rationale and the compelling interest test. *Harvard Civil Rights-Civil Liberties Law Review, 33*, 381–442.

Mayhew, M., Grunwald, H., & Dey, E. L. (2006). Breaking the silence: Achieving a positive campus climate for diversity from the staff perspective. *Research in Higher Education, 47*(1), 63–88.

Milem, J. F. (2003). The educational benefits of diversity: Evidence from multiple sectors. In M. J. Chang, D. Witt, J. James & K. Hakuta (Eds.), *Compelling interest: Examining racial dynamics in colleges and universities*. Palo Alto, CA: Stanford University Press.

Milem, J. F., Chang, M. J., & antonio, a. l. (2005). *Making diversity work on campus: A research based perspective*: Making Excellence Inclusive Initiative. Association of American Colleges and Universities.

Pascarella, E., Edison, M., Nora, A., Hagedorn, L., & Terenzini, P. (1996). Influences on students' openness to diversity and challenge in the first year of college. *Journal of Higher Education, 67*(2), 174–195.

Reskin, B. F. (1998). *The realities of affirmative action in employment.* Washington, D.C.: American Sociological Association.

Roebuck, J. B., & Murty, K. S. (1993). *Historically black colleges and universities: Their place in American higher education.* Westport, Connecticut: Praeger Publishers.

Rudolph, F. (1962). *The American college and university.* New York: Random House.

Saenz, V. B., Ngai, H. N., & Hurtado, S. (2007). Factors influencing positive interactions across race for African American, Asian American, Latino, and White college students. *Research in Higher Education, 48*(1).

Stage, F. K., & Manning, K. (1992). Enhancing the multicultural campus environment: A cultural brokering approach, *New directions for student services.* San Francisco: Jossey-Bass.

Statham, A., Richardson, L., & Cook, J. (1991). *Gender and university teaching: A negotiated difference.* Albany, NY: SUNY.

Thelin, J. R. (2004). *A history of American higher education.* Baltimore, MA: JHU Press

Williams, D., Berger, J., & McClendon, S. (2005). *Toward a model of inclusive excellence and change in postsecondary institutions: Making Excellence Inclusive Initiative.* Association of American Colleges and Universities.

Williams, J. (Ed.). (1988). *Desegregating America's colleges and universities: Title VI regulation of higher education.* New York: Teachers College Press.

PART TWO

Identity Politics on College Campuses

CHAPTER SIX

Women Leaders in Higher Education: Constructions of Organization, Reduction, and Rejuvenation

Penny A. Pasque

Diaries provide an insight into a person's lived experiences. They have the potential to transport us to past centuries, uncover true loves, or move us to tears. There are a number of famous diaries that have been published over the years including Anne Frank's "Kitty," which is one of the most world-renowned diaries ever written. Anne Frank describes her life in hiding with family and four friends in Amsterdam during the German occupation. She chronicles her daily life from June 12, 1942 to August 1, 1944 prior to her death in a concentration camp. It was her father, the only living survivor from the family, who found and published her diary. Virginia Woolf, another famous diarist, wrote numerous personal accounts of her life as an English novelist and writer. Through her later years, she provided evidence of her life of depression, and this information provides great insight into how depression can deeply impact lives. Other famous diarists include Alanis Morissette, Stevie Nicks, Alice Walker, Andy Warhol, Elie Wiesel, General George Patton, Lewis Carroll, and Courtney Love. Blogs, Facebook, MySpace, and Twitter have become current-day diaries that provide writers with an online format and readers with up-to-date information, photos and videos.

From these hard copy and electronic diaries, we have the potential to learn about the intricacies of people's daily lives and the depth of various experiences. This information can be quite instructive as we create inclusive climates in colleges and universities, supervise or are supervised by people with various gender identities, and craft policy that directly impacts the experiences of students, staff and faculty. In a rare opportunity, this chapter explores a diary collectively kept for nine years by women elected to the leadership of a national association in higher education. The women are from various positions across college campuses, represent multiple racial identities, and hold positions at different points in their professional and/or scholarly careers. The women embark on this creative writing process together as they reflect on their experiences as women leaders in higher education and student affairs.

The goal of this chapter is to explore the written narratives of these women leaders and offer findings to help the field of higher education understand the experiences of women and work more intentionally and inclusively with women on college campuses. The orienting research questions for the larger research project are: What do the women leaders mention in this diary? What was important to communicate in this venue? I then considered the goals of this book and reflected on what women leaders communicate about the organizational behavior of this group and their experiences in the field of higher education. In order to address these questions, I share some contextual information including the statistics and experiences of women leaders in higher education and student affairs as found in the literature. Next, I briefly describe the theoretical framework, methodological approach, and the specific methods utilized in this study. Finally, I offer emergent findings from the written narratives of the women leaders and discuss the implication of these findings within the context of diversity and equity on college campuses.

Background on Women Leaders in Higher Education

A feminist conceptual model of leadership "rests on the assumption that leadership manifests itself when there is an action to bring about change in an organization, an institution, or the social system—in other words, an action to make a positive difference in people's lives. Leadership, then is conceived as a creative process that results in change" (Astin & Leland, 1991, p. 116). Over the years, there has been change in terms of the number of women that hold leadership positions and our progression through the academy. For example, Tull and Freeman (2008) replicated and extended Rickard's (1985) study and found that males held 55% of Chief Student Affairs Officers

(CSAO) titles while females held 45%, representing a significant increase for females from 22% in 1984 (to 45% in 2006). Further, in public institutions, males represented 69% of CSAOs while females represented only 31%. In private institutions the ratio was closer where males represented 56% and females 44%. Similarly, in local, tribal, and federal institutions, males represented 54% of CSAOs, females 46%. In community colleges males represented 52% of CSAOs, females 48%.

More specifically, women and people of color do not reach the position of CSAO at similar rates as White males (Reason, Walker, & Robinson, 2002). Women are more likely to be chief diversity officers (56% are women) than chief academic officers or provosts (38% women) (King & Gomez, 2008). Further, only 7% of all senior administrators are women of color, and only 3% of chief academic officers are women of color (King & Gomez, 2008).

Blackhurst (2000) found that the highest rates of career satisfaction may be reserved for White women and women in senior administrative positions. Sixty percent of these same women reported systemic discrimination in the form of salary inequity. Importantly, more subtle forms of discrimination were reported by roughly one quarter to one third of the women: 27% reported being asked to work more or longer hours than men; 33% reported being given less support than men and being assigned less rewarding or less visible tasks, and 26% reported being given less autonomy. Blackhurst also found that White women perceived significantly less sex discrimination than women of color as a group, and less than women in any specific racial or ethnic category, including African American, Asian American and Hispanic American women (specifics for Native American and Middle Eastern American women were not provided).

There has been some progress made over the years in relation to earnings, yet the gender gap remains. For example, women who work full time earn approximately 78 cents for every dollar men earn (U.S. Census Bureau & Bureau of Labor Statistics, 2008). Broken down further, African American women make approximately 67 cents and Hispanic women approximately 58 cents on the dollar, as compared to White men. The American Association of University Women (2008) provides a pay gap table, where gender earnings gaps are accessible by state.

In addition to experiencing systemic and subtle forms of discrimination, the voices of women leaders are not always considered in equal measure to those of men. For example, Talbot (1998) found that "women still do not have equal access to privileged professional discourses or to dominant speaker positions within them ... [and] as a consequence, they still struggle to make themselves heard and to have their interests served" (p. 222). In a similar vein, Wackwitz and Rakow (2004) note that women are too often

> denied access to communicative forums—interpersonal, group, organizational, and mediated—or admitted to them only to have their ideas dismissed out of hand as deviant or irrelevant. To have voice is to possess both the opportunity to speak and the respect to be heard. (p. 9)

Importantly, to be invited to the table is not enough. Voices must be heard and considered. On a related note, I found that women leaders in higher education who share "advocacy" perspectives had their perspectives reframed, redefined, and/or silenced in the higher education discourse (Pasque, in press, a).

These various research findings may appear unconnected yet represent a pattern of institutionalized sexism displayed in a higher education context, even with participants who may have the best intentions to embark upon transformative educational change (an assumption). Resistance to this marginalization by women is found to be a political strategy toward change (Gilligan, Rogers & Tolman, 1991) and provides a foundation from which to explore the complexities of gender in education and alternatives to current paradigms. I have argued elsewhere that if a more thorough understanding of leaders' perspectives is not offered, then dominant perspectives will prevail without consideration of alternative perspectives, which may be useful particularly in this time of dramatic economic and social change in higher education (Pasque, 2007, in press, b). To take this concept one step further, the perpetuation of the current trajectory and the continued marginalization of perspectives offered by women may be detrimental to working toward social justice and educational equity, as we are missing leaders' perspectives that may support positive transformation.

I approach this study with the assumption that, as described above, all things are not equal—or equitable—in terms of gender in higher education. Further, gender identity intersects with other social identities such as race, ethnicity, ability, class, age, religion, nationality, etc. (see Jones & McEwen, 2000; Adams, 1997). I also hold an assumption that allies are vital to education management and the revision of equity on college campuses; we must all work toward interrupting the current status quo and implementing change strategies toward educational equity and social justice. My hope is that the voices of these women are instructive as we move forward with these efforts.

Theoretical Framework and Methods

bell hooks's definition of feminism is one that has transcended generations of theorists. She states, "simply put, feminism is a movement to end sexism, sexist exploitation, and oppression" (2000, 1; Also see hooks, 1984/2000). This study takes a feminist perspective, drawing from feminist epistemology and feminist theory. Feminist epistemology—the philosophical grounding for deciding what kinds of knowledge are possible—addresses the connections between knowledge and its social uses and how patriarchal values have shaped the content and structure of that knowledge. Feminist theory is founded on three main principles (Ropers-Huilman 2002). First, women have something valuable to contribute to every aspect of the world. Second, as an oppressed group, women have been unable to achieve their potential, receive rewards or gain full participation in society. Third, feminist research should do more than critique, but should work toward social transformation.

More specifically, I pull from elements of radical-cultural feminism that argues

> the problem is not femininity in and of itself but rather the low value patriarchy assigns to feminine qualities such as "gentleness, modesty, humility, supportiveness, empathy"... and the high value it assigns to masculine qualities such as "assertiveness, aggressiveness, hardiness, rationality or the

> ability to think logically, abstractly, and analytically, ability to control emotion." (Tong, 1998, p. 3)

This approach asks us to consider the patriarchal nature of the academy and question the very essence of its existence. Radical-cultural feminism lends itself more readily to a constructivist grounded theory approach (Charmaz, 2005, 2006) rather than a post-positivist grounded theory approach that is based on methodological conservativism (Strauss & Corbin, 1999). Charmaz's (2006) approach explores how researchers construct themes through "past and present involvement and interactions with people, perspectives, and research practices" (p. 10), where an interpretive portrayal of the narratives is not necessarily an exact picture of it. This emergent perspective lends itself more readily to radical-cultural feminism in that participants are able to construct their own multi-layered meaning, and researcher positionality is acknowledged and addressed. My goal with this exploratory study is not to define an emergent theory, but to utilize principles of constructivist grounded theory to analyze the written discourse in a useful manner.

Further, Haberman (2000) offers that language is not simply a reflection of thoughts but language is also terms that control perceptions, shape understanding, and lead to building ideas. In this sense, the discourse analysis of these diary entries considers the connection between language, perception, and understanding of experiences in higher education; the discourse implicates lived experiences and interpretations of those experiences. Stated another way, the discourse in the diary provides important information about these lived experiences that help us to further understand higher education contexts and enact change.

Historically, the women were elected each year at the national convention and served a three-year term. Approximately six months after the convention each year, the women convene for a mid-year business meeting where they work for four days (i.e., gather by noon on the first day and depart after noon on the fifth day) and plan the events for the following year, including the next convention. Activities included mentor/mentee activities for women in the association, state-by-state connections, programs at convention, publications, awards, family-friendly initiatives and additional activities of interest each year. The women added to the collectively kept diary during the convention and the midyear business meeting.

The diary holds 108 entries from 41 different women. Each of these women was elected to serve as a leader in a national association and wrote in the diary between September 2000 and April 2008. In terms of researcher positionality (Jones, Torres, & Arminio, 2006), I served as a member of this group, overlapping with some of the women who wrote in the diary but not all. As a snapshot of the group, I pull from my own recollection of diversity within the group one year. I share this information only as an example, as the breakdown across race, position, and age was different each year based on the women who were elected to a leadership position. For example, one year there were a total of 11 women on the committee: four Latina, four White, and three African American. Five were in their 20s, five were in their 30s, and one was in her late 40s or early 50s. One worked as athletics, four in residence life (early and mid-career), two were in positions that straddled student and academic affairs, two were in multicultural affairs, one in academic advising, and one in career advising. Five women went on to obtain doctorates in the field of higher education and/or student affairs; some of them have graduated; others are finishing their degree program.

Consistent with Charmaz's constructivist grounded theory, I uncovered themes from the written narratives of the women leaders. The themes were re-analyzed, recoded, and revised in an iterative process over the course of a number of months. Names are not included for confidentiality. I did not obtain member checks at this early stage of the research project, but the long-term goal is to conduct member checks and longitudinal interviews with the women who have remained in, and departed from, the field.

Findings

There were a number of themes that emerged from the voices of the women who participated as leaders in this national association. A few themes that addressed the question, "What do these women leaders communicate about the organizational behavior of this women's group and their experiences in the field of higher education?" are offered here. Themes include the formal and informal organization of the women's group, which emerged as independent themes but are also inextricably linked in the written narratives. In addition, themes regarding experiences of reduction on college campuses and rejuvenation from participation in the women's group were also expressed.

Formal and Informal Organization

The women describe the formal organizational structure and specific responsibilities of the national association and women's subcommittee as well as the informal, unwritten culture of this women's group. At times, the descriptions of the formal and informal processes are separate, but they are described often as interconnected, crafting the very fabric of the committee culture. For example, one woman describes the specific programs and initiatives which are the products of the women leaders' efforts. The specific initiatives are not named in order to protect confidentiality as much as possible. She states,

> We spent so much time working on new initiatives [named initiative] and continuing the pieces laid out before us [named existing programs started by earlier members]. There is so much to do—and so much this group will become. I feel that for every life-altering friendship made here this year, just as strong of an impact will be made with the work we produce.

This woman mentions the specific initiatives and work of the organization but also connects these formal aspects with the "life-altering" friendships that she has made over the year. She anticipates all that this committee "will become" in the future. This perspective is mirrored throughout the diary, when women describe the importance of various initiatives and link this to the relationships that they have made with women in the group. In this manner, the formal and informal aspects of the committee are described as interconnected.

An important and highly referenced formal element of this committee is the intergenerational aspect built into this committee. Incoming members are paired with outgoing members in order to establish mentoring relationships, support the oral traditions to pass information between the generations, and share information regarding the various tasks and initiatives. One woman relates these relationships to those found in books like *An American Quilt* and *Fried Green Tomatoes;* "strong women sharing an experience between generations."

Another member describes the different roles played by each of the cohorts in the organization.

> This has been a good midyear with much work, ideas and productivity. Our new members have jumped in with enthusiasm and vigor—our rotating off members have kept us on task—and the middle group, my group, is coming into its own.

In this way, the committee follows a medical model of learn, act, and teach. Women are elected to the committee and learn about policies and procedures from women whose terms are expiring. In their middle year, women run the specific initiatives on their own. In their third and final year, the women work with a mentee to share what they have learned and how they have developed the initiative over the last year.

In another example, a woman describes the energy and talents of the incoming cohort and anticipates that this will impact future generations of the group.

> Our new members jumped in not as informed as they would have liked to have been, but they brought several outstanding strengths and talents to [the group] that will set a standard that we should expect from future [group] members.

These words reflect the growth of the committee between generations of cohorts. The committee also has a formal mentoring program where a graduate student or new professional is selected to participate in the committee activities throughout the year. It is expected that she learn about the organization as well as contribute to the committee and national association through programs and newsletter entries about her experience. A mentee describes her experience with the women's group.

> So much has been tackled in these few short days. I guess I always wondered when and how (and by whom) decisions got made. This has given me insight that I couldn't have imagined and conversations that other grads in my program would die to have. I think it's probably a familiar feeling to want and need encouragement and/or wisdom—and I am *so* getting that here.

In this entry, the mentee talks about the organization's decision making process and the amount of work that was conducted in a few days. She acknowledges the "unknown" when it comes to the national organization's decision-making process. What she does not describe is a transparent decision-making process within the organization but did witness the process while participating as a mentee in this committee. From her account, more information about the processes and procedures would be useful to her graduate student colleagues and facilitate more communication with the next generation of practitioners and scholars.

In a related example, one leader describes how much she has learned about the structure and function of the national association. She also connects this to the informal culture of communication in the committee:

> I've learned so much from our meetings about the structure and functioning of [association], but I've also learned that so many of us are challenged by similar situations. One thing that has been so fascinating to me is the way this group of 11 women interacts. Each with her own way of processing and presenting, everyone is given the time and space to voice her thought. We let each other speak, we ask for clarification when needed, we make decisions as a group. This is such an empowering way to work. It confirms my need and desire to work with female groups.

The communication among the women in this organization is described as empowering. Specifically, she articulates the importance of turn-taking, asking questions for deeper understanding, and decision making. Time and space to voice thought is heavily weighted and the antithesis of what Talbot (1998) and Wackwitz and Rakow (2004) find in their research of mixed-gender groups. The telling impact of this informal culture of connection and bond between the women is described throughout the diary. This connection between the women leaders is consistent in the written narratives in eight out of the nine years of entries. One woman writes,

> This experience is priceless—a MasterCard commercial couldn't do it justice—nor would a Women's retreat be the same—as I state this with such empathic fact—because despite the numerous visible and invisible differences we each carry, we share one common goal and purpose. As a result, our different personalities and vantage points provide opportunities to

> reach our amplified goal in a myriad of ways—together! No other place have I found a coalition of women who so willingly congregate for four–five days as strangers and come out friends, partners, colleagues, on a mission. Because of this—the past three years have been filled with constant acts of kindness, encouragement, accountability, love, grace and strength.

This leader describes a coalition of women with "purpose." This purpose connects women with diverse perspectives as they work together to enact their mission. Each adjective used to describe her three years with the group carries with it the weight of experience, meaning, and social construction. Moreover, she addresses a balance of "acts" that are traditionally connected to femininity, such as kindness, encouragement, and love. In addition, she utilizes adjectives that describe acts of high value in contemporary society, that of accountability and strength. For this leader, there is value in both traditionally feminine and traditionally masculine qualities in women, and the inclusion of both supports feminism as defined by radical-cultural feminists (Tong, 1998).

In a similar example of the informal culture, a different woman describes this coalition of women but instead uses language about community.

> "Koinonia"—Hebrew for true community is what I have experienced here. I am thoroughly blessed by the individual and collective wisdom that emanates from [the group] and women in general. May we forever be empowered to speak the truth in love…so that our world made—would be one in which women have been able share her treasure of insight and hope for all the world to benefit from…[the group] is a small step toward this realization! Godspeed to all who join this circle.

As is seen often throughout the diary, this woman connects the skills of the committee members (wisdom) with her experience in this "true community" as an important aspect of the informal culture of the group. She ends with a wish for the women in this circle, where the circle symbolizes connection between the women across generations of the organization. On a related note, another woman ends with a wish or blessing for the group.

> The [group] is for me like a kaleidoscope. Each year a new rhythm and pattern emerges as we honor women who have left and welcome new women.

> Yet, every year the pattern and rhythm deeply reflects the value of women centered process and the diversity of all [the national association]. The process of watching this year's pattern emerge has again been grounding and a poignant reminder of what beauty emerges when people have space for voice. My prayer for everybody here is that they are able to carry with them the knowledge of their beauty and power as an important PEACE [sic] of the puzzle.

One can feel the rhythm and pattern of this woman's experience through the description of her experience. She describes the cyclical nature of the women joining and learning this committee and also mentions the value of diversity to the organization. This intergenerational structure of the organization is one of its strong points, which connects women together and sustains the organization.

The intergenerational discussions mentioned by the women leaders in this study correspond to the year they rotated on or off the leadership committee, however as noted earlier, there was also diversity in the age, race, and position of the women leaders each year. As Kezar and Lester (2008) note, the intergenerational relationships between women in higher education have been "intense" between women raised during different waves of feminism (p. 51). The authors illustrate the impact of these differences and describe a process for negotiating intergenerational leadership challenges in their study published in the first volume of the *Journal about Women in Higher Education*. Further exploration of the impact of intergenerational leadership, and leadership from a diverse group across gender, class, and position, is important in order to more deeply understand the dynamics of women in this organization.

Reduction and Rejuvenation

A number of women, but not all, describe the climate on their home campus. When described, they consistently portray climates of isolation, anxiety and burn-out. Coupled with these descriptions is a sense of reduction in their connections with others, productivity, and feelings of self-worth. For example, one woman shares,

> I am at a professional place that is void of the comfort and connection of women I care about and who care about me in return. This [group] time has given me that connection—how lucky I am to be a part of this—I wish a

> small piece of this feeling would be relayed to so many other women feeling isolated.

In this example, the woman describes a home campus culture that is very unlike the one she experienced with this committee. She describes her work environment as void of comfort, connection, and care—an orientation that Gilligan describes as important to women and "in a different voice" than that of men (1982; 1987; 1988). It is this care orientation that radical-cultural feminist seeks to infuse into the dominant patriarchal culture as a valuable aspect of the socio-political context. In the next example, this discussion continues as a woman shares the importance of being respected and valued, and the need to incorporate some of her experiences with this committee into her work life on campus.

> I'm usually not a fan of large groups, preferring to spend my time in more intimate one-on-one relationships or on my own, but this large group is different. We can be with each other all together, with just a few others, or with ourselves, and all are respected and valued places to be. I have had many moments on this trip where I have felt like I've finally been able to *feel* again. It's that which seems to be lost so easily for me in the academic environment, in the rush of everyday life, and in relationships that aren't given the time, attention and energy they need to make them strong. I am here to find, explore, and express "passion, purpose and power" with these women and it feels like it might be important to figure out how to also incorporate that energy and feeling back into the other parts of my life.

In this example, the intimacy between women in the large group is seen as unique. Engaging in this process has helped this woman to "feel again"—a feeling that has dissipated during her time in the academy. She has found passion, purpose and power within this group and seeks to transfer these feelings back to her home campus. In this sense, the culture of this organization is one that she seeks to replicate or, at the very least, transfer to her home campus.

The most predominant theme in the diary was that of rejuvenation. Many of women write about how their work with this committee was rejuvenating, inspirational and powerful. In fact, the word "rejuvenation" (or a form of rejuvenate) was one of the most commonly used words throughout the diary. A few representative examples are shared below.

> Once I stepped inside the airport to come here, I've felt this positive energy that had been lost recently with many job stresses. . . [This work is] rejuvenating since this is the work I'm passionate about.

> I feel rejuvenated from my time surrounded by such a wonderful community of fabulous, committed women.

> I find myself once again thankful, humbled, and uplifted. Each day I found myself appreciating each woman's talents and individuality. What a privilege to work and learn with these women. It seems like the threads of friendship never stopped weaving.

> Another inspiring, amazing, strengthening, rejuvenating [name] retreat. I am continually amazed at the powerful experience of women gathering together.

> Somehow, even with all it takes to get out the door and come to [convention], it's always worth it! I drove away from [city] both physically and emotionally exhausted, but now I'm only physically tired after being here for a few days, away from campus, work, home, and class. Working with [group], being around these women has an inspirational effect. It gives me new energy to set goals, figure out what I might want to do from here for myself, for the group, and for the profession.

> I feel rejuvenated and at such a different place from last year. . . this amazing group of women has helped recenter me this week. I feel able to contribute in meaningful ways and that our group is making a difference in [the organization] and beyond.

Within this reoccurring theme of rejuvenation, the women talk about 1) the work and 2) their connections to other women. Regarding the work, it inspires, refreshes and recenters. Specifically, this rejuvenation helps the women feel they can contribute to the committee and their home campuses in meaningful ways that make a difference for the field. This was described as a part of a "larger purpose," "dedicate[ing] ourselves to making important change." Regarding the meaningful connections to other women in the group, they mention the "amazing group of women" and the "powerful experience of women gathering together." In addition, a number of women actually thanked other women in the group for such deep and meaningful experiences, leaving one woman "thankful, humbled, and uplifted."

This deep connection between women and the work is indicative of the human resource frame of organizational management as described in Bolman and Deal (2008). People who work from this frame focus on people, attitudes, skills, energy, and commitment. Bolman and Deal also discuss organizations from a Structural Frame, Political Frame, and Symbolic Frame. There are traces of all frames represented in the diary; however the Human Resource Frame was most predominant. Also consistent with this frame, most of the women who wrote in the diary mention the committee as stimulating, rewarding and productive. This frame reflects the radical-cultural feminist perspective as defined earlier and is discussed further in the next section.

Discussion

The women leaders elected to this committee within the national association describe the inner workings of the organization-both the formal and informal culture. In addition, some describe the ways in which there have been a reduction in their efforts or energy on their home campuses. It is the work and connection with this women's committee that has been "rejuvenating", and many seek to transfer this energy and excitement to their home campuses.

The majority of women write quite clearly from a Human Resource Frame (HRF) (Bolman & Deal, 2008) about their experience. There are elements of other frames, Symbolic, Structural and Political, yet HRF is most predominant. This information is quite instructive to leaders and supervisors in the field as the women who wrote in the diary are the women in administrative and faculty positions across the nation. The HRF focuses on people's welfare, in this instance, the welfare of students, faculty, staff, and potential students. If there is not an inherent focus on people's welfare, relationships and connection, the person may withdraw, become apathetic, form coalitions with others who support their perspective, or leave the position. The committee is one such coalition and its relationship to women's persistence in the field should be explored further. Important to note, rewards and empowerment are important to the success of HRF people as was reflected in the narratives in the diary.

Both the work of the committee and the connection between women in the group was viewed as rejuvenating. Many expressed a desire to take this energy back to their home campuses. Yet, what if we created departments and programs on college campuses that utilized a HRF model as a part of the organizational structure in a way that was just as rewarding and rejuvenating for our colleagues? For some who operate from a different organizational frame, it may be difficult to "put on a different hat" or try a different type of organizational style. In this instance, Bolman and Deal are instructive as they offer strategies to reframe the organization, not to entrench managers in one frame but to encourage imagination through the utilization of various frames. Applying this knowledge has the potential to strengthen our organizations through diverse organizational styles that are inclusive of the perspectives of all members.

Moreover, in her study of high-achieving women in higher education, Fochtman (in press) found that a participant had "different mentoring needs at different times in her career, indicating that the necessity and desire for mentors never goes away, but shifts as her career progresses." Providing space for women to create such intergenerational connections on campus could provide an additional opportunity for women to benefit from said connections. Such an opportunity may also foster an opportunity for early career scholars and practitioners to learn more about what goes on "behind closed doors" in order to increase the transparency of organizational decision-making processes.

The women in the diary cannot speak for all women in colleges and universities across the country. However, the experiences the women offer in this diary provide unique insight into their own lived experiences. This information is useful as we strive to create inclusive climates that reflect the perspectives and voices of the many diverse women on campus. Further, we must be intentional as we include a diversity of people and perspectives to the organizational table; however, this invitation is not enough. We must also listen and consider the voices and perspectives, as the content of what is offered is as important as the processes and procedures we use to include all colleagues. The utilization of multiple organizational frames is but one way in which we may work to include multiple voices and colleagues as we work toward educational and social justice. As one woman quoted in the diary from Emily Dickinson, we need to "dwell in possibility."

References

Adams, M. (1997). Pedagogical frameworks for social justice education. In *Teaching for diversity and social justice,* edited by M. Adams, L.A. Bell and P. Griffin. New York: Routledge.

American Association of University Women. (2008). Gender Gap Earnings by State. Retrieved January 18, 2009 from http://www.aauw.org/research/statedata/index.cfm.

Astin, H. S. and Leland, C. (1991). *Women of influence, women of vision: A cross-generational study of leaders and social change.* San Francisco: Jossey-Bass.

Blackhurst, A. E. (2000, Winter). Career satisfaction and perceptions of sex discrimination among women student affairs professionals. *NASPA Journal 37*(2), 399–413.

Bolman, T.E. & Deal, L.G. (2008). *Reframing organizations: Artistry, choice, and leadership* (4th ed.). San Francisco, CA: Jossey-Bass.

Charmaz, K. (2005). Grounded theory in the 21st century: Applications for advancing social justice theory. In *The Sage handbook of qualitative research* (3rd ed., pp. 507–535). Thousand Oaks: Sage.

Charmaz, K. (2006). *Constructing grounded theory: A practical guide through qualitative analysis.* Los Angeles: Sage.

Fochtman, M. M. (in press). High achieving academic women: Navigating multiple roles and environments. In P. A. Pasque & S. E. Nicholson, *Women in higher education and student affairs: Research and practice from feminist perspectives.*

Gilligan, C. (1982). *In a different voice: Psychological theory and women's development.* Cambridge: Harvard University Press.

Gilligan, C. (1987). Moral orientation and moral development. In E. F. Kittay and D. T. Meyers (Eds.), *Woman and moral theory.* 19–33. Totowa: Rowman and Littlefield.

Gilligan, C. (1988). Two moral orientations: Gender differences and similarities. *Merrill-Palmer Quarterly, 34*(3), 223–237.

Gilligan, C., A. G. Rogers, and D. L. Tolman. (1991). *Women, girls and psychotherapy: Framing resistance.* New York: Haworth.

Haberman, M. (2000, November). Urban schools: Day cams or custodial centers? *Phi Delta Kappan, 82*(3). pp. 234–240.

hooks, b. (2000). *Feminism is for everybody: Passionate politics.* Cambridge: South End Press.

hooks, b. (1984/2000). *Feminist theory from margin to center*. Cambridge: South End Press.

Jones, S., & McEwen, M.K. (2000). A conceptual model of multiple dimensions of identity. *Journal of College Student Development, 41*(4), 405–413.

Jones, S. R., Torres, V., & Arminio, J. (2006). *Negotiating the complexities of qualitative research in higher education: Fundamental elements and issues*. New York: Routledge.

Kezar, A., & Lester, J. (2008). Leadership in a world of divided feminism. *Journal about Women in Higher Education, 1*, 49–73.

King, J. & Gomez, G. G. (2008). On the pathway to the presidency: Characteristics of higher education's senior leaders. Washington, DC: American Council on Education.

Pasque, P. A. (in press, a). Women's voices of resistance: An analysis of process and content in national higher education policy. *Forum on Public Policy.*

Pasque, P. A. (in press, b). *American higher education, leadership, and policy: Critical issues and the public good.* New York: Palgrave Macmillan.

Pasque, P. A. (2007). Seeing the educational inequities around us: Visions toward strengthening the relationships between higher education and society. In St. John, E. P. (Ed.), *Readings on equal education. Confronting educational inequality: Reframing, building understanding, and making change.* New York: AMS Press.

Reason, R. D., Walker, D. A., & Robinson, D. C. (2002, Spring). Gender, ethnicity, and highest degree earned as salary determinants for senior student affairs officers at public institutions. *NASPA Journal 39*(3), 251–265.

Rickard, S. T. (1985). The chief student affairs officer: Progress toward equity. *Journal of College Student Personnel, 26*(1), 5-10.

Ropers-Huilman, R. (2002). Feminism in the academy: Overview. In A. M. M. Alemán & K. A. Renn (Eds.), *Women in higher education: An encylopedia* (pp. 109–118). Santa Barbara: ABC-Clio.

Strauss, A., & Corbin, J. (1999). *Basics of qualitative research: Techniques and procedures for developing grounded theory* (3 ed.). Thousand Oaks: Sage.

Talbot, M. M. (1998). *Language and gender: An introduction.* Malden: Blackwell.

Tong, R. P. (1998). *Feminist thought: A more comprehensive introduction* (2nd ed.). Boulder: Westview Press.

Tull, A. & Freeman, J.P. (2008). Chief student affairs officer titles: Standardization of titles and broadening of labels, *NASPA Journal 45*(2), 265–281.

U.S. Census Bureau and the Bureau of Labor Statistics. (August, 2008). Annual Demographic Survey. Washington, DC: Author. Retrieved January 14, 2009 from http://pubdb3.census.gov/macro/032008/perinc/new05_000.htm

Wackwitz, L. A. and L. F. Rakow. (2004). Feminist communication theory: An introduction. In L. F. Rakow and L. A. Wackwitz (Eds.), *Feminist communication theory: Selections in context.* 1–10. Thousand Oaks: Sage.

CHAPTER SEVEN

African American Male Collegians: Race, Class, and Gender Revealed

Fred Bonner
Dave Louis
Chance W. Lewis

Emphasis on the gifted poor is increasing in attention among researchers, scholars, policymakers and concerned education officials who study gifted groups. Although this high-achieving group is receiving attention, particular cohorts within this population are continuing to be overlooked. According to Slocumb and Payne (2000), "...in one typical urban school district, only 8 percent of students identified as gifted come from those classified as economically disadvantaged—mostly black and Hispanic—who make up 58 percent of the school population, compared to 81 percent of white students, who constitute little more than a third of the school population" (p. 1). Further problematizing this lack of focus on gifted poor populations of color is the paucity of literature that focuses on giftedness beyond the P-12 context; an even direr situation exists among the literature specifically highlighting postsecondary gifted students of color (Bonner, 2001; Ford, Grantham, & Bailey, 1999; Ford, 1995).

This chapter will focus on the gifted poor—particularly academically gifted African American male collegians who come from poverty. The authors will discuss topics associated with not only the unique adversities and challenges but also the accomplishments and milestones this population experiences in P-16 contexts. Topics of discussion will include critical issues ranging from family influence and identity development to environmental incongruence and culturally specific mentoring. In addition, the chapter will consider the relevance of intersectionality as a concept that offers promise in "theorizing the relationship between different social categories" (Valentine, 2007, p. 10); namely, the multiple and interlocking categories or statuses as they are referred to in this article (i.e., gifted, African American, male, and poor) and how these statuses work in tandem to influence these males' experiences with academe.

Definitions: Gifted and Giftedness

A major drawback in the identification and subsequent inclusion of African American males in gifted programming is the problems associated with how giftedness is defined. Several scholars (Bonner, 2001; Ford, 1995; Hilliard, 1976; Gardner, 1983; Renzulli, 1981; Sternberg, 1985) have provided empirically grounded evidence reaffirming the need to embrace a more inclusive set of practices in the identification process. Narrow definitions of giftedness have tended to focus almost exclusively on academic ability. According to Matthews (2004),

> Beginning with its origins in the early history of psychology, giftedness was defined primarily in terms of intellectual ability. By the 1950s, however, spurred by factors that included the multifaceted model of intelligence developed by J. P. Guilford and the elaboration by DeHann and Kough of 10 categories of gifts and talents, a variety of efforts began leading toward a broader conceptualization of giftedness (p. 77).

One of the first steps in seeking a means to expand the definition of giftedness was initiated by legislative mandate. Then Commissioner of Education Sydney Marland (1972) who published the first formal definition of giftedness reported that minority children were scarcely being served. Several modifications have been made to Marland's original definition, and it was in the United States Office of Educational Research and Improvement (OERI) 1993 report titled *National Excellence and Developing Talent* that the term *gifted* was dropped and *outstanding talent* was used in its place. Additionally, the 1993 definition included key terms such as *potential* and *capacity* as well as critical statements like *outstanding talents are present in children and youth from all cultural groups, across all economic strata...*this shift in language alone in many ways constituted a watershed in how giftedness was identified. According to the Report,

> Children and youth with outstanding talent perform or show the potential for performing at remarkably high levels of accomplishment when compared with others of their age, experience, or environment. These children and youth exhibit high performance capacity in intellectual, creative, and/or artistic areas, and unusual leadership capacity, or excel in specific academic fields. They require services or activities not ordinarily provided by the school. Outstanding talents are present in children and youth from all cultural groups, across all economic strata, and in all areas of human endeavor. (p. 19)

Still other definitions have been developed by the U.S. Department of Education through the Javits Act, the federally sponsored program fostering the development of talent in the nation's schools, and the National Association of Gifted Children (NAGC), the largest organization in the country aimed at supporting the needs of high-potential learners. Both of these entities serve as powerful forces in framing the extant definitions and discussions related to how giftedness is identified. Notwithstanding the current definitions, what is most encouraging about these successive and oftentimes competing codifications is the increasing recognition that giftedness as a concept is multifarious and multilayered with different views on how it is operationalized across as well as within different cultural groups. Sternberg (2007) reports, "Different cultures have different concepts of what it means to be gifted. But in identifying children as gifted, we often only use our own conception, ignoring the cultural context in which the children grew up" (p. 160). Fortunately contemporary definitions are utilizing more inclusive language and ecumenical phraseology that portends greater opportunities for people of color.

Intersections: Gifted, African American, Male, and Poor

Several factors contribute to the underidentification and lack of inclusion of African American males in gifted and talented programs, with how giftedness is defined representing one of the more formidable barriers. Ford, Harris, Tyson, and Trotman (2002) in their research uncovered three additional factors that too lend credence to this ongoing problem—namely, teacher referrals, low test scores, and student and family choice. This section is aptly titled intersections due to the tenuous borders that gifted African American males tend to navigate within and outside of the school context. For many, the conjoining of the terms *African American* and *male* creates a sense of dissonance and in essence represents an oxymoron. In the opening of his book on gifted African American males in college, Bonner (2010) highlights a conversation that he engages in with a colleague,"You're interested in studying whom?—academically gifted African American males—you know the greater academic community doesn't believe this being exists!"

An even direr gap in the literature is assumed when socioeconomic status is taken in tandem with these above-mentioned terms. For the African American gifted male who comes from a background of meager economic resources, particularly those who come from impoverished upbringings, infiltrating and successfully functioning in P-16 educational enclaves can serve as a formidable challenge. These males are challenged to overcome both the lack and incongruence of the intellectual and social capital accrued during their formative years being ill suited for the education contexts in which they find themselves functioning. According to Noguera (as cited in Fashola, 2005), "The choices made by an individual may be shaped by both the available opportunities and the norms present within the cultural milieu in which they are situated" (p. 59). In addition Noguera goes on to state that, "The effects of poverty can be so debilitating that a child's life chances can literally be determined by a number of environmental and cultural factors such as the quality of prenatal care, housing, and food available to their mothers…" (p. 59).

Given the impact that a trajectory of poverty exerts on any child, for the gifted African American male it becomes ever more important to focus on how their multiple statuses as gifted, African American, male and poor intersect to create a unique experience that defies being distilled or forced into existing frameworks that speak in generalities about gifted students of color, or models that overlook key cultural nuances that are endemic to African American male populations. At the intersection of African American and male statuses Mincy (1994) is very clear in his statement about how it is far from unusual for "…black males to reach adolescence with a basic mistrust of their environment, doubts about their abilities, and confusion about their place in the world." (p. 36). At the intersection of African

American and gifted statuses you find several researchers (Bonner, 2000; Bonner, 2001; Bonner, Jennings, Marbley, & Brown, 2008; Conchas, 2006; Ford & Harris, 1999; Ford, Harris, Tyson, Trotman; Hebert, 2002; Ogbu, 2003), who assert that African American males learn strategies to hide or cover their gifted identity through disassociating or developing oppositional frameworks that allow them to maintain their relative standing within their peer and home communities. The intersection of African American, male, and poverty statuses, also treated in a separate section, is worthy of note; Gordon (2002) purports,

> We explain the overrepresentation of black males among the poor in the following way. First, we demonstrate that black males are more likely than white males are to have no income at all. Further, those black males who do have income are likely to fall into the lower income categories for a variety of reasons. Also, and as important, a nontrivial percentage of black males who are employed work part-time rather than full-time. (p. 128).

What these different combinations and permutations reveal about the multiple statuses of these men is that while each singularly exerts an influence on their experiences and motivations—it is their intermingling that typically provides a more accurate focus on what it means to be gifted, African American, male, and poor in the education setting. This section underscores much of what is said about the research surrounding intersectionality, more pointedly it addresses how critical differences are not situated in spaces between identities but in spaces found to exist within identities (Fuss, 1989). It is in the nexus of these competing identities that community, schools, and peers must be negotiated and affixed in ways that are affirming and growth producing for the gifted African American male. Additionally, a focus on how these identities become functional within these different contexts is also critical. In speaking to how identities should be considered in varying settings, Valentine (2007) posited that the emphasis should be on how identities are operationalized in interactions within specific environments and not on how these identities function as static or given understandings of social difference.

African American Family: Influence, Extension, and Support

For more than a decade, the family has been depicted as a central focus in the success of African American students in general and gifted African American students in particular (Allen, 1992; Fleming, 1984; Ford & Harris, 1999; Hughes, 1987; Bonner, 2001; Bonner & Bailey, 2006; Henfield, Moore, & Wood, 2008; White & Cones, 1999). Fries-Britt (1998) asserts that the changing nature of the family unit, changes in socioeconomic status, and parent(s)' educational levels complicate the family dynamic. In addition, White and Cones state,

> The family, the peer group, and the neighborhood influence the psychological perspectives of African American males as they struggle to come to grips with the issues involved in self-definition, attitudes toward women, coping with racism, discovering adaptive possibilities within the African American way of being, and integrating African American and Euro-American lifestyles. (p. 195)

This mix of developmental processes is often hammered out on an anvil of family support; however, what has served as grist for the discussion mill regarding these support structures is how they are constituted and how they subsequently provide support. Roderick (as cited in Fashola, 2005) highlights research that points to the difficulties African American males in urban settings experience related to their transition to high school. One of the explanations she offers is that these males are less likely to be provided with the type of support that they need to facilitate successful transfer experiences. In offering an explanation of how family constitution plays a role, White and Cones offer a vigorous argument about the report submitted by U.S. Senator Daniel Patrick Moynihan in the 1960s. This report derided the Black family and attributed much of its decline to single parent households—households typically run by women. White and Cones, quoting from Moynihan's report, state that "...the Black family was a tangle of social pathology characterized by an unstable matriarchal structure" (p. 196). Yet, what Moynihan saw in the past, the Black family as a "tangle of pathology," has been replaced by a more contemporary view of these structures as "tourniquets for hemorrhaging." And, for the gifted African American male in poverty, the family provides an even more profound source of support.

Support and support structures are critical for this population of men in that the higher education environments they face have been described as *chilly* and even *hostile* to their participation (Fries-Britt, 1998; Harper, 2003). Fries-Britt and Griffin (2007) contend that "facing a hostile campus racial climate can also adversely impact the achievement, integration, and retention of high-achieving Blacks" (p. 510). The family has served as a means for gifted African American males in poverty to transgress against hegemonic and racially charged higher education structures. Additionally the family unit for these males, despite its inability to provide economic resources, does provide needed emotional and psychological support that is tantamount in their retention. Although he references the relationships that African American males ideally should maintain with academic advisors, Strayhorn's (2008) statement is also illustrative of the importance of familial relationships: "For some Black men, having strong support of an advisor (e.g., encouragement, advice) can offset the socioeconomic disadvantages (e.g., inadequate academic preparation for college, lack of rigorous courses in high school) that may threaten their odds for success in college" (p. 40).

Beyond handling the disadvantages and stressors associated with navigating the higher education terrain, family support structures are critical in the identity development process that gifted African American males undergo during their higher education experience. According to Bonner and Bailey (2006), "the establishment of a positive identity for the African American male student is significant in that it serves as the foundation upon which the student can develop some sense of agency and in turn determine where he 'fits' within the academy" (p. 28). Where identity development and family support intersect is a critical space where African American males are either supported and encouraged or not supported and left to fend for themselves. Noguera (as cited in Fashola, 2005) contends that there are a "number of important lessons about the intersection of identity, school practices, and academic performance" (p. 65) that should be investigated in an effort to ensure the schooling success of African American males. Thus, it is imperative to consider the unique role that the family plays in the lives of these men, and it is also important to determine how the interlocking structures of gifted status, gender, race, and socioeconomic standing are also factors of influence in how family roles are engaged.

Identity Development: Frameworks and Challenges

The gifted African American male in poverty is in many ways much like a jigsaw puzzle with interlocking pieces. While each piece on its own does not provide enough vivid detail to capture the entire picture, each constitutes a necessary part of the whole. It is impossible to develop some form of understanding related to identity and identity development among this population without considering how each one of their statuses impacts how they construct a nuanced "sense of self." While the extant literature has been available in respect to African American (Black) racial and cultural identity development (Hughes & Bonner, 2006; Majors & Billson, 1992), applying the term *gifted* or *gifted and poor* as a filter drastically reduces the number of attendant publications. Rowley and Moore (2002) assert,

> The role of race in the lives of gifted African American students is an understudied phenomenon. The discourse in the literature regarding the influence of racial identity on academic achievement has been relatively narrow, often ignoring such important conceptual issues as the fact that racial identity is dynamic across situations; that race is not important to all African Americans; that the individual's assessment of what is African American is most important; and that racial identity cannot be understood without examining the social context. (p. 63)

Thus, developing some sense of understanding regarding the role and purpose of racial identity development among gifted African American males in poverty becomes ever more important as we attempt to support these individuals as they interface with academe. Significant has been Asante's (1988) *Afrocentricity* and Cross' (1991) *Negro to Black Conversion* models. What these cultural typologies have provided is insight on ways to engage with African American males; however, it was William E. Cross, Jr. who first introduced his theory as a means to frame the racial identity development process found to occur among African American populations in 1971 that has held the most promise. A review of Cross' (1971) model reveals four stages or themes he refers to as pre-encounter, encounter, immersion, and internalization—"each describes 'self-concept' issues concerning race and parallel attitudes that the individual holds about Black and White as a reference group" (p. 169). Without delving into an extensive discussion of Cross' theory, suffice it to say that what each theme is found to represent is an individual's ever-increasing sense of self as a racial being and an ever-deepening sense of understanding regarding the establishment of a healthy racial identity (Bonner, Lewis, Bowman-Perrott, Hill-Jackson, & James, in press).

Gifted African American males find that their identity development, particularly their racial identity development subsequently influences their achievement, motivation, and attitudes toward school (Grantham & Ford, 2003). According to Bonner, Lewis, Bowman-Perrott, Hill-Jackson, & James (in press),

> A prime example of how the intersection and overlap of academic, cultural, and racial identity can impact the development of gifted African American male students is seen in how they address perceptions about their achievement. For this cohort, achievement can be impacted by perceptions of being smart as somehow inferring that they are "acting White" (Fordham & Ogbu, 1986; Ogbu, 2003); as a result many of these males opt to become class clowns (Ford, Harris, Tyson, & Trotman, 2002). Although the concept of acting White is sometimes overextended in its application (Tyson, Darity & Castellino, 2005), it is important to look at how recent research has affirmed the relevance of this concept, particularly as it relates to high achieving African American students.

Again, adding poverty as a dimension to the equation only creates more opportunities for misunderstandings and misinterpretations to develop. What these gifted African American males are many times forced to do is to establish their identities and sense of agency in an environment that at best tolerates and at worst objects to their presence. The fact that they come from backgrounds of poverty only reifies the sense of "otherness" that many feel about them as individuals. Hebert's research (2002), although referencing young children offers much regarding the ways in which gifted African American males in postsecondary settings also contend with attitudes and perceptions of their abilities based on their socioeconomic standing. According to Hebert, "With the understanding that gifted students are found in the culture of poverty, educators must not overlook the fact that these young people have achievement needs that must be addressed..." (p. 128).

Demographics: Opportunities and Threats

African American males are educationally at-risk in the United States; they are especially at-risk in institutions of higher education. This at-risk status for this cohort is heightened when poverty is taken as a factor; their probability for success greatly diminishes. However, resilience is found to serve as one the greatest sources of opportunity to reverse these negative effects (Judge, 2005) and usually results in some measure of success at the P-12 level and beyond. While the most persistent and resilient individuals, given proper exposure and support can enter and successfully navigate college, the quintessential issue for some who lack these resources becomes where to find these support structures if they have previously not been made available. For the gifted African American male in poverty, this resource identification process has even more salience if they are to successfully matriculate.

Developing some sense of understanding regarding the status of the gifted African American male in poverty is pivotal to any discourse pertaining to their academic pursuits. According to the Kaiser Foundation Report on Race, Ethnicity and Health Care (2006) there are 4.5 million African American men between the ages 15 to 29, making up approximately 14% of the U.S. male population. This group also represents 12% of the African American population. The report continues by stating, "...[the] high rates of death, incarceration, and unemployment, and relatively low levels of college graduation rates [of African American males] raise concerns for African American families and the nation's economy" (Kaiser Foundation Report on Race, Ethnicity and Health Care, 2006, p. 1). While these numbers encompass all African American males in this age cohort, they do not distinguish between the various socio-economic levels these African American males occupy.

One must also understand the rarity that African American males who do make it to college represent. For the gifted African American male who is saddled with poverty, this individual represents an even greater anomaly in achieving both academic and personal success.

However, it is important to note, success notwithstanding, that these individuals often experience many more barriers that may work against their matriculation in comparison to their peers. For example, gifted African American males in poverty who manage to successfully matriculate through the P-12 system are truly representative of less than 50% of the total African American male school population; that is, roughly 47% of all African American males graduate from high school in the U.S. as opposed to 75% of their White male counterparts (Schott Report, 2008). When it comes to college graduation, the outlook is even bleaker. Less than 8% of African American males have graduated from college compared to 17% of Whites and 35% of Asians (Kaiser Foundation Report on Race, Ethnicity and Health Care, 2006).

Maxwell (2004) cites the American Council on Education's findings reporting that graduation rates for African American males are the lowest of any college-going population; 35% of the African American males who enrolled in NCAA Division I schools in 1996 graduated within six years. When compared to their White male peers, these statistics paint an even darker picture, with White males' graduation rates being represented at 59%. While these numbers do not specifically focus on the experiences of gifted African American males in poverty, they do intimate the need for interventions that will assist this population to engage with higher education in meaningful ways. In essence, these numbers are indicative of the need for a deeper examination into the education ills that face gifted African Americans males in poverty.

Obstacles and Marginalization: Seeking Viable Solutions

Obstacles facing gifted African American males in poverty extend beyond socioeconomic status and represent a core issue that impacts the matriculation experiences among this cohort. Many of their attendant problems begin well before their admission to college and are found to be deeply entrenched and connected to enclaves in which these males instinctively seek support: Family structures, school systems and peer enclaves represent but a few of these structures. As an example, a common problem for many gifted African American males in poverty is that their families harbor expectations that these males will become the breadwinners for the family, in some instances even before the age of 10 (Hunter, 2001). Generally it is not the case that these families do not value education and the intellectual capital that the male embodies; however, survival becomes the main focus and education, particularly higher education, is relegated to take a distant second place role (Cuyjet, 1997). Additionally the research has been very pointed in underscoring the conflicting feelings that many gifted African American males experience related to their success—success they often perceive that is achieved at the expense of their family and peers. The more successful they become, the more removed they find themselves from the people who serve as their confidants, friends, and mentors—a situation that has been described as "survival conflict" (Whitten, 1992).

Also, realizing that navigational hardships that gifted African American males in poverty endure can at times impact academic productivity and ultimately result in probation or dismissal from the institution. Consequently, the social implications associated with these sanctions lead to social isolation and frustration. Therefore, providing necessary scaffolding experiences through programming and policy initiatives becomes critical; one such set of experiences is achieved through mentoring (Brown, Davis & McClendon, 1999; Strayhorn & Terrell, 2007).

Marginalization is also one of the core issues that tend to influence the poor gifted African American college students' experience. Marginalization is particularly significant among this cohort within Predominantly White Institutions (PWIs). According to the extant literature, African American students report that they feel unwelcome on college campuses, specifically due to their ethnic and socioeconomic status (Johnson, 1993; Malaney & Shively, 1995; Gossett, Cuyjet & Cockriel, 1998). These higher education environments in which the student finds himself do not promote a sense of worth, belonging, connectivity or comfort; all attributes of settings that promote intellectually engaging education experiences. Thus, it is imperative that environments are created that nullify marginalization and encourage inclusiveness—a process that should involve every constituent of the higher education community. Gossett, Cuyjet and Cockriel (1996) state that colleges and universities must ascertain why campus perceptions are different among ethnic groups, mainly because these varying perceptions are what create alternate and sometimes negative realties for some student populations. Not only must institutions determine the genesis of these differences, but they also must seek ways to resolve discord among communities who are being disparately impacted.

In speaking to the role that college and university administrators should play, Cuyjet (1997) states:

> [University] administrators concerned about this issue are presented with a twofold agenda: first, the need to provide a nonthreatening environment for African American men where their higher expectations of success can be nurtured and reinforced; and second, the task of reeducating the majority of the community about the inaccuracy of generally held perceptions about black men. (p. 7)

Therefore it is imperative that intentional interventions and interactions with gifted African American males in poverty become a top priority for institutions of higher education; creating avenues for this population of students to consistently engage with members of the campus community should not be left to chance.

Mentoring: Achieving Success and Balance

Many African American males represent the first generation of members from their respective families to attend college. Often parents, peers, and relatives—the usual suspects in the college-going process—are willing but not capable of providing needed information and support for them to be successful in their higher education endeavors. The support that they are able to offer is at best superficial and at worst non-beneficial. While the typical mantras, "Keep it up" or "It'll get better" are gestures designed to assist the gifted African American male to feel better in the short-run, these gestures lack permanence in the long haul to sustain academic success. Therefore, the support from home these students typically receive, though well intentioned and certainly appreciated, may be of little value to the student.

Specifically many gifted African American males in poverty have never been afforded the opportunity to interact with individuals who pursued or earned college degrees; hence, they do not possess a viable template from which they can mold their higher education experiences. Patitu and Terrell (1997), report that minority students without role models have a substantially more difficult time succeeding in college than their White counterparts. Therefore, creating more opportunities for gifted African American males in poverty to receive mentoring and guidance from aspirant peers and role models is warranted. The opportunities should translate into connections that create opportunities for role models and mentees to engage in sustained and meaningful liaisons.

These mentoring programs can serve as the mirrors in which gifted African American male students in poverty can see themselves as successes and not the tragic figures that many see them as representing due to their poverty status. Hebert (2002) asserts that, "Holding lower expectations for high-ability students from economically disadvantaged backgrounds threatens their growth intellectually and socially. Educators can no longer underestimate what students from impoverished backgrounds are capable of achieving and postpone more challenging and personally relevant work" (p.135). Both Carter (1994) and Patitu and Terrell (1997) assert that the value of mentoring programs as tools to assist college students in their adjustment to higher education and as reinforcement to persistence is key. Mentoring programs and models in essence are support structures designed to serve as a bridge for students to move past failures and to discover contemporary successes.

Mentoring models can range from target groups to peer-mentoring to faculty-student mentoring (Strayhorn & Terrell, 2007). What is important to remember is that the development of mentorship models must be based on clear and concise goals. For example, in a study conducted by Strayhorn and Terrell (2007), they report, "Establishing a research-focused relationship with a faculty mentor has a positive effect on Black students' satisfaction with college while establishing a personal relationship does not" (p. 77). The gifted African American male student in poverty in particular needs a meaningful relationship in which his intellectual acumen, desires, career aspirations and an outlet for understanding the world can meld.

Healy (1997) states in Frierson's *Diversity in Higher Education* text that mentoring should be both dynamic and reciprocal; therefore, not only does the student/mentee find the value in the relationship, but the mentor also finds inherent value in the exchange. Having mentors who understand the significance of the relationship to the overall success of the mentee is vital. That is, the knowledge that the mentors possess can assist these males in acclimatizing to college life (Cawyer, Simonds & Davis, 2002; Carter, 1994). For the gifted African American male in poverty, this constant involvement with the mentor builds connections that allow him to foster his self-worth and develop both personally and professionally. This symbiotic mentoring relationship also is then subsequently reflected in positive and successful higher education community engagements (Gossett, Cuyjet & Cockriel, 1998). African American male students are then validated by their accomplishments and by the feedback they receive from their mentors as well as those occupying the academic context who see this relationship taking form and producing positive results. These relationships also help quell many misconceptions and negative stereotypes that individuals may possess as they relate to his gifted cohort.

What these mentoring programs help to do is not only assist African American males in their adjustment to higher education but also counteract the effects that the poverty may have exacted beforehand. Negative sentiments expressed about higher education environments, the lack of value perceived to be associated with completing a degree, peer detractors and even the unsupportive family members who serve as albatrosses around the neck of these males can all be countered by successful mentoring relationships. In commenting on the importance of mentoring relationships, Jones, Bibbins and Henderson (1994) state:

> Growing up in a hostile world and bombarded with negative images and stereotypes of self, many young African American males find themselves trapped in a cycle of despair.... Internally, many experience low self-esteem, lacking vision for a hopeful future. (p.1)

Through these mentoring programs gifted African American males in poverty can seek ways to redefine themselves and find new paths toward success. The opportunity for growth that these mentoring programs provide these men is invaluable and has the potential change the course of their lives forever.

Conclusion

Meeting the needs of gifted African American males in poverty should begin from a place of awareness. Who are these men and what do they bring to the higher education context? The literature has been quite clear in underscoring the lack of focus, deficit-modeling, and underidentification associated with this population; maladies, many of which are associated with a lack of knowledge of who these men are. Beyond a clarion call that needs to go out to scholars and researchers who devote much of their publication capital to gifted learners of color, a fine-grained focus on gifted African American learners who are both male and poor needs to be aggressively undertaken. Subsequent to initiatives aimed at awareness, it will become ever more important for those who are invested in the gifted identification process, to focus on how giftedness is defined. If we are to remain true to the definition provided by the U.S. Department of Education (1993), then it is incumbent that we do not cherry-pick the parts of the definition that do not defy our practices or challenge our sensibilities. Said differently, part of the definition states, "Outstanding talents are present in children and youth from all cultural groups, across all economic strata, and in all areas of human endeavor" (p. 19) and it is imperative that we uphold this tenet.

Additionally, for the gifted African American male in poverty who interfaces with academe, creating "safe spaces" in which they can fully function and meet their academic goals is a process that should involve the entire campus community. Both academic as well as student affairs units must work holistically to engage and support these men in their learning, growth, and development. This chapter attempted to provide a clear roadmap via discussions related to the importance of critical nuanced components in their college matriculation process. Hence, family support, identity development, and mentoring are topics that all swirl about creating opportunities and possibilities to provide these men with a college-going experience that ultimately leads to their success.

References

Allen, W. R. (1992). The color of success: African American college student outcomes at predominantly white and historically black public college and universities. *Harvard Educational Review, 64* (1), 26–44.

Asante, M. K. (1988). *Afrocentricity.* Trenton, New Jersey: Africa World Press.

Brown, M. C., III., Davis, G. L., & McClendon, S. A. (1999). Mentoring graduate students of color: Myths, models, and modes. *Peabody Journal of Education, 74*(2), 105–118.

Bonner, F. A. II. (2010). *Gifted African American male college students.* Westport, CT: Greenwood Publishing Group.

Bonner, F. A., II. (2001). Making room for the study of gifted African American males. *Black Issues in Higher Education, 18* (6), 80.

Bonner, F. A., II. (2000). African American giftedness. *Journal of Black Studies,* May 2000, *30*(5), 643–664.

Bonner, F. A. II & Bailey, K. (2006). Assessing the academic climate for African American men. In M. Cuyjet (Ed.) *African American Men in College* (pp. 24–46). San Francisco: Jossey-Bass.

Bonner, F., Jennings, M., Marbley, A. & Brown, L. (2008). Capitalizing on leadership capacity: Gifted African American males in high school. *Roeper Review,* (*30*), 2, 93–103.

Bonner, F. A. II., Lewis, C. W., Bowman-Perrott, V. Hill-Jackson, L. & M. James. (in press). Definition, identification, identity and culture: A unique alchemy impacting the success of gifted African American males in school. *Journal for the Education of the Gifted.*

Carter T. (1994). Mentor programs belong in college, too. *Journal of Career Planning & Employment, (5),* 51–53.

Cawyer, C., Simonds C. & Davis, S. (2002). Mentoring to facilitate socialization: The case of the new faculty member. *International Journal of Social Work Education, (37),* 283–93.

Conchas, G. Q. (2006). *The color of success: Race and high-achieving urban youth.* New York: Teachers College Press.

Cross, W. E. (1991). *Negro to Black conversion experience: Toward a psychology of Black liberation. Black World, 20*(9), 13–27. Philadelphia: Temple University Press.

Cuyjet, M. (1997). African American men on college campuses: Their needs and their perceptions. *New Directions for Student Services, (80)*, 5–16.

Tyson, K., Darity, W., Castellino, D. R. (2005). It's not a "Black thing": Understanding the burden of acting white and other dilemmas of high achievement. *American Sociological Review, 70*(4), 582-605.

Fashola, O. (2005). *Educating African American males: Voices from the field.* Thousand Oaks: Corwin Press.

Fleming, J. (1984). *Blacks in college.* San Francisco: Jossey-Bass.

Ford, D. Y., Grantham, T. C. & Bailey, D. F. (1999). Identifying giftedness among African American males: Recommendations for effective recruitment and retention. In *African American males in school and society: Practices and policies for effective education* (Eds.) V. Polite and J. Davis. New York: Teachers College Press.

Ford, D., Harris, J., Tyson, C., Trotman, M. (2002). Beyond deficit thinking. *Roeper Review, (24),* 2, 5.

Ford, D.Y., & Harris III, J.J. (1999). *Multicultural gifted education.* New York: Teachers College Press.

Ford, D. Y. (1995). Desegregating gifted education: A need unmet. *Journal of Negro Education, 64*(1), pp. 52–62.

Fordham, S., & Ogbu, J. U. (1986). Black students' school success: Coping with the "burden of 'acting White." *The Urban Review, 18*(3), 176–206.

Fries-Britt, S. & Griffin, K. (2007). The black box: How high-achieving blacks resist stereotypes about black Americans. *Journal of College Student Development, (48),* 5, 509–524.

Fries-Britt, S. (1998). Moving beyond black achiever isolation: Experiences of gifted black collegians. *Journal of Higher Education, (69)*, 5, 556–576.

Fuss, D. (1989) *Essentially speaking: Feminism, nature and difference.* New York and London: Routledge.

Gardner, H. (1983). *Frames of mind: The theory of multiple intelligences.* New York: Basic Books.

Given Half a Chance: The Schott 50 State Report on Public Education and Black Males (2008). Schott Foundation for Public Education. Cambridge, MA.

Gordon, J. U. (Ed.). (2002). *The Black male in White America.* New York: Nova Science Publishers, Inc.

Gossett, B., Cuyet, M. & Cockriel, I. (1998). African Americans' perception of marginality in the campus culture. *College Student Journal, (32),* 1, 22.

Gossett, B., Cuyjet, M., & Cockriel, I. (1996). African Americans' and Non-African Americans' sense of mattering and marginality at public, Predominantly White Institutions. *Equity & Excellence in Education. 29 (3),* 37–42.

Grantham, T.C. & Ford, D.Y. (2003). Beyond self-concept and self-esteem for African American students: Improving racial identity improves achievement. *The High School Journal, 87*(1), 18–29.

Harper, S. R. (2003). Most likely to succeed: The self-perceived impact of involvement on the experiences of high-achieving African American undergraduate men at predominantly White universities. *Dissertation Abstracts International, A64*(6), 1995.

Healy, C. (1997) An operational definition. In H.T. Frierson, Jr. (Ed.). *Diversity in higher education.* Greenwich, CT: JAI Press.

Henfield, M., Moore, J. & Wood, C. (2008). Inside and outside gifted educational programming: Hidden challenges for African American students. *Exceptional children, (74),* 4, 433–450.

Herbert, T. (2002). Gifted black males in a predominantly white university: Portraits of high achievement. *Journal for the Education of the Gifted, (26),* 1, 25–64.

Hilliard, A. G. (1976). *Alternatives to IQ testing: An approach to the identification of gifted "minority" children* (Report No. PS 009 639). Sacramento: California Department of Education, Special Education Division. (ERIC Document Reproduction Service No. ED 147 009).

Hughes, M. S. (1987). Black students' participation in higher education. *Journal of College Student Personnel, 28,* 532–545.

Hughes, R. & Bonner, F. A. II. (2006). Leaving Black males behind: Debunking the myths of meritocratic education. *Journal of Race and Policy,* 2(1), 76–87.

Hunter, Andrea G. (2001) The other breadwinners: The mobilization of secondary wage earners in early twentieth-century black families. *History of the Family 6*: 69–94.

Jackson, D. M. "The emerging national state concern." In A. H. Passow [Ed.], *The gifted and the talented: Their education and development* [pp. 45–62]. 78th Yearbook of NSSE. Chicago: Univ. of Chicago Press. 1979.

Johnson, R.E. (1993). Factors in the academic success of African American college males. University of South Carolina. (ERIC Document reproduction service no. ED 364 639).

Jones, D. J., Bibbins, V. E., & Henderson, R. D. (1994). Reaffirming young African American males: Mentoring and community involvement by fraternities and other groups. *Urban League Review, 16*(2), 9–19.

Judge S. (2005). Resilient and vulnerable at-risk children: Protective factors affecting early school competence. *Journal of Children & Poverty, (11),* 2, 149–68.

Majors, R., & Billson, J. M. (1992). *Cool prose: The dilemmas of Black manhood in America.* New York: Macmillan.

Malaney, G. D. & Shively, M. (1995). Academic and social expectations and experiences of first-year students of color. *NASPA Journal, (33),* 1, 3–18.

Marland, S., Jr. (1972). *Education of the gifted and talented.* (Report to the Congress of the United States by the U.S. Commissioner of Education). Washington, DC: U.S. Government Printing Office.

Matthews, M. S. (2004). Leadership education for gifted and talented youth: A review of the literature. *Journal for the Education of the Gifted, 28(1),* 77–113

Maxwell, B. (2004). On campus, grim statistics for African-American men. *St. Petersburg Times Online.* Retrieved from http://www.sptimes.com/2004/01/04/Columns/On_campus__grim_stati.shtml.

Mincy, R. B. (1994). Conclusions and implications. In R. B. Mincy (Ed.), *Nurturing young Black males: Challenges to agencies, programs, and social policy* (pp. 187–204).Washington, DC: The Urban Institute Press.

Ogbu, J. (2003). *Black students in an affluent suburb: A study of academic disengagement.* Mahwah, NJ: Lawrence Erlbaum.

Patitu, C. & Terrell, M. (1997). Participant perceptions of the NASPA Minority Undergraduate Fellows Program. *NASPA Journal, (17),* 69–80.

Race, Ethnicity and Health Care Fact Sheet. (2006). The Henry J. Kaiser Family Foundation. Washington, DC.

Renzulli, J. S (1981). The revolving door model: A new way of identifying the gifted. *Phi Delta Kappan, 62*(9), 648–649.

Ronald McNair Post-Baccalaureate Achievement Program (2009) Retrieved May 21, 2009 from http://www.ed.gov/programs/triomcnair/index.html.

Rowley, S. J., & Moore, J. A. (2002). Racial identity in context for the gifted African American student. *Roeper Review, 24*(2), 63–67.

Slocumb, P. D., & Payne, R. K. (2000). *Removing the mask: Giftedness in poverty*. Highlands, TX: RPT Publishing.

Sternberg, R.J. (2007). Cultural dimensions of giftedness and talent. *Roeper Review,* 29(3), 160-165

Sternberg, R. J. (1985). *Beyond IQ: A triarchic theory of human intelligence*. Cambridge: Cambridge University Press.

Strayhorn, T. (2008). The role of supportive relationships in facilitating African American males' success in college. *NASPA Journal, (45),* 1, 26–52.

Strayhorn, T. & Terrell, M. (2007). Mentoring and satisfaction with college and black students. *The Negro Educational Review, (58),* 1–2, 69–83.

Tinto, V. (1975). Dropout from higher education. A theoretical synthesis of recent research. *Review of Educational Research, (45),* 89–125.

Tinto, V. (1993). *Leaving college: Rethinking the causes and cures of student attrition* (2nd ed.). Chicago, IL: University of Chicago Press.

Tyson, K., Darity, W. Jr., Castellino, D. R. (2005). It's not "a black thing": understanding the burden of acting white and other dilemmas of high achievement. *American Sociological Review, 70,* 582–605.

U.S. Department of Education. (1993). *National excellence: A case for developing America's talent*. Washington, DC: Author.

Valentine, G. (2007) Theorising and researching intersectionality: A challenge for feminist geography, *The Professional Geographer, 59* (1), pp. 10–21.

White, J. L., & Cones, J. H. (1999). *Black man emerging: Facing the past and seizing a future in America.* New York: Routledge.

Whitten, L. (1992). Survival conflict and survival guilt in African-American college students. In M. Lang & C. A. Ford (Eds.), *Strategies for retaining minority students in higher education* (pp. 64-74). Springfield, IL: Charles C. Thomas.

CHAPTER EIGHT

Racial and Sexual Identity Politics in College: New Directions in Campus Equity

Terrell L. Strayhorn

Demographic shifts, globalization trends, and efforts to change from an elite system of higher education to universal access have dramatically altered the complexion and characteristics of faculty members, staff, and students in American colleges and universities (Kuh, 2001; Trow, 1992; U.S. Department of Education, 2006). For instance, while only 943,000 African American students enrolled in college in 1976, more than 1.9 million enroll today, representing a 103% increase in just more than three decades (U.S. Department of Education). Additionally, some evidence suggests a larger presence of lesbian, gay, bisexual, and transgendered (LGBT) persons on college campuses today than ever before, although there are no national data available on the number of LGBT persons in American higher education (Leider, 2000). Still, the weight of evidence suggests that American colleges and universities are now much more diverse in terms of race/ethnicity and sexual orientation.

Many scholars agree that structural diversity, as reflected by the demographic composition of the campus, is a significant aspect of the learning environment as it increases the opportunity for interactional diversity (Gurin, 1999; Hu & Kuh, 2003). Interactional diversity refers to the extent to which individuals from diverse backgrounds actually come into contact with others and interact in educationally purposeful ways (see Dancy, Chapter 5, this volume).

Interactional diversity has been linked to important educational outcomes. For instance, Chang (2001) analyzed Cooperative Institutional Research Program (CIRP) data from 18,188 students attending

392 four-year colleges and found that multiracial campus diversity is a significant and positive, though not strong, predictor of students' likelihood of forming interracial friendships and talking about race and diversity, even after controlling for differences in background traits and campus environments. Additionally, he found that socializing with someone of another race/ethnicity is positively associated with educational outcomes, including self-concept, satisfaction, and retention. Similarly, Hurtado et al. (1999) posited that engaging diverse peers in the learning environment could improve intergroup relations and mutual understanding. By engaging persons whose personal and cultural backgrounds differ from one's own, individuals are more likely to develop positive opinions about "the other" and come to understand them in new and culturally relevant ways (Gay, 2000).

There are other ways that historically underrepresented groups, such as racial/ethnic and sexual minorities in higher education, attempt to (a) fashion a positive sense of self both individually and collectively, (b) establish or improve intergroup relations with majority groups, and (c) achieve mutual understanding with others, which, in turn, may reduce or eliminate marginalizing experiences that render minorities as invisible and voiceless. One way in which this occurs is identity politics. Although theoretical literature suggests the various ways in which racial and sexual minorities engage in identity politics—that is, complicated, oftentimes subtle and implicit processes or collective actions toward positive identity formation and cultural transformation—relatively little campus equity research examines this topic directly. This is the gap addressed by the present chapter.

The purpose of this chapter is to focus on race and sexual identity politics on college campuses as a site for current and future equity work. First, a general framework is outlined about identity politics, highlighting three specific aims of social and political processes designed to empower the disempowered. Next, the mechanics of the study, which served as a basis for the chapter, are outlined briefly. Specifically, I describe the study site, participants, and multiple data sources. Then, using information from the study, findings are presented to illustrate how racial and sexual minorities on college campuses engage in individual and collective actions to achieve the aims of identity politics described previously. The chapter ends with recommendations for new directions in campus equity work.

What Is Identity Politics?

Central to this discussion is the work of cultural studies in general and a social definition of identity and culture in particular. To inform this chapter, I draw upon an inclusive social definition of culture whereby "culture is a description of a particular way of life, which expresses certain meanings and values not only in art and learning but also in institutions and ordinary behavior [sic]" (Williams, 2006, p. 32). Analysis of culture, then, is an activity aimed at clarifying the meanings and values implicit in one's way of life; understanding the meanings that individuals attach to experiences; unraveling the complex interplay between social markers (e.g., class), social locations (e.g., gender, race), and ascribed meanings; articulating how particular meanings become embedded in everyday lives; and tracking the production, circulation, and consumption of meanings (Halle, Kurtz-Costes, & Mahoney, 1997). Identity, then, is established, at least in part, by the psychological identification of individuals with the distinguishing values, beliefs, and objective realities of a particular social group.

In many ways, identity politics requires one to be a cultural anthropologist who, through cultural excavations in part, pays attention to the ways in which dominant, hegemonic values disempower and oppress those who occupy a distinctively "different" social location such as African Americans and LGBT persons. Thus, identity politics seek understanding of distinctiveness that challenges normative characterizations, reducing the complexity of many diverse populations to the simplicity of catch-all phrases such as "non-majority," "non-traditional," "other," and even "etc." Furthermore, identity politics closely examine the range of voices that are heard, even amplified, in the dominant discourse in order to force the inclusion of marginalized perspectives that are often silenced and unheard as well as the tapestry of meanings that are often misunderstood or misrepresented. Whereas culture is fundamentally concerned with the production, circulation, and consumption of meanings, and identity is established, in part, by the psychological identification of individuals and groups with particular meanings, meaning making is a fertile site for studying identity politics as a process of cultural transformation through struggle and negotiation, resistance and incorporation (Storey, 2007). And it is the transformative objectives of identity politics—to secure freedom for marginalized groups through transformation of hegemonic, oppressive norms—that makes this wide range of political activity central to the chapter's focus on campus equity work.

A brief description of the study that informed this chapter is presented in the next section, followed by a summary of key findings related to identity politics and its three key concepts: resistance, representation, and incorporation. The balance of the chapter highlights new directions for campus equity work.

The Study

As part of a larger research program that focuses on the experiences of historically underrepresented groups in American higher education, the study that provided the basis for this chapter consists of both quantitative and qualitative data. While the larger study focuses generally on the experiences of students, this chapter presents information provided by several campus constituents including administrators, faculty members, and students.

Research Site

As I was interested in understanding the complicated, oftentimes subtle, and implicit ways that racial/ethnic and sexual minorities engage in identity politics to promote positive identity formation and cultural transformation in spaces that might otherwise render them marginalized, I collected data at a large, public, research-extensive Predominantly White Institution (PWI) located in the southeastern region of the United States. The institution enrolled approximately 27,000 students and employed 1,400 faculty members; 8% of the students were African Americans according to information provided by the institutional research unit. Institutional data did not exist, however, on the number of LGBT persons on campus.

It's also important to note that the institution is located in the proverbial "Bible Belt," which is fairly well known for its conservative religious views and political opinions about homosexuality as well as an unpleasant racist past that indelibly affects the experiences of African Americans in the region and links the present to a history that many would rather forget (Beauboeuf-Lafontant & Augustine, 1996; Feagin & Sikes, 1995). The demography of the institution is important as it largely represents the ethos and prevailing campus conditions for African Americans and LGBT persons. For instance, although *Brown vs. Board of Education* (347 U.S. 483, 1954) called for desegregation in public services including education, this campus remained mostly White, exclusively non-Black, until the late 1960s when the first African American undergraduate enrolled. Due to hostile campus climate conditions, he left the institution without earning a degree. Secondly, even at the time of the study, the campus did not offer same-sex partner benefits, an LGBT resource center, or an undergraduate major in LGBT or queer studies, all of which are considered "best practices" in the LGBT-friendly Campus Climate Index (Windmeyer, 2006).

Participants

To understand the way in which marginalized groups engage in identity politics on a college campus, information-rich participants were selected using a purposeful sampling approach (Patton, 1990). Specifically, all participants shared several important characteristics. Only African Americans and/or self-identified LGBT persons were selected as participants to reduce, if not eliminate, any unforeseen variability in motives and experiences due to differences in personal identity (e.g., LGBT person vs. ally). Second, the study only included individuals who were active members of one of two campus-wide commissions, hereafter referred to as *African American Commission* (AAC) and *LGBT Commission* (LGBTC), which served in advisory roles to the university's chancellor. Members were defined as anyone who had served on the commission for at least one semester prior to the study and, therefore, was listed on the group's official roster. These sampling criteria were employed to increase the likelihood of identifying individuals who were information rich, somewhat skilled in talking about equity work, and involved in the "doing" of identity politics. All participants are referred to by their self-selected pseudonym or position title to ensure anonymity.

This sampling approach yielded 11 participants. Of these, 7 were members of the AAC, 4 were LGBTC members. AAC participants self-identified as African American (n = 4), Haitian (n = 2), and West Indian. LGBTC members included three openly gay White men and an openly gay White woman.

Data Sources

Data were drawn from several sources including one-on-one interviews (ranging from 90 to 120 minutes each) with members of the two sociopolitical groups (i.e., African Americans and LGBT persons) featured in this chapter, anecdotal evidence that individuals shared with the researcher through various conversations, and campus documents. Three groups of campus documents were examined: minutes from administrative meetings, mission statements, and campus policies, especially those designed to affect the experiences of African Americans and LGBT persons.

Data Analysis

Prior to analysis, qualitative data were organized and stored in NVivo®, a qualitative data analysis software. The analytic process began once all interviews had been transcribed, all documents had been scanned and entered into the study's database, and all marginal notes had been compiled and organized. Data analysis proceeded in several stages using the constant comparison method (Glaser & Strauss, 1999).

First, a preliminary set of codes was identified using a form of open coding. Codes were compared within a single transcript or document and across participants. Then, data were reanalyzed using axial coding to determine whether different words or phrases could be combined or collapsed into similar categories. This process also resulted in the elimination of codes that did not prove significant across participants. Hence, fifteen reasonably distinct categories were inductively derived. In the final stage of analysis, categories were then sorted and organized into broader themes, which are presented in the next section.

Findings

Four major themes were identified using the analytic process outlined in the previous section. First, the weight of evidence suggests that *identity politics* is an essential element of campus equity work. Second, identity politics are undertaken by representatives of a collective whose principal interest is *resistance to oppression*. Third, individuals from certain social locations (e.g., LGBT persons) force the expansion of dominant discourses by giving voice to the experiences and perspectives of their group wherever possible; this is labeled "representation through 'voice.'" Lastly, those who engage in identity politics refuse the legacy insisting that (a) the dominant culture changes its exclusionary practices rather than representing itself as generously accommodating the "special needs" of otherwise marginalized groups or (b) the hegemonic norm is transformed into a standard that respects *everyone* as different. The fourth and final theme is "incorporation through transformation." These findings are discussed below, using verbatim quotes from participants to illustrate the meaning and context of each theme.

Identity Politics as Equity Work

Participants spoke at length about identity politics as an essential element of equity work, both nationally and locally. For instance, LGBTC members described how their maneuvering to secure the civil rights of LGBT persons on campus was linked, in many ways, to a larger "LGBT movement in the nation." By advocating for the inclusion of sexual orientation in the university's non-discrimination clause, establishing an LGBT faculty and staff association as well as partnering with the Division of Student Affairs to explore the efficacy of safe zone programs on college campuses, LGBTC members sought to secure rights and freedoms for LGBT persons on campus as a means of redressing, if not eliminating, inequities in society. Consider the following excerpt from Gary (director of academic unit, chair of LGBTC):

> What makes the work of our commission different from say the work of the faculty senate is the fact that it is one's identity--not his or her rank or tenure status—that makes him a target for discrimination and oppression. The commission's work is about making outcomes equitable for individuals who

> share this identity. And that's what we do...fight for the political right even if it's contrary to our own personal belief. So I think we have to stay current on the political rights and goals of our community both within campus and without. On any given day, we may have to speak up for partner benefits, gay rights, or even offer an opinion about recent decisions like Prop 8 in California. To me, that's identity politics...it's about equity.

Historically marginalized individuals often face multiple disadvantages (Lee, Winfield, & Wilson, 1991); consistent with that belief, participants, on average, saw being involved in the work of the commissions as one of many ways to "fight for justice," as Debra put it. She went on to explain:

> At the end of the day, the work of the Commission is about justice...it's our way or vehicle to fight for justice of LGBT persons on campus. I'll give you a good example. A few months ago we discovered that the campus recreation center, which is open to all faculty, staff, and students, offered shared membership options but they emphasized 'spouse' and 'husband or wife' in their advertisements and application forms. I say discovered but really it's realized because it had been that way for a long, long time. Anyway, what if you're gay and work for the university? You don't have a 'spouse' or 'wife' by traditional definitions. That becomes an equity issue because you can't access the same benefits as others, solely on the basis of your sexual orientation. We brought this to the attention of the entire Commission and then started a campaign, which included a series of meetings and campus forums, to not only fight for the right of gays and lesbians to share their rec center membership with their partners but to also change the language on printed forms and ads.

Similar to what Debra pointed out, 6 out of 11 participants talked about how some campus policies not only reinforce Eurocentric, heteronormative categories of difference (e.g., membership policy that uses heterosexist categories [i.e., married, spouse]) but also contribute to the marginalization of groups by determining race and sexual normalcy. In other words, by not using inclusive language (e.g., partner, co-applicant), the campus policy *implies* that heterosexual relationships are normal and, therefore, represented in the policy while non-heterosexual relationships are abnormal, invisible, and unrepresented.

Members of the African American Commission also described identity politics as part of campus equity work. Charlie, past-chair of the commission, paraphrased the AAC's purpose and objective: "We do a lot of stuff but our main goal is to protect and represent the interests of Black people on campus." Throughout the interviews, participants revealed that this was accomplished through a variety of activities. Activities included but were not limited to: meeting with senior/central administrators (e.g., provost, chancellor), hosting social events and educational workshops, and writing "press releases" or op-ed articles that address the specific needs of African Americans on campus.

Whereas LGBTC members saw their work as connected to a broader national movement toward gay rights, AAC members saw their work as a present-day continuation of the 1960s civil rights movement. Melanie (a sociology professor who served as AAC secretary) offered her perspective, which generally reflected that of others:

> I don't think a lot of people believe that African Americans still face a number of formidable challenges on campus and I'm talking about faculty, staff, and students. This isn't new though. What we do on this commission is similar, in many ways, to what African Americans have always had to do…fight. In the 1960s, Martin and others led the fight for our right to vote, to eat in public restaurants, to ride the bus home. And even now in the year 2009, the Commission is leading a similar effort to ensure that Black faculty can be elected to office in senate fairly and that Black students can come and go to class without being harassed, assaulted or feeling like they're the only one here. So I like what you called it…identity politics because that's what we're doing—politicking for our identity.

Indeed, participants agreed that identity politics is an essential aspect of their work for equity and justice on campus. Furthermore, equity work on campus was perceived as being connected to broader, national (LGBTC) and historical (AAC) civil rights movements. Engaging in identity politics and campus equity work provided a mechanism for pursuing justice and fighting for the rights and interests of one's social identity group.

Resistance to Oppression

Many of the participants described identity politics as resistance to oppression; this is the second major finding. Oppression was typically defined as exclusionary policies, practices, and environments that systematically restrict, constrain, or limit opportunities based on involuntary membership in a particular social group, such as African Americans and/or LGBT persons. While participants employed a variety of strategies to resist oppression, two deserve emphasis given the frequency with which they were mentioned across interviews: converting oppression into encouragement/empowerment and intentionally challenging stereotypes/perceptions.

According to participants, identity politics involved resistance to oppression, and one way they resisted oppression was to convert sites of oppression (i.e., events, practices) into source(s) of encouragement and empowerment. The following quotes illustrate how this relates to the work of the AAC and LGBTC, respectively:

> One thing we do very well, I think, is education and consciousness-raising. We try to turn negative, potentially marginalizing experiences into points of pride. You can't do this all the time but we have been successful at doing it every now and again. A lot of campuses saw negative problems on their campus on November 4th when Obama won the White House. Even here on our campus we had a few negative incidents involving Whites and Black students. It was confirmed that someone hung a noose outside the cultural center and, as you can guess, this upset a lot of students—Black, White, Asian, all. We still released a statement condemning that behavior but we also hosted an event on campus talking about the history of racism in the south, lynching, and how historic and inspiring Barack's election is given that history. We like to think we took a sore point and made it a point of pride [laughing]. (AAC member)

> We've come a long way but we're far from done to make this place open and welcoming of all people, especially gays and lesbians. We finally got sexual orientation into the campus non-discrimination statement and we have several committees for LGBT persons on campus. That doesn't mean it's perfect. Last year, a woman was denied tenure seemingly on the basis of her sexual orientation, several people admit to knowing that some applicants aren't hired because of their sexual orientation, and a few years ago a student was beaten badly in the residence hall because he was gay. I'm not saying it's all gloom-and-doom but we've got to do more to make these negative experiences educative. The tenure situation allowed us an opportunity to educate some people about the tenure process, criteria for tenure, and why tenured LGBT faculty add to the richness of the education provided by [said institution]. (LGBTC member)

Intentionally challenging stereotypes and negative perceptions was another way that participants resisted oppression in campus environments. For instance, Jamel (a third-year engineering major, AAC member) recalled instances when negative stereotypes about Black men affected his experiences in the classroom. On one occasion during his first-year, Jamel stayed after class to talk to his "mechanics of engineering professor," Dr. Haas, about switching to mechanical engineering as a major. Jamel's interest was driven largely by Dr. Haas' unusual ability to engage students actively in their own learning. After expressing his interest in majoring in mechanical engineering, Jamel was stopped abruptly by the professor (laughing):

> I encourage you to think seriously about this and perhaps to consider another major. Engineering is difficult and very few minorities pass when majoring in it. It's just hard for them. I think it's the math and science really.

Dazed and confused, especially by Dr. Haas' use of "them" to refer to minorities as if his student was not part of *that* collective, Jamel sought the advice of his mentor (a Black administrator on campus, also an AAC member) who encouraged him to "not only major in engineering but beat the stereotype." Jamel did exactly that—majored in mechanical engineering to challenge prevailing perceptions of African Americans as non-scientific or technical.

Both Jamel and his mentor cited the experience above as identity politics, although it is a bit more complicated than previously understood. "Jamel was fighting on behalf of himself and the entire [Black] race. That's what makes this work so difficult—it's personal and political, selfish and selfless simultaneously." Jamel's story offers a poignant illustration of how racial and sexual minorities resist oppression by intentionally challenging stereotypes and negative perceptions that the dominant culture may hold about them individually or their identity group as a whole.

Several members of the LGBTC also alluded to intentionally challenging stereotypes and negative perceptions that individuals hold about LGBT people through their actions, decisions, and behaviors. For instance, commission leaders stressed the importance of outreach activities and educational workshops to correct misperceptions of gay men and women as promiscuous lovers, flamboyant, materialistic, and sexual predators. They admitted that removing or erasing prejudice and erroneous stereotypes is not easy. "It takes experience and engagement," Ricky noted; "people think those things because they have not had enough interaction with LGBT people for their stereotypes to be challenged by reality...part of our job is to challenge the stereotypes by exposing folks to reality."

Resisting oppression by converting sites of oppression into sources of pride or places from which to draw strength and/or by challenging racist or homophobic stereotypes through one's own actions, participants engaged in a complicated, oftentimes implicit, process of identity politics to reduce erroneous beliefs, interrupt hegemonic characterizations, and promote positive identity formation.

Representation through "Voice"

An interesting observation was made about the ways in which AAC and LGBTC members engage in a wide range of activities to "give voice" to the experiences of African Americans and LGBT people, respectively. Sponsoring campus events (e.g., Black History Month speakers, LGBT monthly concerts), establishing and/or serving on special interest groups (e.g., Black Faculty & Staff Association, LGBT Student Association), and authoring campus publications (e.g., "State of the Black Union") were legitimate attempts to expose others to the realities and lived experiences of their respective community.

Hosting public forums was another way that participants gave voice to the realities and lived experiences of their respective community. Public forums were especially useful as they tended to attract large audiences, provided a means for responding to critical incidents quickly and publicly, and served as one of few mechanisms for working with other identity groups on campus. Cliff (AAC member, former chair) described a public forum that was held after a controversial situation involving the denial of tenure to an openly gay Black lesbian:

> See, we do a lot of the behind-the-scenes work to make sure that Blacks are heard and represented on campus. When they denied tenure to [said professor], we were outraged. She had more than enough publications, excellent teaching evaluations, and her tenure was supported all the way up to the Dean and provost. It's simple...she was denied tenure either because of her race, her sexual orientation, or both. We held a public forum and talked about the details of her case. A lot of people did not know that her colleagues in the department and college supported her. AAC partnered with

> the LGBTC and discussed the nature of her work and how the question seemed to turn on issues of civil rights for Blacks and LGBT persons. It was very well-attended and turned much needed attention to her story, her experience at [said institution].

Lack of representation through which to "voice" the concerns and needs of one's community was a consistent concern across groups. Thomas (student affairs director, LGBTC member) explained:

> Another problem we face is not knowing the needs of our community but rather having sufficient representation on campus to voice our concerns to. We have very, very few openly gay administrators and faculty on campus. So, when it comes to faculty and staff senate, you're virtually invisible because there are not mouthpieces to speak up. The students have the student group but my understanding is that that are still problems there trying to find a spokesman or spokeswoman too [chuckling].

So, a second aspect of identity politics is representation through voice. Racial and sexual minorities engage in a wide range of activities to give voice to the experiences and needs of their community although lack of representation is a major issue that deserves attention.

Incorporation through Transformation

A fourth major finding related to the ultimate goal or intended outcomes of identity politics and campus equity work is incorporation through transformation. This theme recalls information about culture that began this chapter. Without exception, all participants identified transformation—not acculturation or assimilation—as the target of their efforts. Similar to Kruks' (2001) conceptualization of identity politics, participants sought acceptance and inclusion in the campus culture *as* different rather than *in spite of* differences. Kruks pointed out: "What makes identity politics a significant departure from earlier, pre-identarian forms of the politics of recognition is its demand for recognition on the basis of the very grounds on which recognition has previously been denied; it is qua women, qua Blacks, qua lesbians that groups demand recognition" (p. 85).

Several examples illustrate the AAC's and LGBTC's efforts to transform the dominant cultural context or "norm." Members of these two communities engaged in [political] actions, both individually and collectively, to change the dominant discourse and alter the prevailing culture into one that is more accepting and inclusive. Julian described this well:

> About 40 years ago, African Americans could not attend college especially not in the south. Now that we're here at [said institution] our job is more than representing ourselves well and speaking up for others. We have to leave our mark, you know? Leave the place a little different from how we found it. This is what gets us as a campus moving away from tolerance toward true acceptance and inclusion of those who may be different from the dominant culture. To change the place, you have to leave a sign behind. The cultural center is a sign; it changes the culture just by being here on campus. Degree programs in Africana Studies…even the AAC attempt to transform the campus so that diversity and inclusion or incorporation are not just possible but inevitable.

All LGBTC participants echoed the sentiments of Julian's comments and described in elaborate detail the ways in which the LGBTC sought to change the dominant culture on campus. Debra shared the following, while fighting back tears:

> I've been here for 25 years and my service on the LGBT commission started about 12 years ago. We continue to face barriers and sometimes even roadblocks to the progress we hope to achieve. I remember when we started a petition to establish the LGBT commission; it was met with unusual resistance and protests from faculty and staff. At the time, we had a chancellor who was fairly supportive and he agreed to establish the commission without financial support or even a formal policy statement. A few years passed, we were formally recognized through a university resolution and we started our campaign for inclusive policies for faculty and staff…partner benefits and stuff, you know. Well, that was basically World War III…again, met with unusual and vicious resistance. It's just an uphill battle all the time it seems [pausing to wipe tears from her eyes]. Our fight never ends though and we're now trying to establish an LGBT resource center, a queer studies major or minor, and still hammering away at the partner benefits issue. It's not enough to say we're welcome here…the campus has to be transformed and changed to incorporate aspects of our identity, our interests, our community too.

Discussion

Findings presented in this chapter reveal the myriad ways in which racial and sexual minorities on college campuses engage in identity politics as equity work, to resist oppression, and to give voice to the realities and needs of their respective communities. Below, I summarize potential new directions that can be derived from the study's results.

Centering on the experiences of historically underrepresented groups can reveal much about how members of such groups engage in individual and collective acts of resistance to challenge oppression as part of identity politics. And, while useful, the chapter's study is limited in its focus on African Americans and LGBT persons. Future equity work might examine the political maneuvering of other identity groups including Latinos, Asian Pacific Islanders, international students, as well as bisexual and transgendered persons who were noticeably absent in the preceding sections.

Research also is needed that analyzes how individuals and groups use different and often unrecognized forms of resistance in response to domination. For example, recall Jamel's story. Jamel exercised his personal agency to declare a major in mechanical engineering despite discouragement and potential psychological violence (Strayhorn, in press) from his professor. Exercising one's agency through personal decisions that may also reduce, if not eliminate, stereotypes held about the group is one way that minorities resist oppression, although this is infrequently discussed in the literature. Thus, more information is needed, and future equity work should pay attention to these subtle ways of reworking the margin (hooks, 1990).

Those engaged in campus equity work do not need to be members of the respective identity group or to have a personal stake in an issue to recognize erroneous assumptions, ideological traps, and inequitable policies and practices. What's needed are individuals who can offer serious critiques of our campuses, where necessary, that allow us to transform them. In that way, allies make viable partners in the work of identity politics as they may be better able to uncover hidden and unexamined assumptions that operate within and reinforce the dominant structure. Thus, I not only encourage partnerships with allies in future equity work but also commission research that examines the experiences of allies engaged in social justice work on college campuses.

Theory also plays a role in equity work. Critical theory has been found to be an illuminating interpretive framework for analyzing mainstream cultural practices and processes (Stage, 2007). Moreover, critical theories, such as critical race theory, can be used to understand campus policies and beliefs as well as to expose and critique inconsistent assumptions that underlie such practices. Educators and social justice activists, then, are encouraged to maintain a critical theory perspective in future equity work. Casting a critical eye on issues of power and how individual lives are mediated by racism, sexism, and homophobia, we are positioned to find new pathways through the puzzles we face in campus equity work.

References

Beauboeuf-Lafontant, T., & Augustine, D. S. (Eds.). (1996). *Facing racism in education* (2nd ed.). Cambridge, MA: Harvard Educational Review.

Brown v. Board of Education, 347 483 (U.S. 1954).

Chang, M. J. (2001). The positive educational effects of racial diversity on campus. In G. Orfield & M. Kurlaender (Eds.), *Diversity challenged: Evidence on the impact of affirmative action* (pp. 175–186). Cambridge, MA: The Civil Rights Project, Harvard Education Publishing Group.

Feagin, J. R., & Sikes, M. P. (1995). How Black students cope with racism on White campuses. *Journal of Blacks in Higher Education, 8*, 91–97.

Gay, G. (2000). *Culturally responsive teaching: Theory, research, & practice*. New York: Teachers College Press.

Glaser, B. G., & Strauss, A. L. (1999). *The discovery of grounded theory: Strategies for qualitative research*. New York: Aldine DeGruyter.

Gurin, P. (1999). The compelling need for diversity in higher education, Expert testimony in *Gratz et al. v. Bollinger et al. Michigan. Journal of Race & Law, 5*, 363–425.

Halle, T. G., Kurtz-Costes, B., & Mahoney, J. L. (1997). Family influences on school achievement in low-income, African American children. *Journal of Educational Psychology, 89*, 527–537.

hooks, b. (1990). Choosing the margin as a space of radical openness. In b. hooks (Ed.), *Yearnings: Race, gender, and cultural politics* (pp. 145–153). Boston, MA: South End Press.

Hu, S., & Kuh, G. D. (2003). Diversity experiences and college student learning and personal development. *Journal of College Student Development, 44*(3), 320–334.

Hurtado, S., Milem, J. F., Clayton-Pederson, A., & Allen, W. A. (1999). *Enacting diverse learning environments: Improving the climate for racial/ethnic diversity on campus* (ASHE-ERIC Report Series Vol. 26, No. 8). Washington, DC: George Washington University.

Kruks, S. (2001). *Retrieving excellence: Subjectivity and recognition in feminist politics.* Ithaca, NY: Cornell University Press.

Kuh, G. D. (2001). Assessing what really matters to student learning: Inside the National Survey of Student Engagement. *Change, 33*(3), 10–17, 66.

Lee, V. E., Winfield, L. F., & Wilson, T. C. (1991). Academic behaviors among high-achieving African-American students. *Education and Urban Society, 24,* 65–86.

Leider, S. (2000). *Sexual minorities on community college campuses* (No. ED 427 796). Los Angeles: ERIC Clearinghouse for Community Colleges.

Patton, M. Q. (1990). *Qualitative evaluation and research methods* (2nd ed.). Newbury Park, CA: Sage.

Stage, F. K. (2007). Answering critical questions using quantitative data. In F. K. Stage (Ed.), *New directions for institutional research: No. 133. Using quantitative data to answer critical questions* (pp. 5-16). San Francisco: Jossey Bass.

Storey, J. (2007). Culture and hegemony. In M. Reiss, R. DePalma & E. Atkinson (Eds.), *Marginality and difference in education and beyond* (pp. 3–14). Stoke-on-Trent, UK: Trentham Books.

Strayhorn, T. L. (in press). The burden of proof: A quantitative study of high-achieving Black collegians [Electronic Version]. *Journal of African American Studies* from http://www.springerlink.com/content/gg732gw647542117.

Trow, M. (1992). Class, race, and higher education in America. *American Behavioral Scientist, 35,* 585–605.

U.S. Department of Education, National Center for Education Statistics. (2006). *The condition of education 2006* (NCES 2006-071). Washington, DC: U.S. Government Printing Office.

Williams, R. (2006). The analysis of culture. In J. Storey (Ed.), *Cultural theory and popular culture: A reader* (3rd ed., pp. 32–40). London: Pearson.

Windmeyer, S. L. (2006). *The Advocate college guide for LGBT students*. New York: Alyson Publishers, Inc.

CHAPTER NINE

Manhood and Masculinities in College: Connecting Theory and Research to Practice

T. Elon Dancy II

Men know so little of men.

W. E. B. Du Bois (1903)

The concept of diversity is one for which drawing conceptual parameters is difficult. It is common parlance across America to think of diversity as variances across ethnicity and/or race followed by gender and class; however, the diversity concept is far broader than those social categories. In higher education, schools of thought organize the diversity concept in two primary ways for individuals. One way, *structural diversity* refers to the numerical or proportional representation of different races and ethnicities on college campuses. The other, *interactional diversity* describes the ways in which individuals encounter others' differences (Hurtado, Milem, Clayton-Pedersen, & Allen, 1999). While these definitions provide useful frameworks for understanding the diversity concept, we must remain open to how acknowledged and unimagined differences may alter our understanding of diversity.

The diversity concept evokes otherness or human qualities that vary inside or outside groups to which individuals feel they belong. Hence, other dimensions of diversity include but are not limited to: age, ancestry, gender, physical abilities/qualities, educational background, geographic location, income, marital status, military experience, religious beliefs, parental status, and work experience. One dimension of diversity often missing from this list is masculinity and femininity, or diversity of behavior and physical expression as connected (or disconnected) to gender. Masculine diversities, or masculinities, are often marginalized in conversations about diversity in higher education and society writ large. However, these concepts are valuable in broader conversations about gendered trends and futures in higher education (Ropers-Huilman, 2003). Men's issues in higher education are compelling sites to explore these concepts further.

Historically, the large majority of participants in American higher education were White men. Later, American higher education sought to preserve White men's economic, social, and political interests even after minorities and women gained access (Gordon, 1997). Over time, gender gaps are apparent despite diversification of college student bodies. Today, women outnumber men in college participation overall (Snyder, 2009). To be sure, gendered trends do not necessarily hold in the same ways when factors like family income level and ethnicity are considered. Also, collegiate enrollment among diverse groups is disproportionately gendered albeit men of oppressed races and ethnicities are no longer barred from higher education as a matter of policy (Brown & Lane, 2003). Men are enrolling in college and completing college degrees at greater rates than men two decades ago but not nearly as fast as women (NCES, 2009). In addition, men continue to hold a disproportionate majority in many science and engineering majors while women are generally receiving more associate, bachelor's, master's, and doctoral degrees than men (NCES, 2009). Also, women generally receive better grades than men (NCES, 2009). However, gendered trends among collegiate personnel do not reflect those among students.

Men continue to dominate the leadership of colleges and universities. More specifically, a recent report from the American Association of Colleges and Universities (AAC&U) reveals that women are greatly underrepresented in college presidencies (Touchton, 2008). Further, the report notes that 38% of current senior academic administrators are women with only 7% of these being women of color. Women are only 38% of chief academic officers with only 3% of these being women of color. In addition, men faculty continue to outnumber women across academic programs and men are more likely to be tenured and promoted to higher faculty ranks (The Chronicle of Higher Education Almanac, 2009). A large body of feminist work compels us to think critically about gender, gender roles, and relational aspects (i.e., masculinity and femininity) as these shape student, faculty, and administrative lives in higher education. Historical work as well compels higher education as an American institution to develop what it knows about men.

For instance, in the classic *The Souls of Black Folk*, W.E.B. Du Bois (1903/2005) posits the assessment, "men know so little of men." Though over one hundred years have passed, this statement locates its relevance in a dearth of higher education research and scholarship on men as gendered and masculine beings. Therefore, the purpose of this chapter is to engage the topics of college men and masculinities through conceptual and theoretical frameworks of gender, masculinity, and diversity. The chapter first conceptualizes and separates the concepts of gender, manhood, and masculinities. Second, this chapter describes the ways in which various phobias and sexism are shaped and often witnessed in collegiate contexts. In this discussion, the concept of effemophobia is introduced as it nuances higher education's thinking about diverse affects or gender performance among men. In introducing and reviewing concepts, this chapter encourages colleges and universities to think more inclusively about gender and diverse masculinities when shaping diversity initiatives on college campuses. Implications and helpful strategies are offered in this regard.

Social Constructions of Gender, Manhood, and Masculinities

The conceptual frameworks for this chapter draw from social constructivist thinking about gender, manhood, and masculinity. First, it is important to draw distinctions between sex and gender. The term sex describes biological differences between bodies, categorizing individuals as males and females (Schoenberg, 1993). Men's studies scholar Michael Kimmel (1987b) recalls that the historical study of men used a "sex-role" model which detailed the ways in which innate biological differences between males and females encode different social behaviors. However this paradigm is largely critiqued in the literature as too static and oversimplified (Connell, 1995; Courtenay, 2000; Gerson & Peiss, 1985; Kimmel & Messner, 2007). Highlighting the limitations of sex-role models, Kimmel (1987b) writes, "The sex-role paradigm posits a historically invariant model, a kind of static sex-role container into which all biological males and females are forced to fit [and] posits an ideal configuration that bears little, if any, relation to the ways in which sex roles are enacted in everyday life" (p. 12).

In contrast, gender is socially constructed through relationships, teachings, and reminders of appropriateness which are produced and reproduced through the actions of individuals (Kimmel & Messner, 2007). More descriptively, Ropers-Huilman (2003) offers the following conceptualization of gender:

> Girls and boys, men and women, are reminded of their proper sex roles through both formal and informal education. Through the interactions in many contexts, gender is constructed. Although we are each born with a biological sex that is more or less determined, the ways in which our sex is expressed through social practices is known as gender...From the beginning, when boys are encouraged to be active and told not to cry, when girls are praised for their appearance and their quiet and polite behavior, when both boys and girls are given gender-specific toys that implicitly teach them what each gender is "supposed" to find pleasurable, gender is formed. However, gender is not formed only during the early years of our lives. Instead, in our interactions throughout our lives, we subtly (and sometimes not so subtly) let others know what we expect from them as gendered beings (p. 2).

Though men and women are reminded of the proper sex roles, as Ropers-Huilman points out, men are less likely to think about themselves as gendered beings. Kimmel and Messner (2007) argue that men often think of themselves as genderless given that men's gender is a mechanism which affords privilege. Consequently, mechanisms that afford privilege are often invisible to those who possess them (Kimmel & Messner, 2007). Thus, the authors observe, White people rarely think of themselves as "raced" people, and wealthier classes rarely think of themselves as "classed." Individuals belonging to those categories are not socially marginalized, and therefore those identities are non-negotiated in their daily lives. This chapter stands with social constructivist work in arguing that men are gendered in their social lives and experiences.

More easily located in social science literature, the concept of manhood is useful for understanding the varied outcomes of men's gendering process. To become men, males are exposed to gendering processes across cultures that shape their ideas and ideals about social interactions and appropriateness. Ultimately, the lessons men accept comprise their manhood. In a study of Black men, Hunter and Davis (1992) develop a tripod definition: (1) self-expectations (2) relationship and responsibility to family, and (3) worldviews or existential philosophies. In their work, various attributes considered important by men to their manhood were clustered around the three manhood constructs. The following clusters emerged: (1) education/intellectual skills, (2) spirituality and religion, (3) risk-taking, (4) being respected and (5) authority. According to Hunter and Davis, African American men define manhood in multiple arenas and contexts both within and beyond traditional notions of masculinity and the male role.

Manhood is often distinctive along the social categories, or dimensions, of diversity (i.e. race, class, sexual orientation) (Dancy, in press). For example, Du Bois' theory of double-consciousness suggests the ways in which manhood development is nuanced for black men. The theory of double consciousness suggests that African American men face a unique struggle in developing manhood in America. Du Bois' theory posits that African American men are burdened to act in ways that may be different from the manhood lessons they accept. A recent study of Black male college students bears this theory out (Dancy, in press). Gender and manhood, however, are conceptually different from masculinity.

Recall that gender denotes a socialization process to assume sex-roles, while manhood refers to meanings that men accept in their gendered lives. Masculinity, conversely, refers to the socially constructed behaviors, demonstrations or performances of men. These enactments are used across societies and cultures to honor, identify, respect, disguise, and/or to make others aware of their manhood (Alexander, 2006; Kimmel, 2002). The plural form, masculinities, is a way of acknowledging differences among masculine enactments. Scholars point out the relational aspect of masculinity and femininity (Connell, 1995). This chapter notes that masculinity does not exist except in contrast with femininity. Perceptions of men and women as masculine or feminine reflect cultural stereotypes as opposed to psychological realities (Bem, 1987; Constantinople, 1973). Thus, women may be masculine and men may be feminine. Men largely receive social messages, however, that masculine is what men ought to be.

It also important to remember the ways in which manhood and masculinities are intersected with race, gender, class, sexual orientation, age, and other social categories. Given the framework described above, there are Latino heterosexual middle-class manhood and masculinities, Asian educated manhood and masculinities, and White gay religious manhood and masculinities and various other interplays on manhood and masculinity. Thus, fully understanding different manhood and masculinities involves recognizing the intersections of men's many identities as these shape relations with others. In the following section, relations among men and women are considered as they further shape inequities in higher education.

Patriarchy, Hegemony, and Compulsory Heterosexuality in Colleges

Patriarchy is socially reproduced in America and across its institutions (hooks, 2004; Kimmel & Messner, 2007). hooks (2004) defines patriarchy as a political-social system in which men inherently dominate, are superior to everything and everyone deemed weak especially women, and endowed with the right to dominate the weak and to maintain that dominance through various forms of psychological terrorism and violence. hooks further offers the idea that the American patriarchal system is "imperialist White-supremacist capitalist" in scope (hooks, 2004, p. 18). Over time, she argues, men overtly and/or covertly subject women and diverse men to positions of inferiority to maintain power, or, hegemony. American institutions therefore are pressured to evade practices which draw equity into question. Colleges and universities are compromised, however, in light of study findings that instead draw collegiate equity into question.

For instance, Jackson (2001) found disparate college hiring practices of African American and White male faculty. More specifically, the researcher found that both human capital (i.e., education) and merit-based performance measures were good employment predictors for White men but not for African American men. While human capital and merit-based performance mattered for African American men faculty, findings suggest insincere review and/or devaluing of African

American male faculty credentials. Jackson (2001) also conducted additional research studies highlighting additional concerns that included lack of support for administrators of color employed on college campuses.

Another example of how college practice draws questions about equity is found in Glazer-Raymo's (2003) work. She notes that 71% of all male faculty are tenured at their institutions in comparison to 52% of women. In addition, she observes that women comprise the majority of part-time faculty. She contextualizes these trends with reminders of how women faculty are also largely expected to balance their work with family responsibilities (for which differences exist between men and women). She suggests that disrupting patriarchy involves conducting institutional policy analyses which engage gender as a category analytically rather than descriptively. Instituting this idea at the policy level seeks to thwart continued efforts that end in disparate outcomes. The suggestion here is that patriarchy as repeated practice is dangerous as inequity is normalized in colleges in various ways.

Hegemony refers to how ruling groups normalize patriarchal ideologies and marginalize others' ideologies to maintain power and dominance (Gramsci, 1971). Consequently, cultural perspectives are skewed to favor the dominant group. As a result of hegemony, patriarchy is empowered and diverse others excluded. Accordingly, hegemonic manhood ideals align with and maintain the tenets of patriarchy while hegemonic masculinity becomes what men do, perform, or enact to maintain patriarchy (Connell, 1995; Summers, 2004). Hegemonic masculinity may reflect the following behaviors: (1) showing homophobia, or in other words, the fear or hatred of GBT men, (2) behaving in ways that devalue femininity, (3) increasing masculine bravado, and (4) claiming masculine space within spaces deemed feminine or feminized (Anderson, 2007). Hegemonic manhood and masculinity are important in conversations about men college students in groups, fraternities or athletics.

With these notions in mind, Boswell and Spade (2007) studied social interactions between men and women at a private coeducational college in which nearly half of the entire student enrollment was affiliated with Greek-letter organizations. More specifically, the authors asked 40 women students to identify fraternities considered high risk for sexual aggression. In addition, the authors interviewed men from selected fraternities and women who attended fraternity-sponsored parties. In high-risk houses, men treated women as subordinates, men advised each other against relationships in lieu of casual sex, and routinely degraded women. In this study, subordination of women is found to be a tool of patriarchy. Connell (1995) in his theorization largely explores the concept of subordination in relations among heterosexual and gay men. Around the same time, another writer offers a framework specific to relations among men with diverse sexual orientations.

Poet Adrienne Rich (1994) introduced the concept of compulsory heterosexuality to challenge the notion that heterosexuality is a natural expression of human sexuality and other forms are unnatural. The concept of compulsory heterosexuality describes the ways in which the sexual identity leads to social power struggles in America. Compulsory heterosexuality is the assumption that women and men are innately attracted to each other emotionally and sexually and that heterosexuality in America leads to an institutionalized inequality of power not only between heterosexuals and lesbian, gay, bisexual, and transgender (LGBT) persons but also between men and women with far-reaching consequences (Rich, 1994).

Rich (1994) argues that compulsory heterosexuality is patriarchal as men dominate all aspects of women's lives, including their sexuality, childbirth and rearing activities, safety, physical movement, labor, and access to knowledge. Compulsory heterosexuality, Rich argues, also leads to discrimination against, intolerance of, and/or invisibility of LGBT persons in society (Rich, 1994). In this frame, the interests of GBT men are sacrificed under compulsory heterosexuality if they do not conform to heterosexual ideals and behavior. The act of "coming out," or acknowledging a sexual orientation other than heterosexual, in a compulsory heterosexual world represents rebellion and often leads to the marginalization of LGBT persons. Thus, same-sex relationships are taboo and often criminalized while pressure is placed on people to form heterosexual relationships and bonds (Rich, 1994). As Rich conceptualizes the presence and function of compulsory heterosexuality in America, she suggests that the need cultures feel to enforce male-female relationships suggests that heterosexuality may be less of a natural response and more of a social conditioning.

Compulsory heterosexuality works to marginalize sexually diverse men in American institutions of higher education (Case, 1998; Dancy, in press; Dilley, 2002; Rhoads, 1994). Rhoads' (1994) study of eleven GBT male collegians, for instance, suggests the ways in which compulsory heterosexuality works in the lives of gay and heterosexual college students. In this research GBT men describe experiences that affect decisions to come out of "the closet" (proclaiming GBT identity in a unifying sense) or remain in "the closet" (concealing queer, gay, or bisexual identity). Rhoads defines "the closet" as the oppression of lesbian and GBT men who are forced to remain silent about their sexual identity. Thus, Rhoads' work supports the visibility of collegiate programs for college students with diverse sexual orientations. In turn, this disrupts the silence and intimidation around sexual orientation diversity that compulsory heterosexuality intends.

In *The Brother Code: Manhood and Masculinity among African American Men in College,* Dancy (2010) studied twenty-four African American men enrolled across twelve colleges and universities. In his work, one participant described the way in which compulsory heterosexuality shapes his gender, arguing that faculty perceive him as good given his lasting romantic relationships with women. Other participants argued that friendships with women were signs of weakness which were also juxtaposed with gayness. Conversely, participants in this study who were gay or charged with "acting gay" described past experiences in which college men attempted to silence them in their fraternities or other campus groups. As the following section considers, attempts to subjugate others were not necessarily rooted in men's homophobias but their effemophobias.

Nuancing Oppression: Homophobia vs. Effemophobia

Researchers argue that homophobia plays a powerful role in male peer culture (Connell, 1995; Constantine-Simms, 2001; Plummer, 2001). In addition, scholars argue that homophobic reactions create additional challenges in gay men's college experiences (Dancy, in press; Dilley, 2002; Rhoads, 1994). Notwithstanding, homophobia is defined as the "fear or hatred of homosexuals and homosexuality"

(Plummer, 2001, p. 60). Plummer argues that homophobia emerges given men's desires to reinforce values of hegemonic masculinity, which includes separating "real men" and "others" (p. 69). Men's ability, however, to determine who is a real man is often tied to men's masculinities.

Early in their development, boys learn to adhere to a behavior code, or code of hegemonic masculinity, that dictates appropriate ways in which boys act, dress, talk, walk, and otherwise express themselves (Alexander, 2006; Dancy, forthcoming). Thus, young boys learn early to avoid certain foods (i.e., chicken salad sandwiches), certain drinks (i.e., low-alcohol drinks with umbrellas) and certain behaviors (i.e., showing compassion) (Plummer, 2001). Boys and men are often pressured to engage in high-risk behavior (i.e., driving cars dangerously, joining a gang) to construct borders between themselves and those men who avoid these behaviors and are more likely to be labeled gay. Scholars consistently identify homophobia as influential to how men present themselves to others, their social networks as well as their educational, career, life, and other pursuits (Anderson, 2007; Plummer, 2001). In many cases, though, it is unclear whether men who are victims of homophobia are actually gay or have sex with men. Therefore, a need to add to thought in this area emerges.

This chapter offers effemophobia as a way to think about the homophobia phenomenon more clearly. The term, effemophobia, is more readily located in popular media outlets and refers to the fear of feminine behavior and affect (i.e., compassion, vulnerability) among men. Nearly half the men in Dancy's (2007) study acknowledged being labeled as "acting gay" for behaving or engaging in activities deemed feminine. However, only one participant in the study identified himself as gay. Yet this study and others argue that colleges need to mine their institutions for ways to eliminate homophobia but not the phenomenon of effemophobia. An additional study emerges to provide an interesting context for this conversation.

Anderson (2007) studied 68 self-identified heterosexual men who used to play high school football but became collegiate cheerleaders because they were unable to make their university football teams. Using in-depth interviews and observations, Anderson sought to understand how heterosexual men in collegiate cheerleading construct masculinity. Participants in this study shared their views on homosexuality and femininity in men as well as perceptions of women's athleticism and leadership qualities. Additionally, study participants shared how they maintained heterosexual manhood and their management of this varied from when they were football players. In discussing findings, Anderson acknowledges heterosexual men's discomfort with effeminate men but does not indicate this as a phenomenon akin to sexism and homophobia.

Like homophobia, effemophobia is innately linked to sexism or belief that one's gender is inferior. However, as sexism refers to disdain for femininity in women, effemophobia describes disdain for femininity in men. As described earlier, men identified the ways in which they were negatively sanctioned in men's groups as though they were gay albeit these men are not gay-identified. Rather, these men are perceived as feminine or possessing orthodox female sensibilities. Thus, effemophobia is a way of viewing this phenomenon given much scholarship on hegemonic constructions of manhood and masculinity among men (Dancy, in press; Hunter & Davis, 1992; Kimmel, 1987a; Kimmel & Messner, 2007).

Men's Relationships and Campus Diversity: Implications for Research and Practice

Implications for Research

Historically, how White college men used masculinity in negotiating social norms in the broader society was at the center of the research on college men and masculinities. For instance, Komarovsky's (1976) classic, *Dilemmas of Masculinity: A Study of College Youth,* focused on how a sample of college men (most of whom were White) used masculinity in their relationships with women who attended an Ivy League college. The primary purpose of this research was to understand perceived strains in men's gender roles and to better understand how reorganizing these gender roles might bring society closer to its core values. However, Komarovsky avoids offering implications for higher education practice as the intent of her study was broader, informing society about how masculinity may be reconceptualized. Both Komarovsky's study and historical work like Townsend's (1999) *Manhood at Harvard* found college samples of men purposeful in studies of social norms. Only recently are studies envisioning colleges as sites of masculine development or illustrating links between men's gender role development and collegiate achievement and retention (Capraro, 2007; Dancy, in press; J. E. Davis, 2005; T. L. Davis, 2002; Tatum & Charlton, 2008). Moreover, colleges are intriguing sites to study campus diversity given its co-educational spaces, all-male peer groups, and the ways in which these are raced, classed, sexually oriented, religious, and otherwise diverse.

Research investigating gender, manhood, and masculinity phenomena requires more nuanced questions than those that only seek to generally understand pre-college and college experiences. Rather, research is required to discover the multiple ways in which men's lives are shaped in the pre-college and college experiences. Answers to these questions may help colleges funnel orthodox or transgressive masculinities, for example, into social experiences that become stronger predictors for persistence or attrition. Concurrently, research encourages institutions to focus their attention, not only on the availability of good institutional practices, but the applications, deliveries, and behaviors associated with these (Braxton, Milem, & Sullivan, 2000). Additional study of college men and masculinities may potentially inform theories of retention.

In addition, men's relationships with others are also appealing sites to study diversity in colleges. Additional study should also consider the meanings men construct through friendships and informal relationships with each other and other students. These may inform institutions more clearly about male students' attitudes toward diversity and potentially provide insight into the ways in which colleges may shape similar experiences institution-wide. Such an empirical investigation would build upon research which identifies men's friendship groups as sites to study openness to diversity (antonio, 2004). To inform research on classroom diversity, additional study is required to learn the impact of faculty pedagogy and collegiate classroom norms of manhood and gender relations. All-male peer groups (i.e., fraternities, all-male student organizations) in college are particularly rich areas to study intersections among manhood development, diversity, and collegiate gains. Additional work on men in colleges also carries implications for institutional policy and practice.

Implications for Practice

Colleges must work to develop and consistently assess resources used to improve institutional context and climate. Men's studies in higher education can shape existing diversity efforts on college campuses as they involve faculty, staff, and students. With this in mind, this chapter offers ideas to aid colleges in their efforts to manage diversity among men and women students, faculty, and staff.

1. *Colleges must identify spaces where men students may more readily befriend women.* In the studies this chapter reviews, men objectified women in sexualized ways. However, colleges must look for more ways in which these men may befriend women to deconstruct patriarchal plans to sexually conquer, lead, or save. Colleges are reminded in the literature that befriending does not mean being a friend but acting as a friend in order to help, to favor, and to further with openness to learning about this group rather than sexually conquering, pitying, or saving (Laird, 2003). More specifically, faculty must look for opportunities in classrooms to clarify assumptions and biases about student groups. In addition, faculty may choose to structure activities with similar goals. Notwithstanding, faculty who engage in these activities tend to be viewed favorably by students (Milem, 2003). Residential life programs, student organizations, and additional out-of-class activities also have power to challenge men to befriend women where men's intents may be to exploit them.
2. *Men students must be encouraged to utilize women's and gender affairs offices and centers.* Collegiate personnel and students are in positions to disrupt thinking that women's and gender studies centers serve women only. First, though, institutions must know the work of offices of women's and gender affairs. Collegiate personnel and students are encouraged to see the connectedness of the offices of women and gender affairs in the lives of all students. These centers have the potential to shape the work and career readiness of men by developing the following skills: diversity training, assessing others' needs, leadership, team-building, creativity, planning, gathering and analyzing information, organizing ideas, writing, self-discipline, and public speaking. In addition, center activities and offerings are available in which men may learn more about

themselves as gendered beings and gender relations. When possible, student groups and classes should tour these centers to learn more about them. These centers, in turn, may include men by articulating how the centers' work not only furthers awareness of women's issues but men's issues and the intersections of these as well. This fact should be marketed and men enlisted to participate in the office's efforts.

3. *Colleges must create in-class and out-of-class opportunities for men to learn from the narratives of women and men who are different from them.* Studies find that men are more inclusive of diverse others when they participate in activities in which they can form relationships (Anderson, 2007; Dancy, in press). Faculty and student affairs administrators must encourage students to engage with students who are different from them and to reflect on that engagement. Students should be encouraged to enter these conversations with intent to understand, not challenge, ridicule, or intimidate. Though faculty members who teach in the STEM fields may not readily identify ways to do this, STEM faculty are positioned to structure group activity where men have opportunities to engage with diverse students and learn about their lives alongside STEM academic content. STEM faculty may also encourage students to participate in activities and enroll in courses which will develop their worldviews.
4. *Colleges must disrupt norms and behaviors among men's groups that potentially threaten gender relations.* Colleges, particularly college student affairs divisions, must not hold conversations about fraternity hazing, binge drinking, rape, campus violence, and other personal violations without discussing the hegemonic masculine norms from which many of these activities are found to emerge. Colleges must develop gender-sensitive interventions and/or gender-sensitive dimensions of existing programs to disrupt the deleterious effects of oppressive activity sometimes associated with men or men's groups.
5. *Men must receive messages that counseling, tutoring, or related education programs are not signs of weakness.* University services largely offer services for men who pathologically participate in activities (i.e., binge drinking, hypersexual activity, or "hooking up") that

endanger themselves and others. However, the decision of whether or not to participate may be made for reasons connected to manhood. Men who take advantage of these services should be supported even if it involves potentially diffusing others' hidebound assumptions about the identities or masculinities of men who participate in these services or programs. Additionally, all faculty may encourage students to participate in academic support efforts (i.e., tutoring) potentially stigmatized as feminine as well as encourage students to participate in efforts that intellectually awaken their curiosities about living in a global world.

6. *Colleges must center cultural awareness dialogues in students' out-of-class experiences as well as in the work of faculty and staff.* Institutional cultural awareness workshops are mandatory. Diverse issues must inform collegiate conversations about teaching, learning, recruitment, enrollment, retention, persistence, and other strategies. Male student representatives of various backgrounds and cultures must be included. Such work harbors opportunities for men to both teach others about their lives as well as learn about the lives of others. In addition, administrators must thread the importance of diversity through other responsibilities in the division. Mandatory diversity workshops should be required for all collegiate staff to avoid representation by only those who are expected to, or show interest in, participating. Men faculty and staff should serve on diversity committees, and this work should be viewed as essential, not tangential to the work of colleges. Committee work should include developing the cultural awareness of colleagues as they engage each other and students.
7. *Mentoring programs, men's sessions and workshops must evolve.* Mentoring models need to evolve in ways that fit men's constructions of manhood and masculinities more appropriately. Mentors who consider the manhood development of men students can more intentionally mold or impact their futures (Dancy, in press). Concurrently, mentors must seize opportunities to develop inclusive masculinities among men through challenging biases and assumptions about the identities of women and diverse men. Men's sessions, which purport to promote honest social dialogues between men, should diversify panelists in recognition of men's

multiple identities, manhood constructions, and masculinities. Speaker panels should be structured in similar ways if all-male. Occasionally, all-male programs should investigate ways to involve women and other groups with the goals of promoting understanding about difference.

8. *Hiring practices must not privilege races, genders, or any intersections of these and other social categories.* Colleges must develop and/or strengthen systems of assessment and accountability to minimize inequities potentially represented in biased personnel decisions as these decisions are found to separate along race, gender, or various other identity lines. By attempting to engage this work, colleges and universities are also doing the work of inclusion. This type of work is aligned with national policy involving civil rights.

Conclusion

Families, churches, and schools are largely identified as primary sites of boys' socialization. However, colleges become primary sites for the socialization for men upon enrollment and/or collegiate employment. Thus, colleges are spaces in which men learn to reorganize or reproduce their manhood and masculinities. College missions not only articulate commitment to academic teaching and learning but also to shaping students into civically responsible and global citizens. Sexism, homophobia, and effemophobia threaten to disrupt collegiate attempts to manage diversity in the interest of educational benefits of all students.

References

Alexander, B. K. (2006). *Performing black masculinity: Race, culture, and queer identity*. Lanham, MD: AltaMira.

Anderson, E. (2007). Orthodox and inclusive masculinity: Competing masculinities among heterosexual men in a feminized terrain. In M. Kimmel & M. Messner (Eds.), *Men's lives* (7th ed.). Boston, MA: Allyn and Bacon.

antonio, a. (2004). When does race matter in college friendships? Exploring men's diverse and homogeneous friendship groups. *The Review of Higher Education, 27*(4), 553–575.

Bem, S. L. (1987). Masculinity and femininity exist only in the mind of the perceiver. In J. M. Reinisch, L. A. Rosenblum & S. A. Sanders (Eds.), *Masculinity/femininity: Basic perspectives* (pp. 304–311). New York: Oxford University Press.

Boswell, A. A., & Spade, J. Z. (2007). Fraternities and collegiate rape culture: Why are some fraternities more dangerous places for women? In M. Kimmel & M. Messner (Eds.), *Men's lives* (7th ed.). Boston, MA: Allyn and Bacon.

Braxton, J., Milem, J. F., & Sullivan, A. S. (2000). The influence of active learning on the college student departure process: Toward a revision of Tinto's theory. *The Journal of Higher Education, 71*(5), 569–590.

Brown, M. C., & Lane, J. (2003). Studying diverse institutions: Contexts, challenges, and considerations, *New directions for institutional research*. San Francisco: Jossey-Bass.

Capraro, R. L. (2007). Why college men drink: Alcohol, adventure, and the paradox of masculinity. In M. Kimmel & M. Messner (Eds.), *Men's lives*. Boston, MA: Allyn and Bacon.

Case, D. (1998). Breaking the cycle of invisibility. In S. L. Windmeyer & P. W. Freeman (Eds.), *Out on fraternity row*. Los Angeles: Alyson Books.

Chronicle of Higher Education Almanac. (2009). *The Chronicle of Higher Education,* 56(1), 5.

Chronicle of Higher Education. (2005). Number of full-time faculty members by sex, rank, and racial and ethnic group. (Volume *55*, Issue 1), Washington, DC. p. 24.

Connell, R. W. (1995). *Masculinities*. Berkeley, CA: University of California Press.

Constantine-Simms, D. (2001). *The greatest taboo: Homosexuality in black communities*. Los Angeles: Alyson Books.

Constantinople, A. (1973). Masculinity-femininity: An exception to a famous dictum. *Psychological Bulletin, 80*, 389–407.

Courtenay, W. H. (2000). Constructions of masculinity and their influence on men's well-being: A theory of gender of health. *Social Science and Medicine, 50*, 1385–1401.

Dancy, T. E. (2007). Manhood constructions among engaged African American male collegians: Influences, experiences, and contexts. Unpublished doctoral dissertation: Louisiana State University.

Dancy, T. E. (forthcoming). Boys to men: African American manhood, masculinity, and behavior codes in the education pipeline. In J. E. Davis & V. Polite (Eds.), *Manly deeds: Strategies for the academic and social development of African American males*. Alexandria, VA: Association for Curriculum and Supervision Development.

Dancy, T. E. (in press). *The brother code: Manhood and masculinity among African American men in college*. Charlotte, NC: Information Age Publishing.

Davis, J. E. (2005). *Negotiating masculinity in college: African American males and academic engagement*. Paper presented at the Annual Meeting of the American Educational Research Association.

Davis, T. L. (2002). Voices of gender role conflict: The social construction of college men's identity. *Journal of College Student Development, 43*(4), 508–521.

Dilley, P. (2002). *Queer man on campus: A history of non-heterosexual college men, 1945–2000*. New York: RoutledgeFalmer.

Du Bois, W. E. B. (1903/2005). *The Illustrated Souls of Black Folk*. Boulder, CO: Paradigm.

Gerson, J. M., & Peiss, K. (1985). Boundaries, negotiation, consciousness: Reconceptualizing gender relations. *Social Problems, 32*(4), 317–321.

Glazer-Raymo, J. (2003). Women faculty and part-time employment: The impact of public policy. In B. Ropers-Huilman (Ed.), *Gendered futures in higher education: Critical perspectives for change*. New York: State University of New York Press.

Gordon, L. A. (1997). From seminary to university: An overview of women's higher education, 1870–1920. In L. F. Goodchild & H. S. Wechsler (Eds.), *The history of higher education*. Boston, MA: Pearson.

Gramsci, A. (1971). *Selections from the prison notebooks*. London: New Left Books.

hooks, b. (2004a). *The will to change: Men, masculinity, and love*. New York: Atria Books.

Hunter, A., & Davis, J. E. (1992). Constructing gender: An exploration of Afro-American men's conceptualization of manhood. *Gender and Society, 6*(3), 464–479.

Hurtado, S., Milem, J. F., Clayton-Pedersen, A. R., & Allen, W. (1999). *Enacting diverse learning environments: Improving the climate for racial/ethnic diversity in higher education.* ASHE-ERIC Higher Education Report. Washington, DC: George Washington University.

Jackson, J. F. L. (2001). A new test for diversity: Retaining African American administrators at predominantly white institutions. In L. Jones (Ed.), *Retaining African Americans in higher education: Challenging paradigms for retaining students, faculty, and administrators* (pp. 93–109). Sterling, VA: Stylus.

Kimmel, M. (2002). Global masculinities: Restoration and resistance. In B. Pease & K. Pringle (Eds.), *A man's world? Changing men's practices in a globalized world.* London: Zed Books.

Kimmel, M. (Ed.). (1987a). *Changing men: New directions in research on men and masculinity.* Newbury Park, CA: Sage.

Kimmel, M. (Ed.). (1987b). *Rethinking "masculinity": New directions in research.* Newbury Park, CA: SAGE Publications, Inc.

Kimmel, M., & Messner, M. (2007). *Men's lives* (7th ed.). Boston: Allyn and Bacon.

Komarovsky, M. (1976). *Dilemmas of masculinity: A study of college youth.* New York: Norton.

Laird, S. (2003). Befriending girls as an educational life-practice. In E. S. Fletcher (Ed.), *Philosophy of education* (pp. 73–81). Urbana: Philosophy of Education Society.

Milem, J. F. (2003). The educational benefits of diversity: Evidence from multiple sectors. In M. J. Chang, D. Witt, J. James & K. Hakuta (Eds.), *Compelling interest: Examining racial dynamics in colleges and universities.* Palo Alto, CA: Stanford University.

Plummer, D. (2001). Policing manhood: new theories abou the social significance of homophobia. In C. Wood (Ed.), *Sexual Positions.* Melbourne: Hill of Content.

Rhoads, R. A. (1994). *Coming out in college: The struggle for a queer identity.* Westport, CT: Bergin & Garvey.

Rich, A. (1994). *Blood, bread, and poetry.* New York: Norton.

Ropers-Huilman, B. (2003). Gender in the future of higher education. In B. Ropers-Huilman (Ed.), *Gendered futures in higher education: Critical perspectives for change*. Albany, NY: State University of New York.

Schoenberg, B. M. (1993). *Growing up male*. Westport, CT: Bergin & Garvey.

Snyder, T. D., Dillow, S. A., & Hoffman, C. M. (2009). *Digest of education statistics 2008* (No. NCES 2009-020). Washington, DC: National Center for Education Statistics, Institute of Education Sciences, U.S. Department of Education.

Summers, M. (2004). *Manliness and its discontents: The black middle class and the transformation of masculinity, 1900–1930*. Chapel Hill: University of North Carolina.

Tatum, J. L., & Charlton, R. (2008). A phenomenological study of how selected college men construct and define masculinity. *Higher Education in Review*,(5), 99–126.

Touchton, J. (2008). *A measure of equity: Women's progress in higher education*. Washington, DC: American Association of Colleges and Universities.

Townsend, k. (1999) *Manhood at Harvard.* New York: Norton

PART THREE

(In)Equities in Collegiate Contexts

CHAPTER TEN

Underrepresented Minorities in Physics: How Perceptions of Race and Campus Climate Affect Student Outcomes

Sharon Fries-Britt
Toyia Younger
Wendell Hall

National data indicate that although African Americans make up 12.2 percent of the U.S. population, they earned only 8.78 percent of all science and engineering degrees awarded to U.S. citizens in 2004. Similarly, Hispanic/Latino Americans make up 14.1 percent of the U.S. population but earned only 7.65 percent of science and engineering degrees (National Science Foundation, 2006a; National Science Foundation, 2008). The statistics for underrepresented minorities in physics (the focus of this study) are even more daunting. In 2006 African Americans and Hispanic Americans each earned 4 percent of bachelor's degrees in physics with a combined total of 8 percent. That same year African Americans and Hispanic Americans each earned 3 percent of exiting master's degrees with a total of 6 percent. At the Ph.D. level in physics African Americans earned 2 percent of the degrees while Hispanic Americans earned 3 percent (American Institute of Physics, 2008).

Not surprisingly, underrepresentation in the academy impacts the Science, Technology, Engineering, and Mathematics (STEM) workforce. African Americans comprise 5.8 percent of the total number of employed scientists and engineers and Hispanic Americans make up 5.2 percent (NSF, 2006b). These national trends point to a serious underutilization of the nation's increasingly diverse talent pool. Understanding barriers to underrepresented minorities success is imperative. Lewis (2003) observed that an increased empirical study examining the student experience is essential to understanding the cause behind the underrepresentation. Equally important are qualitative studies, such as the one discussed in this chapter, which examine the experiences of students based on their own "lived experiences" (Brown, 2002; Moore, Madison-Colmore, & Smith, 2003; Seymour & Hewitt, 1997) in the sciences.

This chapter reports findings from a larger study focused on the experiences of underrepresented students in physics. The five-year study (2004–2008) sought to understand the academic, social and racial experiences of minority college students succeeding in physics. In this chapter we report the ways in which students' perceptions of race shape their academic experiences in general and, more specifically, interactions with faculty. As might be expected students had different perceptions; however, the overwhelming majority report that race mattered. The findings of this study suggest that it is important to understand the racial experiences of students in higher education and especially in the sciences where underrepresented students continue to be underserved. The chapter begins with a brief review of the literature on racial diversity and campus climate in higher education and factors impacting minorities in STEM fields. We then briefly introduce the conceptual framework and methodology of the larger study from which this study was derived. Next we report the findings on race and conclude with a discussion and implications of this work for managing campus diversity.

Review of the Literature

The 23rd American Council on Education status report *Minorities in Higher Education* observed that, "colleges and universities became more diverse over the past decade, with Whites as a share of the student body shrinking from 70 percent to 61 percent, and the minority share rising from 24 percent to 29 percent." (ACE, 2008). From 1995–2005 racial/ethnic minorities grew from 3.4 to 5.0 million (ACE, 2008). The largest gains were seen in the Hispanic population followed by African Americans. The increasing diversity of college campuses has called for greater attention to the interactions of students, faculty and staff and the increased need to understand the experiences of students in and outside of the classroom (Cabrera, Crissman, Bernal, Nora, Terenzini & Pascarella, 2002; Chang, Astin & Kim, 2004; Chang, Denson, Saenz & Misa, 2006).

Many students enter college from segregated neighborhoods and high schools, often without the opportunity to interact with racially diverse peers prior to entering college. Approximately 90 percent of White students and 50 percent of Black students grow up in racially homogeneous neighborhoods and attend racially homogeneous high schools (Gurin, Dey, Gurin, & Hurtado, 2004). Without a substantial amount of racial diversity within the pre-college environment, students have little opportunity to experience cross-cultural interactions and do not develop the skills necessary to be successful in diverse racial and cultural environments.

While the compositional diversity of students on campus is one way to measure success, as a sole measure it is insufficient. Once campuses have increased the number of diverse students it is important that they engage in activities and programs that encourage interactions across different constituencies. How campuses manage diversity is complex and cannot be measured by an outcome such as the number of racially diverse students on campus or a certain number of diversity related programs to be checked off of a list (Association of American Colleges and Universities, 2005). Instead, managing diversity on college campuses should be seen as a process including multiple facets of diversity: structural diversity, classroom diversity and interactional diversity (Gurin, 1999). As campuses change the composition of their student body it increases the likelihood of conflict, particularly for underrepresented students.

During the 1980s, racial conflicts between students on college campuses were all too common (Hurtado, 1992). An institution's commitment to racial diversity can change student perceptions of the campus' climate (Hurtado, 1992). Research finds a hostile campus climate has a negative impact on minority student grades (Nettles, 1988), and degree completion rates (Fleming, 1984). College administrators attempt to alleviate hostile campus climates by increasing the racial diversity within the student body (AAC&U, 2005). However, such increases alone cannot guarantee that racially diverse students engage in a meaningful way (Chang, Denson, Saenz, & Misa, 2006).

Colleges must be intentional in providing opportunities for students to interact with racially diverse peers. College environments can affect student engagement with diverse peers by addressing diversity from three levels: structural (racial composition of the student body); curricular (placing information about racial diversity within the curriculum); and interactional diversity (providing opportunities for racially diverse students to interact inside and outside of the classroom) (Gurin, 1999; Gurin, Dey, Hurtado & Gurin, 2002; Zuniga, Nagada & Sevig, 2002). While the majority of early initiatives by colleges have focused on structural and curricular diversity, interactional diversity may be the most important. For interactional diversity to be successful, administrators must focus on providing opportunities for diverse students to actually engage with racially diverse peers.

Although Predominantly White Universities have increased their enrollment of racially diverse students, minority students experience the university environment differently than their White counterparts (Hurtado, 1992). Research in higher education has been instrumental in increasing our understanding of the experiences of students (Hurtado, Milem, Clayton-Pederson & Allen, 1998; Hurtado, Dey, Gurin, & Gurin, 2003; LaNasa, Cabrera, Transgrud & Alleman, 2007). This work continues to call for more research to understand the patterns of interaction. One area in need of serious attention is the experiences of underrepresented students in science. Even with the steady enrollment of underrepresented students in higher education and increased research on their experiences; in the sciences, underrepresented minorities lack parity and are often the only one or one of a few in a program.

Research on minorities in STEM reveals that the campus environment can be very challenging for students because of the physical and social isolation which plays an indirect, but powerful contribution to students' decisions to transfer out of STEM and to students' perception of prejudice. In a study conducted by Seymour and Hewitt (1997) underrepresented minority students in STEM majors often felt surrounded by White students who were prejudiced toward them and felt there was no one with whom to share their pain and humiliation. Lewis (2003) building upon the work of Hall and Post-Krammer (1987) identified a broad range of factors that impact the underrepresentation of African Americans in science including 1) academic preparation, 2) career interests, 3) lack of educational and career planning, 4) role models and 5) career opportunities. Campbell (1999/2000) in his work on minorities in engineering notes that,

> Along with the influx of a significant number of minority students came the full range of issues that plague disenfranchised groups: enormous financial need that has never been adequately met; poor K-12 schools; hostile engineering school environment; ethnic isolation and consequent lack of peer alliances; social and cultural segregation; prejudices that run the gamut from overt to subtle to sub-conscious; and deficient relationships with faculty members, resulting in the absence of good academic mentors (p. 22).

One of the more important factors impacting students is their interactions and relationships with faculty. Hurtado et al. (2007) found minority students' odds of engaging in health science research increased along with faculty contact. Brown (2002), in a study of 22 Hispanic students majoring in science, found that they made an important connection between learning and the teachers. Essentially teachers were important to students developing an interest in science. Teachers who were identified as "good" in the study exhibited a number of characteristics, "...a good teacher helps students, cares about students, challenges students, makes students work, uses a variety of teaching techniques, and really wants the students to learn. If a teacher let them simply do minimal work and, therefore, learning was minimal, he or she was not respected by the students" (p. 138). Cabrera, Colbeck and Terenzini (2001), in a study of more than 1,250 students in engineering at seven universities found that the instructional practices, collaborative learning and clarity and organization of classroom materials were positively associated with gains in students' ability to problem solve and group skills and in understanding engineering. Rendon (1985) identified close faculty-student interaction as a key element in successful retention programs designed to retain minority students in science and math. Whitten, Foster and Duncombe et al. (2004) in a study of women in undergraduate physics found that faculty approachability was important to student retention. They also found that the diversity of the faculty was important, especially having women faculty as role models for females in science.

In contrast, negative interactions with faculty can influence underrepresented minority students to enter the proving process to justify their intellectual ability, which may result in psychological and emotional costs (Moore, Madison-Colmore & Smith, 2003). Whitten, Foster, Duncombe, Allen, Heron, McCullough et al. (2004) in a study of nine physics departments found positive interactions with faculty; however, they also found that even with good intentions some faculty were overbearing and created a sense of dependence. They noted that in a few cases students felt harassment in their relationships with faculty.

About the Study

This chapter reports findings from a larger study that included 110 students from underrepresented minority groups who participated in individual interviews or focus groups from 2005–2008. Interviews were audio taped and transcribed verbatim. We used Nvivo software to code and manage the data. The majority of the students identified as Black (e.g., African American, Caribbean, African) with the second largest group identifying as Hispanic. In cases were we did not have demographic questionnaires we used transcripts and field notes to supplement the demographic profile of the group. The majority (65%) of the participants are male with females comprising 35%. Undergraduates and graduate students participated in the study although the majority of the students were undergraduates (approximately 70%). The students attended diverse higher education institutions including private, public, Predominantly White, Historically Black as well as Hispanic-serving Institutions from different parts of the country. Several key questions guided the larger project:

1. What academic and social factors identified in the literature (e.g., faculty, peers, family and finances) as important to minority student success apply to the experiences of minority students majoring in physics?
2. In what ways do minority students in physics characterize their experience?
3. What perceptions do students have about their interactions with faculty in and outside of the classroom?
4. Did race contribute to students' motivation to succeed?

5. How did students' academic experiences shape their sense of self?

In the larger study we utilized concepts across a broad range of theories and bodies of research to construct a conceptual framework and to identify factors important to the experiences of minority physics majors. Briefly this work included college retention and college impact literature (Astin, 1993; Pascarella, 1980; Tinto, 1993), psychological concepts like self-efficacy (Bandura, 1977) and attribution theory (Fishbein and Ajzen, 1975); and the growing research on minority high achievers (Fries-Britt, 1998; Fries-Britt & Turner, 2002; Fries-Britt & Griffin, 2008; Griffin, 2006; Harper, 2005; Hrabowski, Maton & Greif, 1998, 2002). In this chapter we draw upon the literature on the racial climate research (Gurin, 1999; Gurin, Dey, Gurin & Hurtado, 2004; Zuniga, Nagada & Sevig, 2002) and research on minorities in STEM fields (Barr, Wanat & Gonzalez, 2007; Busch-Vishniac and Jarosz, 2004; Cabrera, Colbeck & Terenzini, 2001; Hall and Post-Krammer, 1987; Lewis, 2003; National Action Council for Minorities in Engineering, 2008; Seymour & Hewitt, 1997; Whitten, Foster, Duncombe, Allen, Heron, McCullough et al., 2004).

In the following section, we report findings on race. We start with a brief summary of the findings and then provide examples of how race shaped students' experiences in the study. We offer several examples of how race still matters as well as examples of the types of racial experiences students report.

Findings

Perceptions of Race

Participants shared many stories about their racial experiences and the racial climate on campus. Some students perceived different standards being applied to "minority" students in the classroom. They based these perceptions on what they observed as different attitudes and behaviors conveyed by faculty. They perceived that some faculty responded differently to White students, demonstrating more of an interest in them. They offered as examples invitations White students received to join research teams and the unwillingness of faculty to explain concepts to which their White peers reported obtaining answers. Several students reported that grades seemed to be different for them compared to White peers who had the same answer but calculated it differently. According to these students teachers added or deleted points based on how they derived their answer which they felt was subjective.

Students also shared how they endured racial incidents, how they coped with these incidents, and the pressure they felt to prove themselves based on race. Not all students report racial incidents or have perceptions that they are being treated differently based on race. Some participants believe that it is up to each student to seek out faculty members and to not assume that interactions are about race. Others felt like race simply did not matter. What mattered was one's ability to do science. Several students ascribe to the notion that if you are excellent the faculty will work with you.

The findings suggest a tendency for Black students from the Caribbean or from African countries to have different perceptions about race than African American students. Many of these students did not have the same experiences as African Americans. In several focus groups, non-African Americans observed that African Americans are prone to see racial issues even when they do not exist, and African Americans report that some Blacks from other countries overlook race because they do not understand the full American context. Essentially the two groups tend to see race differently.

A Latino female student who felt that race was less of an issue had a slightly different perspective. She shared, "Race is not a big factor for me because I look White." She grew up in a predominantly White community and consequently she had a number of interactions with Whites. These interactions gave her a degree of comfort with and understanding of the White community. However, as she continued with her story she began to reveal that there were differences from her Latino background that impacted how she engaged in and thought about physics. On the one hand she talked about physics requiring a type of "intensity," but she also needed to combine this intensity with a degree of enjoyment because this was an issue important to her Latino culture.

> ...what I do sense is that there is a different personality that Latinos have, and it's very alive and it's...like wanting to do physics but also in a very intense way...and interested in getting the whole experience and enjoying it

> rather than...sequestering yourself in the little group thing researching by yourself the whole time.

Even though she did not feel treated differently based on race she felt that her cultural background played a role in how she thought about physics and wanting to be engaged within a community of students who were passionate rather than feeling isolated working in a smaller community which tends to be the norm for physics majors.

Pressure to represent the race

Because underrepresented students have such low numbers in physics, some students felt a certain pressure to "represent" their race. They also felt that their personal success was connected to the success of underrepresented communities and to future generations. A typical example was offered a by a female who shared, "I constantly felt like my whole race was on my shoulders and if I did not succeed, then it was like they were not going to let anyone else into the program...I felt constantly like I have to do well, I just have to." Similarly a Hispanic female from a Caribbean island talked about the pressure she felt to represent Hispanics and particularly her island. It was important for her to let people know that they were intelligent; she commented, "...it's a great vacation place [the island she grew up in], but we have to let them know that we have a brain."

Another female student extends this sense of responsibility and commitment. She starts by expressing a connection to the larger community, "I felt like I was going through graduate school just so I can help the race. Just so I can, you know, be another number and say, Okay we had this many Ph.Ds that graduated this particular year." As she continued, she shared how her success was connected to others in the community who did not have the opportunities she was afforded. "...to know that you're getting it for your friends who got pregnant and couldn't make it, for this family member who passed away ....it kinds of instills a sense of pride, a sense of who you are."

While the majority of students expressed a degree of pressure to represent the race, not all students felt this pressure. Some felt a pressure to do well academically but not necessarily because of their race. A male student who did not feel pressure to represent his race shared that he felt people were more surprised that he was studying physics and was Black, but he did not feel that they judged him differently based on race. "...I've found that more often than not people are more interested by the fact that I'm Black and I'm doing physics than...you know trying to put me down because I'm Black and I do physics." In this student's case he felt the focus was on the fact that he was in a field that most felt was difficult. "You go into a party and say, 'yeah, I'm a physicist" they go, "Oh," in fact they're uncomfortable, like they walk away." This student perceived that the major, more than his race, caused the reactions he received from individuals. His example was more the exception and not the rule. Most students felt like they had to prove that they deserved to be admitted into a program and were smart enough to major in physics. The pressure to do well and to be perceived as capable was greater for students who were the only minority or one of a few enrolled in a program.

Examples of racial experiences

Some of the examples that students shared were from experiences prior to college and included stories about the neighborhoods in which they were raised. However, the majority of what they discussed focused on their campus interactions with faculty and peers. While there were different perspectives on race, the majority of students perceive that on occasion they are being judged differently based on race. They describe a certain "vibe" that they picked up in their interactions with some faculty; they offer specific incidents where faculty or peers make comments to them that are blatantly racist. In some cases participants have even filed complaints in their departments.

In their interactions with faculty a number of students report feeling like they were being discouraged from pursuing science as a major. Participants shared how faculty suggested they change their major even if they were doing well in their classes. What was surprising was how often students reported these experiences. We offer part of one African American male's comments about his interactions with a faculty member because his story starts off fairly representative of what students report. Unfortunately in his case the story becomes more extreme: "...and he [the professor] made a statement that I didn't belong in physics, that I should try to switch out and maybe try engineering or switch out and go into business. He was just giving me every opportunity except for completing my physics degree." This student's observations reflect the stories of a number of students who said faculty members made blatant comments, discouraging them and advising them to find a new major. As the student continued to interact with the faculty member, things became worse. "He told me that no matter...if you pass this class or not...I am going to fail you...I am going to give you an F. He took it to the next level, I did fight him, I said okay, he can't do that, I've been sitting in the class the whole time. I went to the exam, passed the exam and he failed me anyway...I had to go through the department chair." While a fewer number of other students shared such difficult interactions with faculty, his story is an important reminder of how damaging some interactions can be for students.

Certainly not all interactions with faculty were negative. In fact many students report very positive experiences with faculty. In a forthcoming manuscript we discuss the nature of students' interactions with faculty in greater detail. Briefly they suggest that these positive interactions occur across a diverse group of faculty. Students report that women faculty tend to give more time to students, and many of the positive interactions occurred with faculty who teach at HBCUs. Students report that some faculty members go out of their way to teach concepts and to work with them directly at HBCUs. They report spending time with faculty members outside of the classroom; oftentimes they invite students into their homes and allow them to share time with their family.

Discussion and Implications

The findings of this study shed light on the research on campus racial climate (Gurin, 1999; Gurin, Dey, Gurin & Hurtado, 2004; Zuniga, Nagada & Sevig, 2002) and research on minorities in STEM fields (Campbell, 1999/2000; Lewis, 2003; Seymour & Hewitt, 1997). The compositional diversity and interactional diversity components are aspects of the campus climate framework that are particularly relevant. In many ways these two components overlap and interact simultaneously. First, the compositional diversity of students in the sciences is important. The low number of minorities in physics has a direct impact on the experiences that students have in the field. The pressure many students feel to represent their race is due to the fact that there are so few students in physics and faculty mentors at their institutions. Given these low numbers students talk about the importance of having a positive environment and climate. Barr, Wanat & Gonzalez (2007) assert that,

> The ethos, or climate of a university, an intangible characteristic that is sensed rather than measured, has to do both with the people at a university and the institutional climate fostered by the university itself. When students have a choice between institutions of similar caliber, and other factors such as level of financial support are equivalent, students appear to favor the institutions where they feel more comfortable and welcome. The importance of institutional climate appears heightened for URM [underrepresented minorities] students. Among URM students, the response to negative perceptions of that environment may be more strident among African American students than among other groups (p. 34)

Similar to Barr et. al (2007) we found that African American students tended to have more negative experiences and perceived more racial discrimination than Blacks from other countries. They felt that it was important to attend universities where there was a community of Blacks studying physics. The component of interactional diversity (Gurin, 1999; Gurin, Dey, Gurin & Hurtado, 2004; Zuniga, Nagada & Sevig, 2002) is very important to the findings of this study. The interactions that students have with faculty are revealing. While faculty cannot be expected to be responsible for the pressure that students feel to represent their race; they can be expected to be aware of how their own behaviors and attitudes may be creating conditions in the classroom that impede the learning of underrepresented groups and contribute to stereotypes. We know from the students in this study that interactions with faculty are important. As shown in other studies (e.g. Brown, 2002; Cabrera et al., 2001; Whitten et al., 2004) faculty members who are aware of the classroom context, practice good teaching techniques and are equitable in how they treat students create the conditions for success. The isolation and prejudice that students in STEM experience are well documented (Campbell, 1999; Lewis, 2003; Seymour & Hewitt, 1997) in the literature. Similar patterns emerged in this study; however it is important to note that not all students had these experiences.

This study reveals that we must continue to understand the racial experiences of students studying physics. In physics the number of underrepresented students is small; consequently the level of institutional scrutiny and responsibility for retaining them should be high in order to ensure their success. Given the underrepresentation of minorities in STEM fields, it is essential for the nation to develop a viable talent pool. This will pose a challenge for the nation given that current data show that most students who decide to switch majors or opt out of the sciences tend to be disproportionately students from underrepresented groups (Vagelos, 2005). This can have a devastating impact on the ability of our nation to compete globally and on the ability of underrepresented minorities to pursue graduate studies and science careers.

Based on the findings of this study we offer the following observations for managing the climate of diversity for students in physics. First, it is important to help students and faculty fortify relationships in and outside of the classroom. Faculty must understand the important role they play in helping students make connections to science. It is important for them to understand that their interactions with students can enhance or impede students' progress. Secondly, it is important for students to have as much exposure as possible to the extended minority science community in order to eliminate the sense of pressure that they feel to represent their race. Each year we collect the data for this project at the NSBP and NSHP annual conference, and we learn how important the conference is to their professional development. At the annual conference they meet physicists who are excelling in their careers, and they learn about research opportunities and interact with peers from around the country who are also studying physics. These interactions are invaluable and often sustain the students when they return to their campuses. Even if campuses can not send students to these conferences, they should be intentional about bringing diverse scientists to the campus as faculty, as participants in departmental programs, as consultants, guest lecturers, and visiting scholars. Essentially, academic programs should seek to enhance interactions with minority professionals and current students.

These professional colleagues are indispensable in their ability to serve as role models and to help socialize students to the field.

References

American Council on Education. (2008). *Minorities in Higher Education* (23rd status report). Washington, DC: Mikyung Ryu.

American Institute of Physics. (2008). *Enrollments & Degrees Report 2006* (Publication Number R-151.43). College Park, MD: Patrick J. Mulvey & Starr Nicholson.

Association of American Colleges and Universities. (2005). *Making diversity work on campus: A research-based perspective.* Washington, DC: Jeffrey F. Milem, Mitchell J. Chang, and anthony lising antonio.

Astin, A. W. (1993). *What matters in college: Four critical years revisited.* San Francisco: Jossey-Bass.

Bandura, A. (1977). Self-efficacy: Toward a unifying theory of behavioral change. *Psychological Review, 84*(2), 191–215.

Barr, D.A., Wanat, S. & Gonzalez, M. (2007). Racial and ethnic differences in students' selection of a doctoral program to attend from those offering admission: The case of biomedical sciences. *Journal of Women and Minorities in Science and Engineering, 13* (1), 23–36.

Brown, S.W., (2002). Hispanic students majoring in science or engineering: What happened in their educational journeys? *Journal of Women and Minorities in Science and Engineering, 8*(2), 123–148.

Busch-Vishniac, I.J., & Jarosz, J.P. (2004). Can diversity in the undergraduate engineering population be enhanced through curricular change? *Journal of Women and Minorities in Science and Engineering, 10*(3), 255–282.

Cabrera, A.F., Colbeck, C.L., & Terenzini, P.T. (2001). Developing performance indicators for assessing classroom teaching practices and student learning: The case of engineering. *Research in Higher Education, 42*(3), 327–352.

Cabrera, A.F., Crissman, J.L., Bernal, E.M., Nora, A., Terenzini, P.T., & Pascarella, E.T. (2002). Collaborative learning: Its impact on college students' development and diversity. *Journal of College Student Development, 43*(1), 20–34.

Campbell Jr., G. (Winter,1999/2000). Support them and they will come. *Issues in Science & Technology, 16*(2), 21-23. Retrieved October 25, 2008, from Education Research Complete database.

Chang, M.J., Astin, A.W., & Kim, D. (2004). Cross-racial interaction among undergraduates: Some consequences, causes and patterns. *Research in Higher Education, 45*(5) 529–553.

Chang, M.J., Denson, N., Saenz, V., Misa, K. (2006). The educational benefits of sustaining cross-racial interaction among undergraduates. *Journal of Higher Education, 77*(3), 430–455 .

Fishbein, M., & Ajzen, I. (1975). *Belief, attitude, intention, and behavior: An introduction to theory and research.* Reading, MA: Addison-Wesley.

Fleming, J. (1984). *Blacks in college: A comparative study of students' success in black and in white institutions.* San Francisco: Jossey-Bass.

Fries-Britt, S.L. (1998). Moving beyond Black achiever isolation: Experiences of gifted Black collegians. *Journal of Higher Education, 69*(5), 556–576.

Fries-Britt, S.L., & Turner, B. (2002). Uneven stories: The experiences of successful Black collegians at a historically Black and a traditionally White campus. *The Review of Higher Education, 25* (3), 420–429.

Fries-Britt, S. & Griffin, K.A. (2008). The Black Box: How high achieving Blacks resist stereotypes about African Americans, *Journal of College Student Development, 48*(5), 509–524.

Griffin, K. (2006). Striving for success: A qualitative exploration of competing theories of high-achieving Black college students' academic motivation. *Journal of College Student Development, 47*(4), 384–400.

Gurin, P. (1999). The compelling need for diversity in higher education, Expert testimony in *Gratz et al. v. Bollinger et al. Michigan Journal of Race & Law 5:* 363–425.

Gurin, P., Dey, E., Hurtado, S., Gurin, G. (2002). Diversity and higher education: Theory and impact on educational issues. *Harvard Educational Review, 72,* 330–366.

Gurin, P., Dey, E.L., Gurin, G., & Hurtado, S. (2004). The educational value of diversity. In P. Gurin, J.S. Lehman, & E. Lewis (Eds.), *De-*

fending diversity: Affirmative action at the University of Michigan (pp. 97–188). Ann Arbor, MI: The University of Michigan.

Hall, E.R. & Post-Krammer, P. (1987). Black mathematics and science majors: why so few? Career Development Quarterly, *35*, 206–19.

Harper, S.R. (2005). Leading the way: High-achieving African American male students. *About Campus, 10*(1), 8–15.

Hrabowski, F., Maton, K. & Greif, G. (1998). *Beating the odds: Raising academically successful African-American males.* New York: Oxford University Press.

Hrabowski, F., Maton, K. & Greif, G. (2002). *Overcoming the odds: Raising academically successful African-American young women.* New York: Oxford University Press.

Hurtado, S. (1992). The campus racial climate: Contexts for conflict. *The Journal of Higher Education, 63*(4), 539–569.

Hurtado, S., Milem, J., Clayton-Pederson, A.R., & Allen, W.R. (1998). Enhancing campus climates for racial/ethnic diversity: Educational policy and practice. *The Review of Higher Education, 21*(3), 279–302.

Hurtado, S., Dey, E. L., Gurin, P., & Gurin, G. (2003). College environments, diversity, and student learning. In J. C. Smart (Ed.), *Higher education: Handbook of theory and research* (pp. 145–190). Norwell, MA: Kluwer Academic Publishers.

Hurtado, S., Eagan, M., Cabrera, N., Lin, M., Park, J., & Lopez, M. (2007). Training future scientists: Predicting first-year minority student participation in health science research. *Research in Higher Education, 49*(2), 126–152. Retrieved November 7, 2008, doi:10.1007/s11162-007-9068-1

LaNasa, S.M., Cabrera, A.F., Transgrud, H., Alleman, N. (2007). *Engagement as a proxy for learning: Testing Pascarella's "model of engagement" with NSSE items.* Paper presented at the Association for the Study of Higher Education, Louisville, KY November 9, 2007.

Lewis, B. F. (2003). A critique of literature on the underrepresentation of African Americans in science: Directions for future research. *Journal of Women and Minorities in Science and Engineering, 9*(3 & 4), 361–373.

Moore III, J., Madison-Colmore, O., & Smith, D. (2003). The prove-them-wrong syndrome: Voices from unheard African-American males in engineering disciplines. *Journal of Men's Studies, 12*(1), 61–73.

National Action Council for Minorities in Engineering. (2008). *Confronting the "new" American dilemma: Underrepresented minorities in engineering—A data based look at diversity*. Retrieved from http://www.cpst.org/NACME_Rep.pdf

National Science Foundation (NSF). (2006a). Women, minorities, and persons with disabilities in science and engineering. A-2 Resident population of United States, by race/ethnicity and age: 2004. Retrieved September 25, 2008 from http://www.nsf.gov/statistics/wmpd/pdf/taba-2.pdf

National Science Foundation (NSF). (2006b). Women, minorities, and persons with disabilities in science and engineering. H-38 Demographic characteristics of employed scientists and engineers, by disability status and sex: 2003. Retrieved September 25, 2008 from http://www.nsf.gov/statistics/wmpd/pdf/tabh-38.pdf

National Science Foundation (NSF). (2008). Women, minorities, and persons with disabilities in science and engineering. C-6 Bachelor's degrees, by field, citizenship, and race/ethnicity: 1996–2005. Retrieved September 25, 2008 from http://www.nsf.gov/statistics/wmpd/pdf/tabc-6.pdf

Nettles, M. (Ed.). (1988). *Toward black undergraduate student equality in American higher education*. Westport, CT: Greenwood Press.

Pascarella, E.T. (1980). Student-faculty informal contact and college outcomes. *Review of Educational Research (50),* 545–595.

Rendon, L. (1985, May 3). *Elements of successful math and science models for Mexican American students*. Paper presented at the Border College Consortium Southwest Region Education Conference, San Antonio, TX. (ERIC Document Reproduction Service No. ED258777)

Seymour, E. & Hewitt, N.M. (1997). *Talking about leaving: Why undergraduates leave the sciences.* Boulder, CO: Westview Press.

Tinto, V. (1993). *Leaving college: Rethinking the causes and curses of student attrition.* Chicago: University of Chicago Press.

Vagelos, P, R. (2005). *Rising above the gathering storm: Energizing and employing America for a brighter economic future.* Presented before the Committee on Science, United States House of Representatives on October 20, 2005.

Whitten, B.L., Foster, S.R., & Duncombe, M.L. (2003). What works for women in undergraduate physics? *Physics Today, 56*(9), 46–51.

Whitten, B. L., Foster, S.R., Duncombe, M. L., Allen, P. E., Heron, P., McCullough, L., et al. (2004). "Like a family": What works to create friendly and respectful student-faculty interactions. *Journal of Women and Minorities in Science and Engineering, 10*(3), 229–242.

Zuniga, X., Nagada, B., Sevig, T. (2002). Intergroup dialogues: An educational model for cultivating engagement across differences. *Equity and Excellence in Education, 35*(1), 7–17.

CHAPTER ELEVEN

Counseling Diverse Students Effectively: Building Cultural Competency Among Collegiate Personnel

Robert T. Palmer

Over the last ten years, the U.S. Census Bureau has predicted a change in the United States' racial demography. Specifically, the Census Bureau (2008) has predicted that African American, Hispanic, and Asian American populations will comprise nearly 50% of the U.S. population, with some groups even doubling their percentage of the population as a whole. In contrast, the Bureau projected that the percentage of White Americans will decline. The change in the country's racial demographics has begun to play out on college campuses, as they are reportedly more diverse than ever (Cook & Córdova, 2007). Changing demographics challenges traditional approaches that student affairs practitioners as well as other institutional support agents have relied on when working with students. As such, institutional support agents need to be proactive in seeking out resources and approaches that will be beneficial in working with diverse college students.

The goal of this chapter is to provide a helpful resource to student affairs practitioners seeking to effectively counsel students from diverse backgrounds. Emphasis is placed on counseling African American, Asian American, and Latino/a populations since these populations are expected to increase in their college enrollment compared to other racial/ethnic groups. This chapter presents demographic information about each of these populations followed by recommendations for counseling. More specifically, background information includes a general overview of each group and subsequent information will delineate their experiences in higher education.

Counseling recommendations are, in many ways, based on the discussions of each minority group. This chapter will first discuss African Americans followed by Asian Americans, and then Hispanics.

An Overview of Ethnic Groups in Education and Society

African Americans

African Americans comprise about 12.2% of the U.S. population (Sue & Sue, 2008). Many African Americans come from families largely headed by single parents. Data from the U.S. Census Bureau show that in 2000, only 32% of African American family households involved married couples. Many African American families can be described as "matriarchal" (Sue & Sue, 2008). Among households headed by females, the extended family and close friends help with the rearing of children. As such, the social system of African American families includes an extended kin network. This network includes the nuclear family as well as relationships—grandparents, aunts, uncles, cousins, and persons who may not be blood relatives (Ennis, Ennis, Durodoye, Ennis-Cole, & Bolden, 2004). For many African American families, church involvement and spiritual beliefs are also important coping components (Sue & Sue, 2008).

The lifespan of African Americans is significantly shorter than that of White Americans (Anderson, 1995; Felton, Parson, Misener, & Oldaker, 1997). The rate of poverty and unemployment is extremely high when compared to their White counterparts. According to Sue and Sue (2008) nearly 12% of African American men, between the ages of 25–29 were in prison or jail compared to 1.7% of White males. Over 20% of African American males have been banned from voting in states such as Texas, Florida, and Virginia because of felony convictions (Cose, Smith, Figueroa, Stefanakos, & Contreras, 2000). The rate of suicide has increased exponentially among African Americans (Day-Vines, 2007). In 1999, suicide was the leading cause of death among African Americans ages 10–14, "the third leading cause of death among those ages 15–24, the sixth leading cause of death among those ages 25–34, and the ninth leading cause of death among those ages 35–44 (Compton, Thompson, & Kaslow, 2005).

Educational Outcomes

African Americans are disparately attending inferior schools, located in high-poverty areas (Jackson & Moore, 2006, 2008). African American males are far more likely to be underrepresented in gifted education programs or advanced placement courses (Jackson & Moore, 2006, 2008) and are overwhelmingly concentrated in special education (Moore, Henfield, & Owens, 2008). Many Black males are disproportionately tracked into low academic ability classrooms (Epps, 1995). African American men are less inclined to invest in education because they are less likely to gain a favorable return on their investment when compared to White men (Epps, 1995). African American males with lower educational attainment are predisposed to inferior employment prospects, low wages, poor health and are more likely to be involved with the criminal justice system (Harvey, 2008). Many of the aforementioned issues impinge upon Black males' ability to finish school, resulting in high rates of illiteracy and unemployment (Hale, 2001; Majors & Billson, 1992). It is important to note that the aforementioned descriptions of experiences for African American males are not true for every African American male. The scholarly work of researchers, such as Shaun Harper (2005), Sharon Fries-Britt (1998), and Fred Bonner (2003) highlights the diversity that exists among African Americans.

Although there have been an increasing number of African Americans pursuing higher education, this increase has been due primarily to the number of African American females enrolling in higher education (Cook & Córdova, 2007). Once the province of men, females are increasingly dominating college campuses. This gender disparity is not endemic to African Americans. Surprisingly, however, gender disparities are most pronounced among Blacks (Cuyjet, 2006; Polite & Davis, 1999).

African American men in higher education lag behind their White counterparts with respect to college-going, retention, and degree completion rates. African American men account for only 4.2% of the total enrollment of four-year higher educational institutions in the U.S. (Strayhorn, 2008). Most African Americans face significant challenges in their attempt to attain their degrees, and two-thirds will never graduate (Harper, 2006). Among the problems that hinder the participation and success of African American males in higher education are lack of financial support, lack of academic preparedness, pride, which may impede their ability to seek support, and the campus climate at Predominantly White colleges (PWIs) (Nelson-Laird, Bridges, Morelon-Quainoo, Williams, & Holmes, 2007). Research has shown that African Americans encounter chilly and hostile environments at predominantly White institutions (PWIs), prompting many to drop out or transfer to Historically Black Colleges and Universities (HBCUs) (Fries-Britt & Turner, 2002).

Issues to Consider for African American Students

Because much of the aforementioned information has focused exclusively on African American males, it is important to discuss some important issues, such as racism, issues of aggression and control, cultural alienation, and self-esteem, to consider when working with African American males. According to Lee and Bailey (2006), while African Americans differ significantly in terms of socioeconomic status, educational attainment, lifestyles, and value orientations, all African Americans share a commonality with racism. Although the ways in which African Americans react to racism may differ, this oppressive dynamic significantly affects the quality of life for all African American men and "should be considered as a significant factor in both etiology and counseling intervention" (p. 101). The issue of racism has significantly affected the mental health of African American men. "African American men have developed a number of ways of coping with and adapting to the dynamics of racism and its inherent challenges, many of which may manifest themselves as presenting issues in counseling" (p. 101).

Aside from racism, another issue that needs to be considered when working with African American males is aggression and control. The problems that African American men experience with aggression and control often manifest in various ways. First, African American males may try to exert too much control over their emotions, which may result in repression or suppressions of affection. Second, "African American men may engage in inappropriate channeling processes in which they direct strong emotions inward. Such channeling processes can lead to stress-related illnesses, such as hypertension, or maladaptive behavior including substance abuse" (Lee & Bailey, 2006, p. 101).

A third issue to consider when working with African Americans is marginalization or oppression and how it shapes isolation. Because African American men are marginalized, some may cope with their anger, frustration, and bleak outlooks by "disconnecting from meaningful personal relationships or roles valued by society" (p. 101). "With a limited sense of interconnectedness and a perceived sense of rejection by many sectors of society, the attitudes, behaviors, and values of many African American men often reflect significant disengagement from the world of work, family, and community" (Lee & Bailey, 2006, p. 101). Such alienation may lead to an "outcast" image among many African American males.

Counseling African Americans

Research has shown that many African Americans typically have a fairly negative view of counseling services because of historical treatment of racism and oppression (Sue & Sue, 1999; Vontress & Epps, 1997). According to Vontress and Epps (1997), African Americans' viewpoint about counseling may be aggravated if a non-Black counselor attempts to counsel African Americans. Nevertheless, they recommend that counselors, regardless of race, should consider "interpretation of the influence of historical hostility as a necessary part of effective psychotherapy of African Americans" (p. 180, as cited in Sue & Sue, 1999). It is important to note that the attitude that African Americans have toward counseling is not completely negative. Many African Americans genuinely believe in the helping process and realize the benefits of engaging in a counseling relationship (Sue & Sue, 2008).

Sue and Sue (1999) point out that several factors must be considered when working with African Americans. The first factor centers on racial oppression. They posit that most African Americans have experienced racism, "and the possibility that this factor might play a role in the present problem should be examined" (Sue & Sue, 1999, p. 246). Vontress and Epps (1997) characterize this factor as "historical hostility," or a reaction and a response to the social injustices that African Americans have endured and continue to endure. The second factor focuses on the importance of being non-judgmental. Sue and

Sue explain that it is important to recognize that some African Americans' behaviors may be strongly rooted in African American culture and others may not. Therefore, it is important for helpers to be open-minded when working with African Americans. The final factor, which overlaps with the previous factor, is to try and understand the personal experience of the individual. Sue and Sue note that this is significant because African Americans are not monolithic. Each person is shaped not only by his/her experiences but also by how he or she interprets and responds to them.

Because religion and spirituality play an important role in the lives of many African Americans, Sue and Sue recommend that the helper try to assess the extent to which the person they are counseling is involved in religion. If the person is heavily engaged in church activities and has strong religious beliefs, the helper might consider using resources (pastor or minister) to deal with the problem or pressing issue. Ahia (2006) reinforces the importance of involving religion and spirituality in the counseling process. He notes "as appropriate and effective, counseling approaches should incorporate aspects of the multifaceted African American religious/spiritual experience" (p. 60).

Stages of Racial identity Development: Implications for Counseling African Americans

Research has shown that minorities go through several stages of racial identity (Atkinson, Morten, & Sue, 1989; Cross, 1995). According to Sue and Sue (1999), "there is some controversy over whether racial identity is a linear process and whether individuals at the earlier stages can be mentally healthy" (p. 237). While there are several Black identity models, the Cross model of psychological nigrescense—the process of becoming Black—has garnered the most attention (Cross, 1991, 1995). Cross' model consists of a five-stage process, which explains how African Americans move from a White frame of reference to a positive Black frame of reference. Pre-encounter is the first stage of Cross' model. During this stage, African Americans consciously and unconsciously engage in a process of self-loathing while simultaneously valuing White values and ways. Encounter is the subsequent stage of Cross' model. During this stage, a two–step process occurs. First, African Americans may encounter a significant crisis or event that challenges them to change their thinking and behavior; second, African Americans may begin to reinterpret the world, resulting in a paradigm shift. During the third stage—immersion-emersion, African Americans disengage from the White culture and become immersed in African American culture. Sue and Sue (2008) note that while African Americans may begin to take pride in their culture, the internalization "of positive attitudes toward one's own Blackness is minimal" (p. 237). In the immersion-emersion phase, "feelings of guilt and anger begin to dissipate with an increasing sense of pride" (p. 237). In the next stage—internalization—conflicts between inner security stemming from the old and the new self are resolved. "Global anti-White feelings subside as the person becomes more flexible, more tolerant, and more bicultural/multicultural" (p. 237). The final stage, internalization-commitment is characterized by the commitment that African Americans have toward social change, social injustice, and civil rights.

The stage of one's racial identity has implications for counseling. Sue and Sue (2008) explain that African Americans at the pre-encounter stages are least likely to report racial discrimination, and those in the immersion stage tend to be younger and less content with societal conditions. Pierre and Mahalik (2005) contend that African Americans at the internalization stage report the greatest level of self-esteem. Atkinson and Lowe (1995) note that the stage of racial identity for African Americans shapes their racial preference for counselors. Parham and Helm (1981) indicates that African Americans at the pre-encounter stage may prefer a White counselor, and those in the other stages may prefer a counselor who is African American. Notwithstanding, Sue and Sue advise that the most important characteristic a counselor should possess when working with African American students is cultural sensitivity (Sue & Sue, 2008).

General Recommendations for Counseling African Americans

(1) When a counselor's race or ethnicity differs from that of African American clients, it may be helpful to assess the client's level of comfort. Sue and Sue (2008) recommend this approach: "Sometimes clients feel uncomfortable working with a counselor of a different race. Would this be a problem for you?" (p. 342). (2) Explore the degree that clients have responded to racism and discrimination; determine

whether they responded to these issues healthy or unhealthy. In addition, assess issues pertaining to client's level of racial identity; if someone refers a student to you, assess his or her feelings about counseling and how the process can benefit them. Assess their conceptualization of counseling and determine how they understand the pressing concerns and possible solutions. (3) Assess the assets of African American clients, such as family (extended kinship), community resources, and church. (4) Work collaboratively with the client to form and achieve goals. Whatever the problem, examine whether the client's family or friends have dealt with similar issues successfully.

Asian Americans

The Asian American population is growing significantly (Sue & Sue, 2008). As of 2007, the Asian American population was a little over 10 million. The Asian American population consists of at least 40 distinct subgroups, which differ in language, religion, and values (Sandhu, 1997). The largest Asian American groups in the United States include Chinese, Filipinos, Koreans, Asian Indians, and Japanese as well as refugees and immigrants from Southeast Asia (Vietnamese, Laotians, Cambodians, Hmongs), and Pacific Islanders (Hawaiians, Guamanians, and Samoans). While within group differences make it difficult to make generalization about Asian Americans, variables, such as mitigation or relocation experience, degree of assimilation or acculturation, identification with the home country, facility in native languages and English, family composition and togetherness, level of education, and religion, help to facilitate common bonds among them (Sue & Sue, 2008).

The families of Asian Americans tend to be family and group oriented compared to America's emphasis on individualism (Sue & Sue, 1999). "Asian American families tend to be hierarchical and patriarchal in structure, with males and older individuals occupying a higher status" (p. 363). Asian men are expected to carry on the name and tradition of the family, and even when Asian children marry, "their primary allegiance is to their parents" (p. 363). Displaying strong emotion, particularly in public, is considered to be immature and lacking control. In Asian families, the father is an authoritative figure and is generally not emotionally involved with his children (Sue & Sue, 2008). His primary function is to provide for the emotional and physical needs of the family. On the other hand, the mother is responsive to the emotional needs of the children and acts as an intermediary between father and children. As with African Americans, suicide is a leading cause of death among Asian Americans (Day-Vines, 2007).

Asian Americans and Model Minority

Asian Americans have been described as the model minority (Bell, 1996). According to Wong and Halgin (2006), Asian Americans have been portrayed in this context since the 1960s. They note Asian Americans are often depicted in the media sources as restaurant or store owners who arrived in the United States with meager amounts of money and worked long hours to achieve a piece of the American dream. Further, they note that the media have touted Asian Americans "as eyeglass-wearing, awkward nerds who spend countless hours in the library reading math and science books" (p. 38). As such, "they are especially acclaimed for their academic success, often portrayed as geniuses or science/math wizards" (p. 38). Research has shown that characterizing Asian Americans as the model minority is harmful to Asian Americans (Crystal, 1989; Min, 1995; Takaki, 1996). These researchers note that the success of a few Asian Americans has negative effects on the collective group. Researchers, such as Hurh and Kim (1989) indicated that since the dominant society has categorized Asian Americans as successful and problem free and not in need of traditional society programs or services to benefits disenfranchised minorities, it places unfair expectations upon them and denies them individuality (Wong & Halgin, 2006). One woman delineated the pressure to live up to the model minority image:

> [Whites] will have stereotypes, like, "we're smart—they are so wrong; not everyone is smart. They expect you to be this and that, and when you're not [shakes her head]. And sometimes you tend to be what they want you to be, and when you just lose your identity—you just lose being yourself. Becoming part of what someone else want[s] you to be. And it's really awkward too! When you get bad grades, people look at you really strangely because you are sort of distorting the way they see an Asian. It makes you feel awkward if you don't fit the stereotype (as cited in Wong & Halgin, p. 43)

Investigations by Toupin and Son (1991) and Ying et al. (2001) corroborate the young woman's story about not all Asian Americans earning good grades. These researchers found that Asian Americans do not perform better academically than Whites and other racial/ethnic groups. Sue and Sue (2008) further challenge the model minority for Asian Americans. Citing 2004 U.S. Census data, they note that while the median income of Asian American families was $59,300 compared to $50,000 for families in general, many Asian American households have more than one wage earner. Further, they explained that despite the higher median household income of Asian Americans, the poverty rate among Asian Americans is high.

Sue and Sue also note that in terms of education, there is a disparate picture of high educational attainment and large number of Asian Americans who are undereducated. They also note that while many think of places, such as Chinatowns, Manilatowns, and Japantowns in San Francisco and New York as tourist attractions, these areas "represent ghetto areas with prevalent unemployment, poverty, and juvenile delinquency" (p. 361). Additionally, Sue and Sue note that Asian Americans have been exposed to racism and discrimination throughout the centuries. They explain that many Asian Americans continue to experience anti-Asian American sentiments. Sue and Sue explained that the number of hate crimes against Asian Americans rose in 1995, "with assaults increasing by 11 percent and aggravated assaults by 14 percent" (p. 361). Although many Asians are fourth- and fifth-generation Americans, many still identify them as "foreign" and view them with suspicion. They advise that it is important for counselors, academic advisors, and educators to look beyond the model minority image associated with Asian Americans and to understand the historical and current experiences of Asian Americans.

Counseling Asian Americans

When counseling Asian Americans, counselors should be directive but encourage the active involvement of Asian Americans in developing goals and intervention strategies. Counselors should present varied options to clients regarding treatment approaches. Thus, Asian Americans are able to select what they believe to be the most effective approach to handle the problem. Consequently, Asian American clients should be encouraged to develop their own solutions to the problems (Sue & Sue, 2008).

Sue and Sue advise that, when counseling Asian Americans, it is important to take into consideration the family and community context during assessment and when framing the issue. "It is important to be open to different family orientations and not automatically consider interdependence as a sign of enmeshment" (Sue & Sue, 2008, p. 363). After assessment, the counselor might want to broach such questions as "How does your family see the problem?" For some Asian Americans, focus on individual needs may encroach upon the values of collectivism. As such, it is important to determine whether the client is aware of conflicting expectations. If so, goals and therapeutic approach may have to include a family focus. Broaching questions (e.g., "How important is consideration of your family in deciding how to deal with the problem?" and "How would achieving the different goals affect you, your family, friends, and social community?" will allow the counselor the opportunity to explore the degree of collectivism in the client. Sue and Sue note that Asian Americans, who have been acculturated or assimilated and who have adopted America's emphasis on individuality versus collectivism, can benefit from this counseling style.

Because Asian Americans who are not acculturated into American culture are not encouraged to display their emotions, counselors should employ approaches that focus on emotional behavior in a nondirect way. For example, Sue and Sue point out that if an individual looks uncomfortable, a counselor might acknowledge their discomfort by responding, "This situation would make someone uncomfortable." By the latter approach, a counselor recognizes the emotion indirectly (Sue & Sue, 2008).

Sue and Sue (2008) explain that since Asian Americans may present emotional difficulty though physical complaints, counselors should treat physical or somatic complaints as real by inquiring about medical and other physical treatment. "This approach legitimizes the physical complaints but allows an indirect way to assess psychosocial factors" (p. 366). Additionally, because of Asian Americans' historical and present experiences with racism and oppression, Sue and Sue encourage counselors to assess the impact of racism on the mental health of Asian Americans.

General Recommendations for Counseling Asian Americans

As with other minority groups, when counseling Asian Americans, counselors should a) display awareness of cultural differences and how they might affect the counseling process; b) assess the extent to which clients are acculturated; c) when completing an assessment, focus not just on the individual perspective but also family, friends, and societal influences. Be certain to pay attention to the worldviews and ethnic differences of the Asian American client; d) when counseling Asian Americans, focus on the strength, skills, problem-solving abilities, and support systems of individuals and families; e) take an active approach, "but allow Asian Americans to choose and evaluate suggested interventions" (Sue & Sue, 2008, p. 372); f) use approaches that are problem focus oriented and time limited that have been adjusted to incorporate cultural factors; g) consider the need to advocate or use appropriate intervention when counseling clients that are experiencing institutional racism or discrimination.

Hispanics/Latinos

The terms Latino and Hispanic include individuals in the United States with ancestry from Mexico, Puerto Rico, Cuba, El Salvador, the Dominican Republic, and other Latin countries (Sue & Sue, 2008). The terms Latino and Hispanic are not acceptable to all groups. Some individuals prefer to be referred to as La Raza (the race) (Sue & Sue, 2008). While some Hispanics from Mexico refer to themselves as Mexicano, Mexican American, Chicano, or Spanish Americans (Sue & Sue, 2008), the official term adopted by the U.S. government to refer to persons of Spanish-speaking descent is Hispanics. Nevertheless, the term Latino has grown in popularity as an alternative identification for Hispanics (Gonzalez, 1997).

As of the 2004 U.S Census Bureau, Hispanic Americans comprised well over 35 million. Thus, Hispanics are the largest minority group in the United States. Similar to Asian Americans, much heterogeneity exists among the groups of Hispanics. For example, while some Hispanics are "oriented toward their ethnic groups, others are acculturated to U.S. values" (Sue & Sue, 2008). While Hispanics populate every state, many live in metropolitan areas. A disproportionate number of Hispanics are poor, unemployed, and live in substandard housing. Many Hispanics hold blue-collar jobs and have semi-skilled or unskilled occupations (Sue & Sue, 2008).

Family cohesiveness or (familismo) and respect and loyalty are very important to Hispanics (Nelson-Laird, et al., 2007). Hispanics are more likely to stress cooperation rather than competition among family members. Interpersonal relationships are developed and maintained "with a large network of family and friends. The development and maintenance of interpersonal relationships are very central to Hispanic families. There is deep respect and affection among friends and family" (p. 377). According to Sue and Sue, typically Hispanics live in households with five or more members. "Traditional Hispanic families are hierarchical in form, with special authority given to the elderly, the parents, and males" (p. 378). Generally, the sexual behaviors of adolescent females are restricted, while males are afforded greater autonomy. Hispanic children are expected to listen to their parents and support the family whenever possible. Furthermore, parents are expected to provide for their children through young adulthood and marriage. It is assumed that older children take care of their siblings when away from home; for example, the "older sister may function as a surrogate mother" (p. 378). Suicide is also a major issue among Hispanics, as it is for other racial and ethnic minorities discussed in this chapter (Day-Vines, 2007).

While research has shown that Hispanic families adhere to strict gender roles, with the man viewed as dominant (machismo) and the female viewed as submissive (marianismo), According to Gonzalez (1997), Hispanics who are acculturated into the American culture may display a preference for more egalitarian attitudes in their relationships. Sue and Sue (2008) supports the notion that traditional gender roles may be declining among Hispanics. Factors serving as the impetus for this decline include the fact that many women are forced to become the primary wage earner and are required to act independently in the work setting and to deal with schools and other agencies.

Education Attainment

Hispanics are not performing well in K-12 (Nelson-Laird et al., 2007). Over one-third of Hispanics fail to complete high school. According to Moore (2001), more Hispanics drop out of high school than African Americans and Whites. Sue and Sue notes (2008) "more than two of five Hispanics 25 or older have not completed high school, and more than a quarter have less than a 9th grade education" (p. 385). One issue that might be posing a problem for the underperformance of Hispanics is that many attend schools with inferior academic, financial, and physical resources (Brown, Santiago, & Lopez, 2003). Additionally, Sue and Sue indicated that language issues are the culprit in the educational problems of Hispanics. Gonzalez (1997) supports this by noting that many Hispanics prefer to maintain their fluency in Spanish because it is important to their identity. While Sue and Sue (2008) explain that most second-generation Hispanics are bilingual, their command of both English and Spanish is limited because many are exposed to Spanish in the homes and English in the schools.

Many Hispanics in higher education are first-generation college students and are generally low-income (Brown, Santiago, & Lopez, 2003; Nelson-Laird et al., 2007). Fry (2002) notes that Hispanics lag behind every other major population group in attaining college degrees, especially bachelor's degrees. Research from Brown, Santiago, and Lopez agrees with Fry's assertion about the status of Hispanics in higher education, but they explain that "the college going rate for Hispanics between the ages of 18 and 22 has increased to 35 percent and their enrollments in undergraduate education by over 200 percent in the last 25 years" (p. 40). The low college attendance among Hispanics, to some extent, has been attributed to the difficulties Hispanic youth have in completing high school and the influx of adult less-educated Hispanic immigrants (Fry, 2003a, 2003b). Furthermore, similarly to African Americans, financing college remains a barrier to a college education for many Hispanic families. Some Hispanic families know little about the cost of a college education or the financial aid available to them. As such, some families conclude that a college education is not an option for their children (Brown, Santiago, & Lopez, 2003). While many Hispanics opt to enroll in community colleges, they do so only part-time, and others put off their college education into their mid-20s and beyond. Further, Fry (2002) explains that approximately 44% of Hispanics between the ages of 18 to 24 attend community colleges compared to about 30% of White and African Americans of the same age.

According to Harvey and Anderson (2005), there were more Hispanic females in higher education than Hispanic males. In 2002, approximately 36% of Hispanic females, between the ages of 18–24, were enrolled in higher education compared with 28% of Hispanic males of the same age. While both sexes have experienced increases in the number of bachelor's degrees conferred, the number of Hispanic females receiving bachelor's degrees has increased more rapidly than their male counterparts.

One initiative that has been implemented to help increase enrollment and success of Hispanic students is Hispanic-Serving Institutions (HSIs). These institutions were born out of the Higher Education Act of 1992 (Nelson-Laird et al., 2007). HSIs are accredited institutions of higher education that enroll a large percentage of Hispanic students, many of whom are low income (Brown, Santiago, & Lopez, 2003; Nelson-Laird et al., 2007). Brown, Santiago, and Lopez note that in 2000, there were 220 HSIs in the United States and Puerto Rico. There are a large number—about 30% or 66 institutions—in California that serve approximately 130,000 undergraduate students. About three quarters of HSIs are two-year institutions, and many are public (Brown, Santiago, & Lopez, 2003). While HSIs were not created to exclusively serve Hispanics, except in Puerto Rico, many are located in communities where there is a large population of Hispanic students. As such, these institutions create vehicles to inform Hispanic students throughout the educational pipeline about resources, services, and information about higher education (Brown, Santiago, & Lopez, 2003). Moreover, although HSIs are relatively new to the landscape of higher education, there is some evidence that suggests that faculty, administrators, and programs at HSIs positively affect Hispanic students (Dayton, Gonzalez-Vasquez, Martinez, & Plum, 2004; Nelson-Laird et al., 2007). Specifically, Laden (2004) noted that HSIs offer a wide array of academic and social support programs aimed at enhancing the retention and completion rates for Hispanic students.

Counseling Hispanic Americans

Because of the structure of Hispanic families, Hispanics may be less inclined to seek counseling until resources from the extended family and close friends are maximized. Allegiance to the family is of great importance, and it takes precedence over any outside concerns. As such, when counseling Hispanics, try to understand the influence of family on individuals' decisions and choices. In addition, during initial assessment, assess the influence of religion or spirituality. If an individual believes in fatalism, instead of trying to change it, a counselor might acknowledge this perspective and help the individual determine the most effective response. For example a counselor might say, 'Given that the situation is unchangeable, how can you and your family deal with this?' You are attempting to have the client develop problem-solving skills within certain parameters. The strong reliance on religion can be a resource" (Sue & Sue, 2008, p. 382).

In addition, when counseling Hispanics, Sue and Sue recommend that counselors assess their level of acculturation. This can be done by inquiring about the "specific Hispanic group that the individual is from, generational status, primary language, religious orientation, strength of religious beliefs, where they live, the reason for immigration (if immigrants), the extent of family support, and other information related to acculturation" (p. 384). Further, similar to other minority groups discussed in this chapter, it is important to take into consideration racism and oppression and the impact that they have on the mental health of Hispanics when counseling them.

General Recommendations for Counseling Hispanic Americans

When counseling Hispanics less acculturated into American culture, it is important to a) engage in a respectful, warm, and mutual introduction with the client. Sue and Sue note that less-acculturated Hispanics expect counselors to engage in a more formal counseling relationship. In this sense, "the counselor will be seen as an authority figure and should be formally dressed" (p. 387). b) Briefly describe the counseling process and the appropriate goals and have the client explain the problems as he or she views them. Determine the influence of religious or spiritual beliefs. c) Encourage the client to paraphrase and summarize the information so you know that they understand you. d) Assess the extent that clients are acculturated. e) Determine whether "there are cultural or societal aspects to the problem" (Sue & Sue, 2008, p. 388). In addition, explore the impact of racism, poverty, and "acculturative stress on the problem" (p. 388). f)

Determine whether a translator is needed. Furthermore, be sure not to interpret slow speech or long silence as indicative of cognitive dysfunction. The client might be struggling with English. g) Focus on the strength, skills, problem-solving abilities, and support systems to individuals and families. h) Use approaches that are problem focused and time limited and have been adjusted to incorporate cultural factors. i) Help the client prioritize the issues and explore what they view as important. j) Discuss the impact of achieving counseling goals on individuals, families, and communities. k) Explain the selection of a psychotherapy, why you selected it, and how it will be used. k) Frequently assess the clients' or family's response to the psychotherapy that you chose. l) Remember that although Hispanic clients who are less acculturated may prefer the counselor to engage in a formal counseling session, once trust has been established, the client may develop a personal bond and perceive the counselor as a family member or friend. Such behavior is cultural and not an indicator of dependency or "lack of boundaries" (Sue & Sue, 2008, p. 388).

Conclusion

The purpose of this chapter was to present counseling strategies that student support agents in higher education may find beneficial in working with African, Asian, and Hispanic college students. With the White college-going population expected to decrease and the minority population expected to increase, it is important that student affairs practitioners increase their familiarity regarding how to best assist minority students on campus. Hopefully, student support officials will find this chapter helpful in this endeavor. While initially, the strategies presented may not seem to be applicable to every student affairs practitioner, there are various aspects that they may find important and effective in helping minority students in various ways. Regardless of the strategies discussed, the most important aspects when working with any students, despite their physical differences, is to see them as individuals and not through the lens of their culture.

References

Ahia, E. C. (2006). A cultural framework for counseling African Americans. In C. Lee (Ed.), *Multicultural issues in counseling* (pp.

57–61). (3rd ed).Alexandria, VA: American Counseling Association.

Anderson, N. B. (1995). Behavioral and sociocultural perspectives on ethnicity and health: Introduction to special issue. *Health Psychology*, 14, 589–591.

Atkinson, D. R., & Lowe, S. M. (1995). The role of ethnicity, cultural knowledge, and conventional techniques in counseling and psychotherapy. In J. G. Ponterotto, J. M. Casas, L. A. Suzuki, & C. M. Alexander (Eds.), *Handbook of multicultural counseling* (pp. 387–414). Thousand Oaks, CA: Sage.

Atkinson, D. R., Morten, G., & Sue, D. W. (1989). A minority identity development model. In D. R. Atkinson, G. Morten, & D. W. Sue (Eds.), *Counseling American minorities* (pp. 35–52). Dubuque, IA: W. C. Brown.

Bell, D. A. (1996). America's greatest success story: The triumph of Asian Americans. In R. C. Monk (Ed.), *Taking sides: Clashing views on controversial issues in race and ethnicity* (2nd ed.). Guilford, CT: Dushkin.

Bonner, F. A. II (2003). To be young, gifted, African American, and male. *The Gifted Child Today*, 26(2), 26–34.

Brown, S. E., Santiago, D. & Lopez, E. (2003). Latinos in higher education: Today and tomorrow. *Change, 35,* 40–46.

Compton, M., Thompson, N., & Kaslow, N. (2005). Social environment factors associated with suicide attempt among low-income African Americans: The protective role of family relationships and social support. *Social and Psychiatric Epidemiology, 40,* 175–185.

Cook, B. J., & Córdova, D. I. (2007). Higher education: Twenty-second annual status report: 2007 supplement. Retrieved on November 16, 2008, from http://www.acenet.edu/

Cose, E., Smith, V. E., Figueroa, A., Stefanakos, V. S., & Contreras, J. (2000, November 13). American's prison generation. *Newsweek,* 42–49.

Cross, W.E. (1991). *Shades of Black: Diversity in African American identity*. Philadelphia: Temple University Press.

Cross, W. E. (1995). The psychology of Nigrescence: Revisiting the Cross model. In J. G. Ponterotto, J. M. Casas, L. A. Suzuki, & C. M.

Alexander (Eds.), *Handbook of multicultural counseling* (pp. 93–122). Thousand Oaks, CA: Sage.

Crystal, D. (1989). Asian Americans and the myth of the model minority. *Social Casework, 70,* 405–413.

Cuyjet, M. J. (2006). African American college men: Twenty-first century issues and concerns. In M. J. Cuyjet (Ed.), *African American men in college.* (pp. 3–23). San Francisco: Jossey-Bass.

Day-Vines, N. L. (2007). The escalating incidence of suicide among African Americans: Implications for counselors. *Journal of Counseling and Development, 85,* 370–377.

Dayton, B., Gonzales-Vasquez, N., Martinez, C. R., & Plum, C. (2004). Hispanic-serving institutions through the eyes of students and administrators. *New Directions for Student Services, 105,* 29–39.

Ennis, W., Jr., Ennis, W., III., Durodoye, B. A., Ennis-Cole, D., Bolden, V. (2004). Counseling African Americans clients: Professional counselors and religious institutions. *Journal of Humanistic Counseling, Education, and Development, 43*(2), 197—210.

Epps, E. G. (1995). Race, class, and educational opportunity: Trends in the sociology of education. *Sociological Forum, 10*(4), 593–608.

Felton, G. M., Parson, M. A., Misener, T. R., & Oldaker, S. (1997). Health promoting behavior of Black and White college women. *Western Journal of Nursing Research, 19,* 654–664.

Fries-Britt, S. L. (1998). Moving beyond Black achiever isolation: Experience of gifted Black collegians. *Journal of Higher Education, 69*(5), 556–576.

Fries-Britt, S. L., & Turner, B. (2002). Uneven stories: Successful Black collegians at a Black and a White campus. *Review of Higher Education, 25*(3), 315–330.

Fry, R. (2002). Latinos in higher education: Many enroll, too few graduate. Washington, DC: Pew Hispanic Center.

Fry, R. (2003a). Hispanics in college: Participation and degree attainment. ERIC Digest. New York, NY: ERIC Clearinghouse on Urban Education.

Fry, R. (2003b). Hispanic youth dropping out of U.S. schools: Measuring the challenge. Washington, DC: Pew Hispanic Center.

Gonzalez, G. (1997). The emergence of Chicanos in the twenty-first century: Implications for counseling, research, and policy. *Journal of Multicultural Counseling and Development, 25*(2), 94–106.

Harper, S. R. (2005). Leading the way: Inside the experience of high-achieving African American male students. *About Campus, 10*(1), 8–15.

Harper, S. (2006). Reconceptualizing reactive policy responses to Black male college achievement: Implications from a national study. *Focus.* Washington, DC : Joint Center for Political and Economic Studies.

Hale, J. E. (2001). *Learning while Black: Creating educational excellence for African American children.* Baltimore: The Johns Hopkins University Press.

Harvey, W. B. (2008). The weakest link: A commentary on the connections between K-12 and higher education. *American Behavioral Scientist, 51*(7), 972–983.

Harvey, W. B., & Anderson, E. L. (2005). *Minorities in higher educationl 2003–2004. Twenty-first annual status report.* Washington, DC: American Council on Education.

Hurh, W. M., & Kim, K. C . (1989). The "success" image of Asian Americans. Its validity and its practical implications. *Ethnic and Racial Studies, 12,* 512–538.

Hurtado, A., Hayes-Bautista, D. E., Burciaga Valdez, R., Hernandez, A. C. R. (1992). *Refining California: Latino social engagement in a multicultural society.* Los Angeles: UCLA Chicano Studies Research Center.

Jackson, J. F. L., & Moore, J. L., III. (2006). African American males in education: Endangered or ignored. *Teachers College Record. 108*(2), 201–205.

Jackson, J. F. L., & Moore, J. L., III. (2008). The African American male crisis in education: A popular media infatuation or needed public policy response. *American Behavioral Science, 51*(7), 847–853.

Laden, B. V. (2004). Hispanic-serving institutions: What are they? Where are they? *Community College Journal of Research and Practice, 28*(3), 181–198.

Lee, C. C., & Bailey, D. F. (2006). Counseling African American male youth and men. In C. Lee (Ed.), *Multicultural issues in counseling* (pp. 93–112). (3rd ed).Alexandria: VA: American Counseling Association.

Majors, R., & Billson, M. (1992). *Cool pose: Dilemmas of Black manhood in America*. New York: Simon & Schuster.

Min, P. G. (Ed.). (1995). *Asian Americans contemporary trends and issues.* Thousand Oaks, CA: Sage.

Moore, K. A. (2001). Time to take a closer look at Hispanic children and families. *Policy & Public Human Services, 59*, 8–9.

Moore, J., L. III, Henfield, M. S., Owens, D. (2008). African American males in special education: Their attitudes and perceptions toward high school counselors and school counseling services. *American Behavioral Scientist, 51*(7), 907–927.

Nelson-Laird, Bridges, Morelon-Quainoo, C. L., Williams, J. M, & Holmes, M. S. (2007). African American and Hispanic students engagement at minority serving and Predominantly White Institutions. *Journal of College Student Development*, 48(1), 39-56.

Parham, T. A., & Helm, J. E. (1981). The influence of Black students' racial attitudes on preference for a counselor's race. *Journal of Counseling Psychology, 28*, 250–257.

Pierre, M. R., & Mahalik, J. R. (2005). Examining African self-consciousness and Black racial identity as predictors of Black men's psychological well-being. *Cultural Diversity and Ethnic Minority Psychology, 11*, 28–40.

Polite, V. C., & Davis, J. E. (1999). Introduction: Research focused on African American males. V. C. Polite, & J. E. Davis (Eds.). *African American males in school and society: Practices and policies for effective education.* New York: Teachers College Press.

Sandhu, D. (1997). Psychocultural profiles of Asian and Pacific Islander Americans: Implications for counseling and psychotherapy. *Journal of Multicultural Counseling and Development, 25*, 7–22.

Strayhorn, T. (2008). The role of supportive relationships in supporting African American males' success in college. *NASPA Journal, 45*(1), 26–48.

Sue, D. W., & Sue, D. (1999). *Counseling the culturally different: Theory and practice.* (3rd ed). New York: John Wiley and Son, Inc.

Sue, D. W., & Sue, D. (2008). *Counseling the culturally diverse: Theory and practice.* (5th ed). New York: John Wiley and Son, Inc.

Takaki, R. (1996). The myth of the "model minority." In R. C. Monk (Ed.), *Taking sides: Clashing views on controversial issues in race and ethnicity* (2nd ed,). Guilford, CT: Dushkin.

Toupin, E. S. W., & Son, L. (1991). Preliminary findings on Asian Americans: The model minority in a small private East Coast college. *Journal of Cross-Cultural Psychology, 22*, 403–417.

U.S. Census Bureau. (2008). *Projections of the population and components of change for the United States: 2010 -2050*. Retrieved on February 5, 2010 from http://www.census.gov/population/www/projections/summarytables.html

U.S. Department of Education. (2004). *U.S. interim projections by age, sex, race, and Hispanic origin*. Retrieved on December 22, 2007 from http://www.census.gov/ipc.www/usinterimproj/.

Vontress, C. E., & Epp, L. R. (1997). Historical hostility in the African American client: Implications for counseling. *Journal of Multicultural Counseling and Development, 25*, 170–184.

Wong, F., & Halgin, R. (2006). The "model minority": Bane or blessing for Asian Americans? *Journal of Multicultural Counseling and Development, 34*, 38–49.

Ying, Y. W., Lee, P.A., Tsai, J. L., Hung, Y., Lin, M., & Wan, C. T. (2001). Asian American college students as model minorities: An examination of their overall competence. *Cultural Diversity and Ethnic Minority Psychology, 7*, 59–74.

CHAPTER TWELVE

Beyond Structural Diversity: Centering "Place" Among African American Students in Predominantly White Campuses

Lorenzo DuBois Baber

A century ago, W.E.B. Du Bois, in an inquiry about the experiences of African American students at Predominantly White institutions (PWIs) in the North, asked administrators to respond to the following question, "In general, what has been their success and what is the attitude of the institution and student body toward them?" (Du Bois, 1910, p. 22). While the vague answers Du Bois received have been enlightened by decades of research, the spirit of his question continues to remain relevant—African American students attending Predominantly White Institutions are facing unique challenges that may inhibit academic success. The continued gap in achievement outcomes among African American college students and their White peers is indicative of the failure to resolve this issue of equity. Longitudinal data show that, among students who begin at a four-year institution, the six-year graduation rate of African American students remain significantly lower than White students (U.S. Department of Education, 2003). Further, the largest graduation rate gaps are observed at Predominantly White Institutions, where the majority of African American college students are enrolled (Carey, 2008; Strayhorn, 2008).

Research has established a connection between campus environment and persistence outcomes for African American students attending Predominantly White Institutions (Allen, 1992; Carter, 2003; Fries-Britt and Turner, 2001; Hurtado, Milem, Clayton-Pedersen, & Allen, 1998; Sedlacek, 1987; Swail, Reed, and Perna, 2003). African American students are less likely to persist if they feel alienation and prejudice because of their ethnicity. The legacy of historical exclusion, a lack of structural representation among the student body, and discriminatory incidents on campus contribute to heightened levels of stress for African American students at PWIs, thereby influencing their desire to stay involved and persist. To cope, African American students often turn to formal African American student organizations on campus (Solórzano, Ceja, and Yosso, 2000; Guiffrida, 2003; Jones, Castellanos, and Cole, 2002; Patton, 2006). These organizations often provide a community of support and encouragement within the larger institutional environment. They provide a counter-space for inclusiveness grounded in a healthy self-concept of ethnic identity. These organizations also supply students with connections to networks of peers who provide social and cultural support.

Previous studies examining the importance of ethnic-centered student organizations for African American students attending Predominantly White Institutions have focused on their role in facilitating social connection to the institution. However, most studies do not address how African American student organizations address the increasing socio-cultural diversity among African American students. African American ethnicity is not a monolithic experience (Brown, 1997; Celious and Oyserman, 2001; King, 2005) but converges with other forms of identity—gender, socioeconomic background, religion—to produce cultural variations among African Americans. Therefore, among a heterogeneous African American population, the social space developed by an African American student organization may not be inclusive of all the within-group cultural variations. Consequently, these counter-spaces can offer, at one moment, supportive environments which honor equality and inclusion while challenging pervasive dominant ideology. At other moments, these organizations can become sources of conflict, supporting exclusionary practices based on within-group differences among the African American community.

As a result, African American students may interpret and reinterpret perceptions of socio-cultural spaces offered by African American student organizations as inclusive or exclusive based on their perceptions and experiences within both the specific organizational and the general campus space. The purpose of this chapter is to consider institutional practices which promote transcendence of campus spaces at PWIs to culturally inclusive places for African Americans. Specifically, this chapter addresses two main questions:

1. How do students view African American student organizations upon initial entry into the campus environment? How do these perspectives change as students experience other social and academic settings on campus?
2. In what ways do African American student organizations acknowledge the heterogeneity among the African American student body? If they do not, what are the socio-cultural characteristics which define inclusion (and exclusion)?

While African American student organizations create important *space* for African American students, a specific meaning of *place* is developed by individual perceptions. *Place* is what *space* becomes when the gathering of people, objects, and interpretations interact within a specific boundary to create structures, practices, and norms (Bourdieu and Passeron, 1998; Gieryn, 2000). Using a place-sensitive sociology framework, one may view African American organizations as both a catalyst for development of culturally inclusive places and as avenues which struggle to maintain security and identity for growing cultural heterogeneity within the African American community.

Evidence suggests that institutions rarely move beyond initiatives which target structural diversity goals (Chang, 2007; M. Chang, J.Chang and Ledesma, 2005). While access for individuals from diverse backgrounds is a critical step towards progress, numerical representation alone does not create inclusive environments. As administrators and educators reconsider diversity issues on campus, it is critical to challenge the monolithic assumption of African American students attending PWIs and reveal the less visible issues of within-group sociocultural stratification which are often stimulated by the overall institutional climate. The movement from 'space' to 'place' is critical to challenging traditional notions of cultural dominance and exclusion at PWIs and as an opportunity for development of proactive strategies which support equity and inclusion for all African American students attending Predominantly White Institutions.

Conceptual Framework

From Integration to Inclusion: African American students at PWIs

Much of the early literature on student retention stresses the importance of non-cognitive factors, including the degree to which students become involved and integrated into various social and academic systems of the institution (Astin, 1975; Pascarella and Terenzini, 2005; Tinto, 1993). Students who perceived congruency between their norms and values and those of the institution will likely establish a connection and persist while those who perceive incongruence will likely feel isolated and leave the institution. Initial conceptual models of student attrition, most notably Tinto's theory of student departure, were criticized for overlooking issues of power and cultural dominance in the exchange between students and the subsystems of the institution (Tierney, 1992; Braxton, 2000; Rendon, Jalomo, & Nora, 2000: Swail, Reed, & Perna, 2003). Institutional experiences that lead to departure may be contextually dissimilar for different groups, limiting the use of traditional student attrition models for nontraditional students in higher education. Elaborating this point, Rendon et al., (2000) conclude that "absent from the traditional social integrationist view are the distinctions among cultures, differences among students with regard to class, race, gender, and sexual orientation, and the role of group members and the institutions in assisting students to succeed" (p. 139).

A social conflict perspective on student retention suggests that connections within the institutional system require not just congruence with cultural norms but a conformity to cultural rules grounded in explicit expectations, values, and practices within the institution (Bourdieu & Passeron, 1998; Braxton, 2000; Braxton, Hirschy, & McClendon, 2004; Carter, 2003; Rendon, Jalomo, & Nora, 2000). Bourdieu suggests that education structures *assume* possession of specific forms of cultural competence and awareness rooted in the dominant culture of the society. This cultural capital provides advantage for individuals from certain backgrounds, increasing likelihood of congruence and persistence in the educational structure. Over time, success at educational institutions become less about meritocracy and more about 'inhereditocracy'—educational achievement rooted in intergenerational transmission of dominant cultural capital forms.

In Predominantly White Institutions, these coded cultural norms are often rooted in White, upper-class ideology. This is not to suggest that students from traditionally marginalized backgrounds do not possess unique, valuable forms of cultural capital, but these non-dominant forms are often devalued or ignored within the institution. Therefore, PWIs become hostile places for certain students, by both their distant position to dominant perspectives and a possession of a culture that goes institutionally unrecognized. Faced with this challenge, underrepresented students, African Americans in particular, seek connection to sociocultural spaces within the institution. Students anticipate formal and informal support and (perhaps) a collective challenge to the deficient view of African American culture.

African American student organizations have traditionally provided opportunities to gather and share knowledge and information useful for navigating through hostile campus climate (Fries-Britt and Turner, 2001; Guiffrida, 2003; Jones, Castellanos, and Cole, 2002; Solórzano, Ceja, and Yosso, 2000). Particularly in the absence of a critical mass, African American students attending PWIs turn to African American student organizations to combat subtle and overt acts of racism within the academic and sub-communities of the institution. Subtle acts of racism include individual perceptions of being stereotyped by peers and faculty as being less academically qualified; direct experiences of unchallenged behaviors which situate African American culture as monolithic and inferior to dominant ideology; observations of systematic cultural bias within institutional policies and procedures. Overt acts of racism, while less prevalent today than a generation ago, still exist on college campuses (one may look no further than the recent rise in racialized theme parties on college campuses). Overall, African American student organizations provide formal and informal counter-spaces where, as Solórzano et al. state, "deficit notions of people of color can be challenged and where a positive collegiate racial climate can be established" (p. 70).

Having confirmed the continued importance of these organizations for African American students, it may be valuable to consider the degree to which these counter spaces defy or conform to exclusionary practices based on sociocultural diversity within the African American collectivity. Researchers have recently paid closer attention to the increasing heterogeneity among African American students (Alford, 2000; Allen, Jayakumar, Griffin, Korn, and Hurtado, 2004; Nichols and Harper, 2008). In particular, African American students who attend PWIs may perceive African American student organizations very differently over time based on their evolving ethnic identity development, their personal experiences within the larger academic and social systems of the institution, and the shifting cultural dynamics of the institution. Consequently, it becomes important for administrators and educators to consider whether these important counter-spaces account for the sociocultural diversity or are biased toward a particular variation of African American culture. Further, we should question how students, based on their individual experiences with both African American organizations and other units on campus (both academic and social), contribute to the practices within these counter-spaces. Finally, we need to consider our responsibility in ensuring the inclusiveness of these spaces for all students.

Place-Based Sociology and Campus Climate

The transformation of space from a physically bounded location to a socially interactive setting involves both individual and collective action (Simmel, 1950; Gans, 2002). Simmel describes the development of space as including exclusivity of use by participants, frequency and pace of interactions among participants, and isolation from a more complex environment for participants. However, the definition of space is limited to measurable objective aspects of geography, while place describes aspects of human territorial experience. "To have root in a place is to have a secure point from which to look out in the world, a firm grasp of one's position in the order of things, and a significant spiritual and psychological attachment to somewhere in particular" (Gans, 2002, p. 36).

Gieryn (2000) suggests that 'place' is what 'space' becomes when the gathering of people, objects, and interpretations interact within a specific boundary to create structures, practices, and norms: "Places are endlessly made…when ordinary people extract from continuous and abstract space a bounded, identified, meaningful, named, and significant place" (p. 471). A sufficient feature of place is the individual and collective investment of meaning and value of the space they occupy— flexible in the company of diverse people, dynamic over time, and inevitably contested. Gieryn warns that the meaning of place is difficulty to quantify, for an attempt to reduce subjective matters to objective measures is ill-conceived reductionism: "Here, place becomes a stand-in for clusters of variables located in spaces chosen for their own analytic utility but generally denuded of…actors' own narratives" (p. 466). Further, as places bring people together in a co-presence, an identity of place is formed, and two possibilities become apparent for individuals—engagement or estrangement. If identity of place harmonizes with personal identities, place becomes interactive and cohesive. However, if individuals encounter an identity of place which clashes with personal identities, identity of place becomes a source of marginalization and detachment. Gieryn concludes that "debates over the conditions for one of the other outcomes constitute perhaps the most celebrated and enduring contributions of sociologists to the study of place" (p. 476).

At a Predominantly White Institution, the identity of place created by the African American student organization is inescapably flexible, dynamic, and contested through responses to internal and external environmental shifts. Internally, participation in African American student organizations as place is altered by new students entering the organization, returning students assuming leadership positions, and older students exiting the organization (via graduation, transfer, or dropout). External environmental shifts may include increases (or decreases) in structural diversity and frequency (or infrequency) of racialized incidents on campus. Often the identity of place for African American student organizations is connected to the environmental characteristics in the institution. For example, if there is a widely reported racialized incident on campus, African American student organizations may be identified as a place to plan for collective action. In the absence of major racialized incidents, African American student organizations may be identified in less collective ways. From this perspective, we may use a placed-based conceptual framework to consider both micro and macro organizational influence of campus culture—examining factors which directly and indirectly shape 'place' and influence individual and collective behaviors in the community.

Methodology

To consider the centrality of campus 'place" in shaping experiences of African American students at Predominantly White Institutions, I use qualitative data collected from students attending a PWI in the mid-Atlantic region during the 2006–2007 academic year. Purposeful sampling procedures identified fifteen traditional-aged (18 to 20 years old), residential students who were first-time freshmen at the same postsecondary institution. Pseudonyms were assigned to each student, as well as the institution, in order to ensure participant anonymity. All students described themselves as African Americans, and every participant was born and socialized primarily in the United States. The sample includes nine females and six males.

The institution selected for this study is a public, four-year, doctoral research extensive institution located in the mid-Atlantic region of the United States. With a campus located just outside a major metropolitan city, Coastal University (pseudonym) has an overall enrollment of 12,000 students, drawing students from the inner city as well as the suburbs. The university enrolls approximately 1,400 first-year students in the fall, with over 70% residing in campus housing. In 2006, the ethnic profile of students was 61% White, 19% Asian American, 13% African American, 5% international students, 2% Hispanic American, and .4% Native American.

Two sources of data are used—individual interviews and journal entries. The primary source of data for this study was individual interviews. In order to assess the meaning participants make of their experience, a set of semi-structured, open-ended questions during interviews at three points during the academic year—October, December, and March—were employed. Additionally, journal entries were used to provide an indication of the thought process of the individual in their personal language, uncovering events with lasting impact, stimulating further questions from the researcher. Students were asked to complete at least one journal entry between October (first interview) and December (second interview) and two entries between December (second interview) and March (final interview).

Pattern-matching logic, through development of a coding system, is the specific technique used for within-case and across-case analysis. Pattern-matching logic compares a theoretical-based pattern with an empirically based pattern (Yin, 2003). Coding is often based on description of setting, definition of particular situation, and ways of thinking about specific aspects of a situation. Developing a list of coding categories outlines emergent themes, reducing the data to patterns for comparison.

Findings and Discussion

In this chapter, I present patterns from discussions with participants related to their evolving perceptions of African American student organizations and how their perspectives were altered by experiences within the organization and the general campus environment. Overall, three main themes emerged. First, initial impressions of African American student organizations by new students were confounded by uncertainty over their purpose. Secondly, students who participated in organizations found them to be rigid sociocultural places. Lastly, students tended to settle on involvement in smaller African American student organizations which allowed expression of multiple aspects of their identity.

Uncertainty over Purpose

During initial interviews, many students discussed uncertainty over the purpose and mission of African American student organizations. Kristina, who initially identified herself a member of the Black Student Caucus (pseudonym), stated that she often is left wondering what the purpose of the organization is after attending a meeting. "I don't even know what it's supposed to do on campus. We get together and you just have a lot of Black people in the room. Is that what we're supposed to do? I have no idea what the purpose of that organization is." Will was equally direct, "I guess it's to bring Black people together, I guess, or to raise awareness or something. I don't know." Jada also touched upon the unclear mission statement of the Black Student Caucus and other African American student organizations she considered joining:

> I went to one meeting of (Black Student Caucus). They weren't doing much. I went to (a Female Student Organization), which is supposed to be a predominantly African American organization. They weren't doing much either. I was like, what am I doing here, just socializing? Aren't we supposed

> to be doing community service or something? Something. Anything. But they don't really do anything. If I'm going to join a club, I'm joining to have fun or to do community service or work or something. Not just sit around and chat about…what do they chat about?

For students in this study, initial disassociation with African American organizations as a community place was rooted in their lack of awareness of the historical and contemporary mission. It did not appear that the members of the student organizations, particularly the Black Student Caucus, were proactive or explicit in stating their value to new members of the campus community. As a result, students did not feel any need to invest in the organizations and, in some cases, questioned their usefulness or existence on campus. As Will states, "I don't think they are necessary organizations. I mean, if they got rid of them I don't think anything would go wrong…."

African American identity models suggest that African American students, until directly encountering overt acts of racism in their immediate settings, tend to absorb many of the Eurocentric beliefs and values of the dominant culture (Cross, Parham, and Helms, 1991; Cross, 1995). While students in this study appeared initially attracted to African American student organizations, without evidence of an explicit purpose or reason to invest the sociocultural place developed by the organization, they tended to dismiss their usefulness. Indeed absent from these initial discussions with students was acknowledgement or discussion of experiences with racialized incidents within the larger campus. Hence, from their perspective, without understanding of the historical or potential threats of racism in the social and academic settings of the institution, students placed little or no value on a social place centered on African American ethnicity. In fact, their meaning of ethnic-centered place appeared to be rooted in self-marginalization from other places on campus. As Imani states, "I think race is important, but they had this Black student orientation and automatically that put me off because it was like, 'orientation for us,' and they had 'us' in bold letters and I was like, I don't know, separating yourself, and I didn't like that."

The initial rejection of African American student organizations did not seem rooted in an internal desire to seek a Eurocentric identity but rather a lack of explicit definition about the potential value of place provided within African American organizations for African American students on this campus. As participants experienced the larger campus environment, many began to experience and acknowledge the impact of racism in their social and academic lives and many reconsidered their initial rejection of ethnic-centered places African American organizations provide. However, students were often motivated to make an investment in the sociocultural place as a reaction to negative experiences in the hostile institutional environment rather than through proactive supportive encounters. New students did not find much connection in the historical role of African American student organizations or through the declaration that it was an organization for 'us.' Rather, as they developed perceptions of the larger institutional environment and, perhaps, had personal experiences with racism, they sought supportive environments. As students develop investment in ethnic-centered environments as a response to negative encounters, there should be a concern about whether students are further isolated during their interactions within the organization.

Rigidity of African American Student Organization as a Social Place

At some point during the academic year, most students, despite initial uncertainty over mission and hesitation about participation in ethnic-centered place, attended a Black Student Caucus meeting or event. As Tara explains, "I wanted to establish more Black pride or something, you know, heritage." Most students felt that the Black Student Caucus could be a place that could meet that need for 'something.' However, for the most part, students describe a place of exclusion rather than inclusion. Jada states:

> So I went to the first meeting (of the semester) and another meeting after that...I thought it was something that I was going to do, that I would stick with. But I stopped going....Why? The first meeting, they were talking about something that I had nothing to do with. This thing they do before, they go somewhere and they get to know each other. I didn't go to that. So, they were talking about that the entire meeting and I was kind of lost, like, 'Why am I here?' And every now and then they have discussions about topics or whatever. And I signed up to be on one of the committees for volunteer efforts, but I stopped going.

The Black Student Caucus slogan is 'Embracing Others to Create a Cultural Identity.' However, Eric disagreed with the suggested inclusiveness: "(Black Student Caucus) seems to cater to the urban, hip-hop, trendy crowd. (Black Student Caucus) kind of shuts out the Black kids who are into anime (Japanese animated art) or rock music, or anything else. What would they talk about when they go there? They would more than likely not be accepted." Bridgette agreed, defining BSC as "the clique of the century." She continues:

> I think it's become more of a social thing...sI've heard about some of their topics and they're really superficial and they don't even delve that much into the Black community so it seems like a group that doesn't even care about its message, they just labeled it the (Black Student Caucus) because that would get them maybe sponsoring or...I don't know...they're not really doing that much for themselves or the campus.

Students perceived the meaning of the Black Student Caucus on this campus as a purely social place. Additionally, this social place has established cultural norms that, they feel, were not flexible enough to include a wider sociocultural heterogeneity. African American identity models suggest as individuals experience negative 'encounters' which challenge Eurocentric notions of ethnic identity, they seek 'immersion' into sources of African American culture (Cross, Parham, and Helms, 1991; Cross, 1995). While participants in the study expressed a desire to connect with an ethnic-centered place on campus as a result of marginalization in dominant culture spaces, they also described a place which held conditional inclusion based on specific sociocultural values. This distinction included congruence with specific fashion and musical taste. During the spring semester, a number of participants described an incident at a Talent Show sponsored by the Black Student Caucus. As Bridgette described "All the Black people were there, I mean every Black person on this campus." Bridgette reported that a mix of talent was presented, but only those performances that "delivered it in this, this certain...what I say 'way'...were supported by the crowd and Black Student Union judges." Bridgette describes the reaction of an act she was impressed with: He was playing piano with his spoken word, and he was kind of more, he was cool with it. "He was cool with his words and they said it sucked...I don't think they were open...they weren't open to anything else so, that kind of frustrated me a little bit." In a separate interview, Imani discussed the same event in response to a question about student organizations on campus. She offered a similar observation about the piano act:

> The guy who was um playing piano…it wasn't fair what they said about him, and others were just like oh yeah, he sucked. I don't know. I didn't think it was right what they said. And they, they go in with this image of like…I don't know, Black people playing drums and doing stomp and stepping and all that. You don't necessarily (pause)… that's fun to have, but you don't need that for it to be good.

It appeared that this incident represented the Black Student Union as a place in which definitions of African American identity were contested. Many students who participated in the study felt estranged rather than engaged by the cues of the social norms within the Black Student Union place—whether it was at general meetings or social events. Because students perceived this ethnic centered student organization as primarily social, they saw limited opportunity for connection if their social interests were not congruent with the established community. Ultimately, those students who were estranged or marginalized found support through informal connections and multidimensional student organizations.

Focus on Smaller Organizations

Through initial perceptions and personal experiences, students developed a perspective on the Black Student Caucus as a primary social organization. As such, they did not feel the need to utilize the organization to establish social connections. As Eric states, "It's easier to just make friends with people on your floor than to go through the hassle of signing up with a group, going to all the meetings, keeping up with everything. So it's better when it's more informal." Tara describes the process of establishing her network without involvement in formal organizations:

> I guess maybe every once in a while in (Residence Hall), we'd just come across each other and we'd talk about a few things, and then from there, I guess we talked about more things that were less chit-chatty stuff that you say, like 'How was your day? What are your classes?' We talked about stuff that meant more to us….

Natalya adds, "We all just kind of click and support each other. It's like a community within a community. I think we get along because we are the same in certain ways and different in others." Perhaps the structural diversity present at Coastal University (39% non-White student body, including 13% African American) provided more opportunity for African American students to connect with each other outside of the Black Student Caucus. A critical mass of African American students on campus allows sub-cultures to emerge among the population, offering valuable support to members (Fries-Britt & Turner, 2001). The presence of a critical mass reduces the role of main ethnic-centered student organizations to provide sociocultural counter-spaces on campus. Instead, students are able to create a community of place, infusing a more personal investment of meaning based on identities which include, but are not limited to, their African American ethnic identity.

Absent from these discussions with students was acknowledgement or discussion of the role of the Black Student Caucus as a counter-space to overt and subtle racism within the larger campus. This is not to suggest that students did not have perceptions or experiences, both in social and academic environments, of a racially hostile environment. When students describe finding formal support during challenging personal moments, they were more likely to mention smaller organizations which were ethnic centered but also multidimensional. In other words, these organizations connected to identities beyond their ethnicity—Gospel Choir, support organizations for males of color such as Brother 2 Brother , support organizations for females of color such as Sister 2 Sister, academic organizations such as National Society of Black Engineers, etc. Malik states "I know a lot of people in Gospel Choir are really dedicated to it, and also the Brother 2 Brother program. It depends on your priorities. If you want more on academics and make sure you do good at it, or you still want to focus but also want something on the side," Ron added, "Guys in Brother 2 Brother were like…they stayed on you about coming to meetings and letting you know how important it was…and also, it was a smaller group, so you didn't feel like…it was just easier to fit in." Kristina states:

> I feel that that's what (Black Student Caucus) kind of was, like, 'You're Black. You're Black. You're Black. You're Black.' I know. I grew up being it.

> I still am it. I plan on being it for the rest of my life...people are going to see me as being Black first enough, I want to be known as more than that...as a Christian, as a woman...I can be more than just Black in (other organizations).

In addition to perceiving the Black Student Caucus as a social organization, students also viewed the organization as one-dimensional, a focus on ethnicity void of other dimensions of their identity—spiritual and gender for example. Rather than experience social isolation in 'non-dominant' culture place on campus, students in this study chose to commit to organizations that offered place for expression of multiple identities. This is not to suggest that a main ethnic student organization cannot provide a similar place, but in the case of the Black Student Caucus at Coastal, there was little explicit recognition, at least from the perspectives of the participants, that their multiple identities would be acknowledged and recognized.

Implications for Practice and Further Research

Previous research suggests that African American students often turn to formal African American student organizations to battle perceived prejudices at PWIs (Solórzano, Ceja, and Yosso, 2000; Jones, Castellanos, and Cole, 2002; Guiffrida, 2003). These organizations serve to facilitate cultural connections and social integration by exposing and connecting students to African American culture. The information presented in this chapter proposes that the role of African American student organizations in supporting transition of African American students is influenced by centrality of place through clarification of value to individuals, sociocultural inclusiveness, and acknowledgment of multiple identities for participants. It should be noted that this study is limited in several ways. Foremost, this is an in-depth study of one institution during one academic year. Additionally, data were collected from a select group of first-year students. Perceptions from other students, particularly leaders of the Black Caucus, were not included. However, we may draw some valuable lessons from the narratives of these students for future administrative practices.

First, perceptions of place are related to mobility of identity for African American students attending Predominantly White Institutions. As students experience the campus as a social and academic place, they are also uncovering multiple identities grounded in gender, socioeconomic background, and spirituality. The degree to which they can feel comfortable revealing their multiple selves is related to their perceptions of an inclusive or exclusive place. Students recognize the opportunities provided by African American student organizations, but they also struggle with concerns about whether, as a sociocultural place, the organization limits their mobility of identity. For example, they may ask themselves 'What identity, if any, must I suppress to be recognized in this organization?'

In acknowledging the interplay between self-conceptualization of identity and influence of sociocultural place, current administrative practices underestimate the influence of the latter on the development of the former. In particular, African American organizations are often viewed as stagnant places where meaning is grounded in a monolithic perspective of African American culture. From this perspective, a 'authentic' African American experience is narrowly defined and supported, producing degrees of marginalization from within. This viewpoint is particularly damaging at Predominantly White Institutions, where African American students are still likely to face hostility and discrimination based on their ethnicity. Hence, African American students are faced with the ridiculous paradox of being 'too Black' in some places while 'not Black enough' in other places.

Therefore, the challenge lies in how African American student organizations present themselves to new members of the campus community and project themselves to the larger community. A mission statement should be grounded in historical, cultural, and intellectual meaning rather than just having a social meaning. Additionally, inclusiveness and respect of heterogeneous African American identity must not be just words on a page but be present in the actions of student members and administrative advisors. Future research should investigate ways African American organizations identify, clarify, and revisit their purpose. Administrators should work with students to consider whether messages are constructed with the diverse interest of the African American student population in mind.

Second, structural diversity and presence of a critical mass remain an important features of the institutional environment. Fortunately for students at Coastal, the struggle for engagement of multiple identities was largely muted by presence of a critical mass of African American students on campus. Without a critical mass, African American students at PWIs may be more likely to be marginalized because of their ethnicity in 'dominant cultural' spaces on campus and socially isolated in the limited 'nondominant' culture spaces on campus. A critical mass of students creates varied sub-cultures where students may find opportunities to interact with other African American students in smaller organizations or through informal interactions. Conversely, a lack of structural representation of African American students at PWIs stresses the importance of maintaining inclusive student organizations overall but particularly among the African American student organizations.

However, just as administrators cannot support monolithic perspectives of African American culture, they must be equally cautious about reducing development of culturally inclusive places to quantitative measures such as numerical representation of ethnicity. Presence of diversity does not necessarily lead to cultural inclusiveness for all students although it does provide increased opportunity for associations. However, there cannot be the assumption that all students will have the knowledge to navigate through the complex processes of identifying and connecting with supportive sub-communities. If these assumptions are made, many students will quickly get lost along the way.

Consistently, it has been observed that African American students will inevitably look for supportive places at PWIs to develop self-concepts of ethnic identity, process the congruence of ethnic identity with other forms of identity and express the significance of their ethnic culture. Therefore, administrative practices should include not just development of culturally inclusive places but visibility of these places to students. Additionally, future research should consider how presence or absence of a critical mass influences the formal role of African American student organizations in creating counter-spaces on campus. In investigating outcomes for sub-groups within the African American student population, we should consider which sub-groups are finding difficulty with navigating the larger campus environment and why. It is also critical to identify what institutions are successful in creating more visible opportunities for inclusion.

Finally, it is important to note that African American student organizations continue to hold value as a sociocultural place within PWIs, particularly during difficult periods for individuals and the community. They often become the place to go when overt acts of racism spark outrage and tension on campus. If ethnic-centered student organizations did not exist, they would likely have to be created. However, it appears that in many cases, these organizations have been defined as a reactionary place, with no particular attention paid to their continued development by administrators (and, perhaps students) until that moment of crisis.

Normalizing these organizations as places of reaction rather than proactive communities that can influence the transformation of PWI communities as inclusive places is a significant issue. When this occurs, African American student organizations become more about maintenance of space until they are 'needed' by the larger community. Further, the physical boundaries these organizations occupy, as part of a cultural center for example, are challenged and often reduced because they are no longer deemed valuable or necessary. This is not exclusive to African American organizations, as similar trends are observed among Latino, Asian American, and Native American student organizations. These disputes are heightened when overall campus space is limited, increasing conflicts over usage of space.

As the dominant culture finds it convenient to categorize African American students and the sociocultural meaning of place provided by African American student organizations in homogenous terms, it becomes increasingly important to develop and document their value to individuals and the collectivity beyond response stations to racial issues. It is important for administrators to consider whether African American student organizations at their institutions are reduced to places for reaction rather than consistent communities which proactively contribute to inclusiveness. Further, practitioners should not wait until they are challenged to prove the value of African American students organizations but be proactive in documenting their consistent and continued value to issues of inclusiveness.

Conclusion

A place is remarkable and what makes it so is an unwindable spiral of material form and interpretative understanding or experiences (Gieryn, 2000, p. 472).

In this chapter, I have tried to provide examples of the centrality of campus 'place' in shaping experiences of African American students at a Predominantly White Institution, paying particular attention to the role of African American student organizations. As the narratives of the students suggest, understanding the cultural and social heterogeneity which exists among African Americans is just as important in shaping experiences as observing the physical presence of African Americans. Recognition of the diversity among African Americans allows students to consider their position along the broad spectrum of African American culture rather than subscribing to monolithic notions of African American culture that limit individual perspectives. African American student organizations, developed and maintained aptly, provide valuable sociocultural places for students to engage in the dynamic process of identity development in "individual and communal, conscious and unconscious, positive and negative, past and present, cognitive and emotional, expressive and symbolic dimensions" (Gay and Baber, 1987, p. 35). Without emphasis on the salience of place within a larger context of diversity and inclusiveness, there is a tendency to detach, devalue, and void individual experiences from any historical, cultural, and social meaning. As educators move forward towards a recommitment to equity on college campuses, we must continue to emphasize the centrality of place and its capacity to influence inclusion and connection or exclusion and domination.

References

Alford, S. M. (2000). A qualitative study of the college social adjustment of Black students from lower socioeconomic communities. *Journal of Multicultural Counseling and Development, 28* (1), 2–15.

Allen, W.R. (1992). *College in Black and White: African American students in Predominantly White and Historically Black public universities*. Albany, NY: State University of New York Press.

Allen, W.R., Jayakumar, U.M., Griffin, K.A., Korn, W.S., & Hurtado, S. (2005). *Black undergraduates from* Bakke *to* Grutter. University of California at Los Angeles: Higher Education Research Institute.

Astin A. (1975). *Preventing students from dropping out.* San Francisco: Jossey–Bass.

Bourdieu, P. & Passeron, J.C. (1998). *Reproduction in education, society, and culture.* London: Sage Publications.

Braxton, J.M. (ed.) (2000). *Reworking the student departure puzzle.* Nashville, TN: Vanderbilt University Press.

Braxton, J. M., Hirschy, A. S., & McClendon, S. A. (2004). Understanding and reducing college student departure. *ASHE-ERIC Higher Education Report, 30*(3).

Brown, M.C. II (1997). Revising Nigrescence theory: Racial identity development among students attending Historically Black Institutions. *Journal of the Pennsylvania Black Conference on Higher Education,* 12, 17-31.

Carey, K. (2008). *Graduation rate watch: Making minority student success a priority.* Education Sector Report. Retrieved from http://www.educationsector.org/usr_doc/Graduation_Rate_Watch .pdf

Carter, P. (2003). Black cultural capital, status, positioning, and schooling conflicts for low-income African American youth. *Social Problems 50* (1), 136–155.

Celious, A. & Oyserman, D. (2001). Race from the inside: An emerging heterogeneous race model. *Journal of Social Issues, 57,* 149–165.

Chang, M. J. (2007). Beyond artificial integration: Re-imagining cross-racial interactions among undergraduates. In S.R. Harper & L. D. Patton (Eds.), *Responding to the realities of race.* San Francisco, CA: Jossey-Bass.

Chang, M. J., Chang, J., & Ledesma, M. C. (2005). Beyond magical thinking: Doing the real work of diversifying our institutions. *About Campus, 10* (2), 9–16.

Chavous, T.M., Harris, A., Rivas, D., Helaire, L. Green, L. (2004). Racial stereotypes and gender in context: African Americans at Predominately Black and Predominantly White Colleges. *Sex Roles, 51*(1), 1–12.

Cross, W. (1995). The psychology of Nigrescence: revisiting the Cross model. In J. Pontero, J. Casas. L. Suzuki, & C. Alexander (eds.), *Handbook of multicultural counseling* (pp. 93–122). Thousand Oaks, CA: Sage Publications.

Cross, W. E., Parham, T, & Helms, J. (1991). The stages of Black identity development: Nigrescence models. In R. Jones (Ed.), *Black psychology*, 319–338. Berkeley: Cobb & Henry.

Du Bois, W.E.B. (1910). *The college-bred Negro American: A study made under the Atlanta University under the patronage of the trustees of the John F. Slater Fund*. Atlanta: Atlanta University Publications.

Fries-Britt, S. & Turner, B. (2001). Uneven stories: Successful Black collegians at a Black and a White campus. *The Review of Higher Education, 25*(3), pp. 315–330.

Gans, H. J. (2002). "The sociology of space: A use-centered view," *City & Community 1*(4), 329–340.

Gay, G., Barber, W. L. (1987). *Expressively Black. The cultural biases of ethnic personality*. New York, NY: Praeger Publishers.

Gieryn, T. F. (2000). A space for place in Sociology. *Annual Review of Sociology*, 26, pp. 463–496.

Guiffrida, D. A. (2003). African American student organizations as agents of social integration. *Journal of College Student Development, 44*, 304–319.

Hurtado, S., Milem, J. F., Clayton-Pedersen, A. R., & Allen, W. R. (1998). Enhancing campus climates for racial/ethnic diversity through educational policy and practice. *Review of Higher Education, 21* (3), 279–302.

Jones, L., Castellanos, C.,& Cole, D. (2002). Examining the ethnic minority student experience at Predominantly White Institutions: A case study. *Journal of Hispanic Higher Education, 1*, 19–39.

King, J. (Ed.) (2005). *Black education: A transformative research and action agenda for the new century*. Washington, DC: American Educational Research Association/Lawrence Erlbaum.

Nichols, A. & Harper, S. (2008). Are they not all the same? Racial heterogeneity among Black male undergraduates. *Journal of College Student Development, 49* (3), pp. 247–269.

Pascarella, E.T. & Terenzini, P.T. (2005). *How college affects students: A third decade of research.* San Francisco: Jossey-Bass.

Patton, L. D. (2006). "The voice of reason: A qualitative examination of Black student perceptions of Black culture centers." *Journal of College Student Development, 47*(6), 628–644.

Rendon, L. I., Jalomo, R. E., & Nora, A. (2000). Theoretical considerations in the study of minority student retention in higher education. In J. M. Braxton (Ed.) *Reworking the student departure puzzle* (pp. 127–156). Nashville, TN: Vanderbilt University Press.

Sedlacek, W. (1987). Black students on white campuses: 20 years of research. *Journal of College Student Personnel, 28*: 484–495.

Simmel, G. (1950). The stranger. In K. Wolff (Ed.), *The sociology of Georg Simmel*, 402–408. New York: Free Press.

Solórzano, D., Ceja, M. & Yosso, T. (2000) Critical race theory, racial microaggressions and campus racial climate: The experiences of African-American college students, *Journal of Negro Education, 69* (1/2), 60–73.

Strayhorn, T. L. (2008). Influences on labor market outcomes of African American college graduates: A national study. *Journal of Higher Education, 79*, 29–57.

Swail, W.S., Reed, K.E., & Perna, L.W. (2003). *Retaining minority students in Higher Education: A framework for success.* San Francisco: ASHE-ERIC Higher Education Report Series.

Tierney, W.G. (1992). An anthropological analysis of student participation in college. *The Journal of Higher Education, 63* (6), 603–618.

Tinto, V. (1993*). Leaving college: Rethinking the causes and cures of student attrition*. Chicago: University of Chicago Press.

U. S. Department of Education, Digest of Education Statistics (2003*). Beginning postsecondary students longitudinal study, second follow-up (BPS:96/01),* Table 10. Washington, DC: National Center for Education Statistics. NCES Pub Num2003-151.

Yin, R.K. (2003*). Case study research: Design and methods.* Thousand Oaks, CA: Sage Publications.

Yosso, T.J. (2005). Whose culture has capital? A critical race theory discussion of community cultural wealth. *Race, Ethnicity and Education, 8*(1), 69–91.

CHAPTER THIRTEEN

Researching for Justice: Using One's Role as Faculty Member to Fight for Equity in Higher Education

Marybeth A. Gasman

> "You can't do research and also be an activist."
>
> – Dean, Ivy League Institution

> "I don't want to be a faculty member because you can't really have an impact. I want to make change; research can't do that."
>
> – Countless Students, Every College and University

The two quotes above are messages that I continually hear in academic settings. Interestingly, the very reason that I became a faculty member was to make change—to transform minds, to provide knowledge to larger audiences, to write a more inclusive and empowering history, and to shape and reconstruct the future of the professoriate. The very thought of faculty members conducting dispassionate research from which they are "completely" detached doesn't make any sense to me and, in fact, runs counter to the way I am built. Perhaps this approach works for someone who has not felt oppression or been discriminated against, but there's a disconnect for someone like me who has had less than perfect experiences or has experienced circumstances in which others have endured extreme struggle.

In this chapter, I discuss my personal background and how it has shaped my research as I think all of us are fashioned by our identities whether we want to believe it or not (Lincoln, 2000). I also discuss the ways in which faculty members can use their role to make systemic change across their departments, schools, and institutions. In fostering this discussion, I draw from my personal experience and that of other faculty members and students. In addition, I discuss ways in which faculty members can instill a commitment to justice in their students—those who plan to pursue faculty and practitioner careers (hooks, 1994). Lastly, I discuss the possible negative ramifications of pursing a research agenda dedicated to justice.

Personal Background

I grew up in a family of ten children in a very rural area of the Upper Peninsula of Michigan. We were horribly poor. I often tell people, "We were so poor that when my mom made chipped beef on toast, there wasn't any beef." My mom did the best she could on about $7,000 a year. People often ask how ten children and their parents could survive on so little money—the answer—we grew and made everything. As a child, I learned how to can fruits, make jelly, wax vegetables for winter, cut sides of meat, and bake pies. Ironically, as an adult I don't eat meat and my husband is the cook in the house (enough is enough). As children, we entertained ourselves. We didn't have a television or any fancy games; we made up games. We shook apple trees for fun, flooded the backyard to make an ice rink during winter, played "kick the can" and rode the tractor for sport.

We had no idea that we were poor. Of course our parents knew but we kids thought everyone lived this way. It wasn't until eighth grade when our house burned to the ground and we had to live in temporary housing in a nearby city (10,000 people—some city!) that we realized we were poor. I noticed what others had and the access that money gave people. It was then that I discovered that I was on free lunch and that my school uniforms had been worn by my brothers and sisters before I wore them. I wondered why my shirts weren't white and why my tights had holes in the knees. I didn't say much about my thoughts and feelings to anyone because I knew it would hurt my mom and dad.

My mom was lovely although she cried a lot. She tried her best to hide her tears but her struggle was hard. My father was an adequate husband. He was resentful and jealous of the accomplishments of others. He was bitter and this emotion resulted in very little love shown toward my mother. She did what she needed to raise her children and get through the madness that had her trapped in a life she had never envisioned. Perhaps what I admire most about my mom and why I am talking about her in an essay about researching for justice is that she spoke up and pushed back. In a provincial town where most people conformed and took part in hatred and bigotry, my mom did not.

Sadly, my father did. When I wrote that he was bitter earlier, I was referring to his hatred of others, be they Blacks, Latinos, or Asians. Native Americans were spared for some reason (more than likely, my mother says, because my father was actually part American Indian). I grew up hearing my father say nigger, spic, jap, and chink. But, I also grew up with a mother who told me that these words were wrong and hurtful. She washed our mouths out with soap if we ever repeated these words. I saw my older brothers endure the Zest or Dove bar many times. She told us that hatred of someone based on race, or color, or wealth was wrong. Of note, there were NO African Americans, Latinos, or Asians living in our town or within 150 miles from us at any point during my childhood (and even today—the town hasn't changed much). But, that didn't stop my father or many of the other residents of our town from hating these racial and ethnic groups. They were easy targets. Oh, they were fun to laugh at on *Sanford and Son* and *Chico and the Man,* but you wouldn't want "those people" as friends.

My father did anything he could to convince us that African Americans were bad and that we should always hold them suspect. "Martin Luther King was a rabble rouser and didn't really believe in peaceful protest." "Malcolm X was anti-American." "Blacks were dirty and lazy; they just wanted a handout." Ironically, my father was always trying to get government cheese. Many of my school teachers reinforced these stereotypical racist ideas. I learned nothing about African American history and culture with the exception of slavery (and that was whisked over and romanticized and, of course, there was no blame to be had). I heard teachers say derogatory things about Blacks. My Catholic grade school had a slave auction and wasn't apologetic about it. As a small child, I didn't see a problem. I didn't even know what slavery was, let alone the horrors of Jim Crow. The local coffee shop was called "Little Black Sambos" and had a young African boy being chased by a tiger on the sign and on the menus. I thought Sambo was cute. The bakery had big fat cookie jars decorated like

Black women. I dug my hand in for a cookie, never thinking twice about the image on the jar. I went to "Sambos" and the bakery with my father; my mother never took me to these places.

As my mom saw my father's influence on her children, she worked to counter it—ever so patiently. She told us not to listen to him. She confided in us—telling us how my dad blamed minorities for his lack of success, for his problems. She told us that she had grown up in Flint, Michigan, living next door to a Black family and that they were "exactly like you and me." When she married my father she had no idea that he held such racist views. Many times these views don't surface for years and by that time she had too many kids to make it on her own. She felt trapped. And as a result, she endured his hostile and shameful verbiage. Through our mother, some of us learned that prejudice is wrong and that we should speak up for others and confront injustice. Unfortunately, not all of my siblings learned this lesson—some of them harbor horrible thoughts and school their children in racist ideas. I no longer speak to these siblings—a choice I had to make when I had my own child.

Because of my mother, despite growing up in a racist and exclusionary environment, I chose to pursue a research agenda and scholarly life dedicated to issues of race. It makes sense to my mother. My father couldn't understand until very late in his life why his daughter would care so much about equity. In the spirit of true irony, my father had a stroke and we placed him in a nursing home near my sister in Tennessee. Unlike in the Upper Peninsula of Michigan, there are African Americans in Tennessee, and my father's roommate in the nursing home (he had a roommate because he couldn't afford a private room) was an African American man. Although disgusted and belligerent about the idea at first, my father grew to love the man and the man's family. They became close friends and when I would visit him, the two of them would be sitting in rocking chairs, laughing and sharing stories. A few months before my father died, he told me that he had been wrong about Blacks. He cried in my arms about the life of anger and hatred he had lived for over 80 years; he was proud of me for standing up against his racist beliefs. Sadly, he never acknowledged the work of my mother to push back against his influence over her children; he continued to resent her.

Given the example of my mother (and my father for that matter), my interest in race and equity might make sense. Despite not knowing anyone of another race or ethnicity (outside of Native Americans) until graduate school, I felt compelled to make a difference in the world. I idealistically believed (and still believe) that we should "be the change we want to see." I make no apologies for having this perspective. Yes, it might color my viewpoint—it might make a difference in what I choose to research. But, it doesn't mean that I will cover up findings to appease my ideology. It doesn't mean that I'll avoid asking questions that run counter to my hopes. I believe that it's entirely possible to pursue a research agenda steeped in a commitment to justice.

Making Change as a Faculty Member

Push with Your Research

I am a firm believer in doing research about which you are passionate and with which you can make a difference. For me, issues of race, class, and gender have been salient in my life. Growing up in poverty with a trapped mother and a racist father gives me a unique insight into these issues—not the only insight but an interesting one.

I chose to focus my research in three major areas. First, I do work related to the history of Black colleges, and while doing this research, I focus on uncovering examples and stories of agency or action on the part of African Americans. Sometimes this agency is positive and other times it is less than flattering. However, overall, my research gives a voice to African Americans because they are not merely depicted as victims in history. Yes, Blacks were the victims of brutal racism and apartheid; however, they also played a significant role in uplifting their own lives and shaping society at large. I never thought much about the idea of agency until I read James Anderson's (1988) book *The Education of Blacks in the South*.

In this book, Anderson details the efforts of Blacks in local communities to raise money for schools and libraries. Interestingly, those same schools and libraries eventually bore the names of wealthy White philanthropists and not those of African Americans. In some cases, Blacks raised half of the money for the buildings. When you read about these schools and libraries, you assume that their namesake paid for their establishment, and you miss the efforts of local Blacks completely—you miss the action and agency of these African Americans to shape and better their own existence.

My research draws upon Anderson's identification of agency and works to uncover the role of individual African Americans—students, faculty, and administrators—to craft and bolster African American higher education within the Black college setting. As I have moved along in my career, I've become aware of how historical incidents shape our actions in the current day, and as a result my research on Black colleges has taken on a more present-day manifestation. It is here that I have been able to shape policy and practice. For example, historical inquiry shows us that Black colleges have been much maligned by the media and scholars alike. A lack of understanding of these venerable institutions and a constant need to deny their individuality and treat them as a monolithic entity continue to permeate the media (Gasman, 2007). To counter this trend, I started to "educate" reporters every time they called me. As these reporters always begin with the same question—"Why do we still need Black colleges in an era of integration?"—I immediately stop them and spend a few minutes explaining the diversity among Black colleges. After almost 9 years of doing this with reporters, I can see a difference in the stories about Black colleges—with the exception of the *Atlanta Journal Constitution*, which doesn't seem to want to change. In fact, reporters will now often begin the conversation with, "now I know that not all Black colleges are alike…" when they call me. Although I am certainly not single-handedly responsible for changing the media's perspective, along with other researchers studying Black colleges, I have worked to counter the prevailing notions in the media. I do this by using empirical evidence to change the minds of those in the media, higher education, and policy arenas. One must not only conduct research but distribute it to various audiences and venues—those that have the potential to facilitate change.

It should be noted that I have also been critical of Black colleges when they invoke that criticism. Recently, for example, I wrote a controversial op-ed article that called for a new solution to the problems that Atlanta's Morris Brown College has been facing for decades. The institution has been limping along for years, asking alumni to pony up whenever there is a funding crisis. Although I have supported Morris Brown in the past, taking on the institution's critics, I think that the small college needs to reflect upon its future in creative ways and consider merging with one of the nearby Black colleges in the Atlanta University Center or becoming the junior college of the Center. It now faces insurmountable debt and has frustrated its loyal donors with its inability to find suitable leadership and financial assets despite considerable assistance. Holding on to an institution merely for the sake of holding on helps no one—especially the 100 African American students who are being led to believe that their degree from an unaccredited institution is valuable. Based on my historical knowledge, a good grasp of politics and policy, and my understanding of Black colleges, I decided to take a risk and recommend that the hopes and dreams of the former slaves who built Morris Brown College manifest in another form (Gasman, 2009).

The second area in which I do research is African American philanthropy. While I was conducting research related to Black colleges, I noticed that all of the philanthropic contributions discussed in the literature pertained to White philanthropy. African Americans and their efforts did not appear. Of course, one could assume that Blacks have not had and don't have access to wealth, but that would be a faulty assumption (Meizhu et al., 2006). Regardless of their access to money, African Americans have been philanthropic since the days of slavery. In fact, in the current day, African Americans are more philanthropic than the majority population in terms of the proportion of their discretionary income given to charity (Gasman & Sedgwick, 2005). My research in this area has sought to reshape the nation's views of African Americans. I want Blacks to be viewed as active participants in the betterment on our country and not as the mere recipients of philanthropy. Moreover, I want African Americans to view themselves as philanthropic because seeing one's impact on the world can be empowering.

My last area of research focuses on African American graduate students at elite, historically White institutions. This research interest grew out of my experience at the University of Pennsylvania, an elite, Ivy League institution with a dismal percentage of African American students (interestingly, Caribbeans and Africans are counted in this group). When I first arrived at Penn, I encountered a barrage of students who sought solace from their past experiences within my department. Faculty members, who have long since retired, drove them crazy. One young woman, who now teaches at another Ivy League institution, was told she was "dead in the water" upon admission—that she would never make it at Penn. Of course, when she graduated with distinction, she was a "phoenix rising from the ashes." Other African American students were discouraged from studying topics related to race. Classes revolved around White, Eurocentric ideas and rarely did anyone notice. Above all of that, admissions decisions were made with no commitment to bringing in a diverse class and as a result, I found myself looking out upon a sea of Whiteness in the classroom.

For me teaching a diverse student body and providing a nurturing and empowering community in which students can develop are essential (I have learned a lot from studying Black colleges). Although I will discuss the actions that I took to make change of a practical nature within my school below, I pursed research related to African American graduate students at elite institutions as well. Interestingly, there is little research in this area as faculty members tend to focus on undergraduates. However, the path to graduate school and graduate student experiences for African Americans at elite institutions is absolutely crucial to understanding the dearth of African American faculty at these same universities (Tierney & Salle, 2008).

I care deeply about the future make up of the professoriate because I believe firmly in equity. I also believe that a diverse professoriate is the responsibility of all faculty and not just faculty of color. As such, I have focused much of my scholarly efforts on issues that will help bolster the future professoriate. Interestingly, my actions here are connected to my historical work on Black colleges. My dissertation was on an African American leader of a Black college named Charles Spurgeon Johnson. One of his goals was to change the face of the academy and to prepare future scholars and leaders. I decided to follow his lead. Of course, making a decision to change the status quo is not without its critics.

Push with Your Voice and Actions

Those who want to protect the status quo guard it with their lives. And taking on these individuals can mean coming to terms with your sense of integrity. Although I am fortunate to have, for the most part, good colleagues at Penn, there have been times during which I had to assert my perspective on equity in order to stop the extreme perpetuation of privilege.

One of my first efforts to make change at Penn related to admissions decisions. As mentioned, I was uncomfortable teaching an all-White class, and as such, I banded together with one of my White male colleagues to make much needed change. I knew that we would have more power working together. We conspired on ways to increase not only diversity in the applicant pool but how to push back against our senior colleagues who wanted to maintain the status quo. When the time came for the meeting in which admissions decisions were made, we pushed back at our colleague who had separated the candidates into acceptable and non-acceptable. Of course, the majority of the non-acceptable students were students of color. Together, we forced our colleagues to review each candidate in a holistic way, emphasizing the need for a diverse class and our commitment to access for more than merely White students from the Northeast. Our efforts started out slowly, with some success, but today, we have the most diverse programs in our school. Our cohorts are truly representative of the nation as a whole. Moreover, our faculty is now committed to enrolling a diverse class. We no longer have to push with such intensity.

Based on my knowledge of higher education and especially the experiences of African American students both within Black colleges and historically White institutions, I know that learning in an environment that embraces one's ideals and culture is beneficial. In addition, as someone who also wants to be part of an environment that cares about issues of race and tries to move forward in the ability to understand and manage these issues, I wanted to create an open conversation around race. With the help of the dean of students in my school, we started a Race in the Academy series that showcased research on race and also highlighted films and plays pertaining to race. Although the attendance was slow in the beginning, it picked up and students began to look forward to the events. They saw the gatherings as a safe space in which they could share their thoughts and frustrations. Of note, White students participated in these events as often as African Americans and saw them as a supplement to their classroom instruction. When the Race in the Academy series started there was some backlash from a few faculty and staff members who "didn't think race was a problem" or "wanted to see more talks on Whiteness because that is a race as well." We tried our best to embrace these faculty members and offer programs that met their needs too. Unlike some scholars, I believe that people who are resistant to change and the infusion of conversations around race should be included in discussions. The only way for learning to take place is through exposure. That said, with some faculty, we just could not change their minds.

Over time perhaps we have changed minds. Shortly after the launching of the Race in the Academy series, with the support of our dean at the time, we began a series of informal discussions about race among the faculty. We met once a month over breakfast and talked about issues of race in our research, teaching, and interactions with students and each other. Interestingly, different people showed up for the discussion every month. Sometimes those people who we knew were committed attended; we knew they were committed from student comments, from their research, and from their actions in the school. Other times those people who never spoke up in a meeting or never attended any race-related events showed up. They didn't talk, but they listened to the conversation. I think that just listening to others talk about the manifestations of race was helpful to those who live in fear of taking a risk. These monthly conversations about race and the Race in the Academy series bring the conversation to the surface and it bubbles up, and from time to time there is a breakthrough.

Recently, I feel that we had a breakthrough in terms of an individual's understanding of her own perpetuation of oppression. During a faculty meeting, we had a discussion about issues of race in the classroom, and one professor who is notorious for ignoring these issues, silencing others, and making deeply insensitive comments to students, spoke up. She said, in a trembling voice, something so important—"How do I know if I am one of the people making our African American students feel uncomfortable? I think I might be but how will I know unless someone tells me." Interestingly, this professor is one of the most powerful faculty members in our school and commands immense respect externally and within the university—yet, she doesn't know how to manage her thoughts about race and doesn't know how to facilitate conversations around this issue in the classroom. She did, however, take the first step and admit her inability. Bringing issues of race (as well as class, gender, and sexuality—which is something we do) out into the open is vital and creates an environment in which people (eventually) feel comfortable asking for help, admitting fault, and expressing a desire to change. For those of us doing research related to race, it is crucial that we create these opportunities in our local environments. It's not JUST enough to do research—the research should engender change.

Push with Your Teaching

Perhaps the area in which a professor and researcher can have the most impact is in his or her teaching. Of course, this is a choice. One can merely present information and let students take from it what they want and move forward. Or, one can present information and ask probing questions to make students think—critically think. Or, one can teach with a particular ideological approach and ignore other perspectives. I want to make it clear that although I believe in discussing issues of race in the classroom, I do not believe in jamming an ideology down students' throats. I use the second approach I described above.

For example, in my History of American Higher Education course, I provide students with readings that speak to issues of race, class, gender, sexuality, ethnicity, and religion. Within these readings, I present many sides of each issue and a variety of perspectives. So, if I am teaching about the civil rights and student protests of the 1960s, I present readings from the right, left, and center. I want students to analyze these readings and understand the various perspectives. I want them to study the language—there is a difference between calling students "activists" and "radicals," for instance. Why are the different words used and how does the use of one word rather than the other color the reader's perspective?

In addition to presenting different perspectives, I try to push students to understand their role in the world and more specifically, in

American history. So often, students think that they are powerless. Not true! I provide my students with many examples of how students have changed many aspects of academe as well as the larger society. One need look no further than the Black college students who sat at a lunch counters in Greensboro, North Carolina and endured ridicule and abuse in order to desegregate eating facilities (and so much more) (Branch, 1989). Students have had a great impact on the makeup of the faculty at many colleges and universities, pushing for greater diversity. They have also shaped the curricula, asking for offerings that represent their perspectives and serve their needs. Sometimes students doubt the ability of one person to make change. In response, I talk about those well known individuals who have led movements for change—Nelson Mandela, Martin Luther King, Jr., Cesar Chavez, among others. But, I also talk about those leaders, many people of color but also Whites, who have made change on a daily basis within their local communities, schools, and universities. The readings I provide to students focus on these people and their efforts. Of course, regardless of one's politics, all of my students now have a contemporary example of how one person can make a difference and make great change—Barack Obama—a person who started out making change in local communities and is now the leader of the United States. And, of note, students at colleges and universities across the country are partially responsible for Obama's success—students who many assumed were passive and lacked any inclination to step up and take responsibility for their country.

Although I only tell the students once that I want them to live their lives for something bigger than themselves, I secretly hope that my message will get through to them. I hope that they will choose to fight for justice in many areas—some do, some don't.

From time to time, students don't like my approach to teaching history. They are angered that I don't teach the traditional "White men and wars" curriculum. When I was younger, those students who disagreed with my approach got on my nerves—got under my skin. However, now I just let people know on the first day of class that my approach to teaching history is an inclusive approach. I let them know that I want each student to see him or her self represented in the readings. And, I bluntly let students know that they might want to drop the class if they aren't comfortable with this approach. Rarely do people drop. Rumor has it that my class pushes people to think differently—that students leave feeling refreshed and energized about making change. They may not agree with everything I say, but they understand that "to be educated is to be conscientiously uncomfortable" (Peterkin, 2008, n.p.).

Concluding Thoughts

My identity has shaped the way that I approach scholarship, teaching, and service within the academy. Rather than merely pushing paper and pencil, I aim to push students, my colleagues, and the policies of the academy that exclude, oppress, and discriminate. I aim to push for change and progress regardless of the "sage" advice from older colleagues that researchers should be just that—researchers, keeping their noses out of activism. I urge future scholars to consider pushing back against the status quo. When you use empirical research to back up your opinions and perspectives, you can rest assured and feel confident that your actions are justified.

References

Anderson, J. (1988). *The education of Blacks in the South, 1860–1935.* Chapel Hill: NC, University of North Carolina Press.

Branch, T. (1989). *Parting the waters: America in the King years, 1954–1963.* New York: Simon & Schuster.

Gasman, M. (2007). Truth, generalizations, and stigmas: An analysis of the media's coverage of Morris Brown College and Black colleges overall, *Review of Black Political Economy, 34*(2), 111–135.

Gasman, M. (2009). Much ado about Morris Brown College. *Diverse Issues in Higher Education Blog.*

Gasman, M. & Sedgwick, K. (2005). *Uplifting a people: African American philanthropy and education.* New York: Peter Lang.

hooks, b. (1994) *Teaching to transgress.* New York: Routledge.

Lincoln, Y. S. (2000) The practices and politics of interpretation in N. K. Denzin & Y. S. Lincoln (Eds.) *The handbook of qualitative research* Thousand Oaks, CA: Sage Publications.

Meizhu, L., Leondar-Wright, B., and Robles, B. (2006). *Color of wealth: The story behind the U.S. racial wealth divide.* New York: The New School.

Peterkin, D. (2008). Entry made on Teagle Foundation Blog.

Tierney, W.G. & Salle, M. (2008). Do organizational structures and strategies increase faculty diversity?: A cultural analysis. *American Academic, 4*(1). 159-184.

AFTERWORD

Beyond Managing Diversity: Shaping Collegiate Environments of Respect and Empowerment

Lemuel Watson

Our society has been struggling with issues of diversity, equality, and social justice from the point of genesis. Our American forefathers dealt with so many of the same issues that trouble contemporary society, including sociocultural, political, and economic differences. Notwithstanding, my personal belief is that effectively managing diversity across institutions first requires deeply rooted conviction about the work of diversity as an important challenge to the general work and health of institutions. Since this is an afterword, I will briefly and directly reflect on the content of the book within the context of my experiences and the body of research on how colleges manage diversity.

During my years in the academy, I have attended many training experiences that claimed to do the work of diversity. Largely, these activities dealt with issues of respecting and valuing differences when attempting to get along with each other. As a faculty member, I have been taught (and talked at) by various "professionals" on the topics of diversity, multiculturalism, nationalism—you name it—and the intent of such training and professional development has been to bring about a change in behavior, understanding, or disposition in order to create a better work environment. It is necessary to keep issues of diversity in front of professionals who work with the public, yet the methods of the last few decades have proven less effective in diffusing behaviors that exclude, oppress, and disenfranchise. The chapters in this volume provide proof of past training and its ineffectiveness.

I must admit that twenty years ago there seemed to be some enthusiasm for diversity training. People appeared to tolerate it and mildly allow themselves to enter the process of "diversity" training. Administrators believed that calling in the experts du jour would be one step to show that "we, the institution and administration," understand and are committed to eliminating discrimination and prejudice. The Translation is, "We are doing something to appease those who believe they are victims."

Over the last twenty years, we have also seen a change in professionals' dispositions toward training appropriate for specific groups' needs. Institutions are not so easily convinced that they need training anymore regarding our differences. The chapters in this text, however, clearly demonstrate that more work is required even after thirty-plus years of multicultural training of professionals in higher education institutions. In this volume, we were exposed to various ways that diversity matters across campus environments, how policies and those who create policy and procedures are challenged by the organization's structure and political nuances of place and time and how such factors continue to disrupt possibilities for change and enlightenment toward a new 21st-century mindset of cultural proficiency.

The chapters in this text also reminded us of the pain and frustrations that faculty, students, and administrators face in engaging different-race institutions. This text placed front and center the needs to expand our notions of managing diversity in ways that are inclusive beyond race to underrepresented groups such as lesbians and gay students. In fact, there has been a void in the discourse about managing diversity in a very specific and practical way. This volume did not shy away from that discourse but entered it willingly and compellingly.

Although we have written, trained, researched, and experienced various "good natured" products, programs, and services related to diversity within higher education, I believe that little has changed in how we empathize with equity doctrine and modify behavior in the workplace. Continually, I am amazed at how search committees operate despite affirmative action officer efforts for transparency and accountability. Although we spend an enormous amount of time, money, and talent on advertisement, selection of committee members, time at conferences recruiting, and time in discussion of candidates, the selection process remains flawed unless all involved evince commitment to diversity or unless one lonely member stands up, "reminding" people about the ways in which diversity matters. Likely, these reminders identify the value added to institutions, the faculty guild, and to student learning.

The same is said for managing diversity within the curriculum. Many faculty proudly offer the following rationale, "We don't have a course in diversity because we infuse it throughout our curriculum in all classes." I have found that if diversity topics are addressed in these classes, they are not engaged but glossed over, rushed, and superficial. More importantly, ask students where or what they learned about best practices in managing diversity for themselves or with others, and you are likely to discover that they have no idea about what you are speaking.

I bring the above issues to light not to criticize but to argue that there are lots of good-intended people who believe their dispositions model appropriate behavior for respecting and accepting differences. Professionals in institutions of higher education seem committed to "getting it right" on issues of diversity by obtaining knowledge about diversity. However, possessing the most salient skills needed to effectively manage diversity or create an environment where people feel they matter requires additional skill sets. I believe we must take the recommendations, ideas, and strategies in these book chapters and push further. We must go beyond merely "managing" diverse environments to "creating" and "orchestrating" environments where all are welcomed at the table and can speak from their unique experiences, through whatever pain, in sharing perspectives. At the same time, we need not find offensive genuine mistakes (i.e., individuals who inadvertently use the "wrong" words or labels) or sincere attempts to understand the experiences of people who we deem diverse. We need to develop our senses of empathy, sympathy, and interest.

We must go into discussions with the assumptions that people are at the table because they really want to see real change and are committed to such. The discussion need not focus on a liberal agenda of "I feel so guilty because I am European decent"; it should not be about

"I am Black and I am mad as hell at White people" to be effective in managing diversity, we should accept the premise that this is bigger than all of us. Managing diversity is not new, and we will continue to struggle as a civilization to add to the knowledge of building community together through our differences. Yet, there is a place for the emotions; however, to get beyond what we have done over the last thirty years, we must approach managing diversity from the intellectual-rational stance while considering our historical, social, and cultural context within the national nuances which define our current society.

Unfortunately, the world has been dealing with the complexity of managing diversity a very long time. We are not unique with regard to this issue. Great civilizations long before us have had to deal with the issues of diversity; some have been extremely harsh, others not so much. In *How Minority Students Experience College* (cited earlier in the text), one emergent in the book and through most all of the chapters in this book is that students want to be treated as unique individuals. They do not embrace the notion that just because we look alike we are the same. They do not want to be put in categories. They accept the fact that society treats them a certain way due to the color of their skin and understand exactly what action or disposition that is; however, they refuse to let it define them.

What does this mean for managing diversity? It means that we need to get to know the context for which we would like to bring about change in the culture, tradition, and behaviors. We need to not make assumptions about students based on any categorical definition. We need to always evaluate policies and procedures that affect our work lives related to diversity. We should also convey to higher education professionals that we are all responsible for the success of every students, faculty, and professionals.

As a faculty member, I stated to my students, "Say what you will, just help us understand why you feel a need to be the way you are"; hence, this taught empathy and created a sense of depth for understanding one another. As a practicing administrator, I simply say that certain unacceptable behaviors are not permitted and the consequences that will accommodate a breach of that code of ethic or policy. I am successful in creating environments of respect and empowerment because I have been put through the tests of many situations and have been consistent, fair, honest, and diligent. Simply stated, I have built trust with my colleagues. Yet, I must say, although I have high expectations and have tried to manage and create a positive space for diversity, I am realistic and accept the fact that humans have limitations. Those limitations have been displayed in many of our historical documents. Although I continue to believe in the spirit of the human race and know that all things are possible, I will accept the basic behavior of respect in the workplace if nothing else is possible. Respect opens the door for trust, and trust is the cornerstone for managing diversity.

ABOUT THE EDITOR

Dr. T. Elon Dancy II is Assistant Professor of Adult and Higher Education at the University of Oklahoma in Norman (OK). He received his Ph.D. from Louisiana State University (LSU) with an emphasis in Higher Education. His research agenda investigates the intersection of race, gender, and culture in colleges and universities as well as other educational settings. More specifically, his scholarship addresses boys and men in schools and colleges and the ways in which these gendered constructions intersect with race, class, sexual orientation, and other social categories. His work also considers how identity constructions, pipeline issues, and environmental norms influence, improve, and contest Black males' retention, persistence, experiences, and socio-cognitive outcomes. Dr. Dancy has written scholarly publications that engage the sociology, history, and politics of schooling/postsecondary education. He was named Emerging Scholar by the Association for the Study of Higher Education Council on Ethnic Participation (2006). He also was the AERA-J 2008 Outstanding Dissertation Award Runner-Up and the LSU College of Education Dissertation of the Year Award Honoree (2007–2008). Dr. Dancy is the author of *The Brother Code: Manhood and Masculinity among African American Men in College* (2010) and editor (with M. Christopher Brown II and James Earl Davis) of *Educating African American Males: Contexts for Consideration, Possibilities for Practice* (2010).

CONTRIBUTORS

Lorenzo DuBois Baber is Assistant Professor in the Department of Educational Organization and Leadership at the University of Illinois, Urbana-Champaign. He received his Ph.D in Higher Education from Pennsylvania State University. His scholarship focuses on experiences of traditionally underrepresented students in postsecondary education and the role of higher education in reducing social, political and economic stratification among racial/ethnic minorities and individuals from low-income backgrounds.

Fred A. Bonner II is Professor of Higher Education Administration and Educational Psychology and Associate Dean of Faculties at Texas A&M University—College Station. He received an Ed.D. in higher education administration and college teaching from the University of Arkansas-Fayetteville. Dr. Bonner has published articles and book chapters on academically gifted African American male college students, teaching in the multicultural college classroom, diversity issues in student affairs, and success factors influencing the retention of students of color in higher education.

Kirsten T. Edwards is a doctoral student in Higher Education at Louisiana State University. Areas of specialization include curriculum theory and women and gender studies. Her current research interests include race, class, and gender in higher education and the ways in which these social categories shape faculty and student epistemologies in colleges and universities.

Kathryn A. E. Enke is a doctoral student in Higher Education at the University of Minnesota-Twin Cities. She earned her B.A. degree in History at the College of Saint Benedict and her M.A. in Educational Policy and Administration at the University of Minnesota-Twin Cities. She has worked as an institutional researcher at the College of Saint Benedict and Saint John's University, a women's college and a men's university, both located in central Minnesota.

Sharon Fries-Britt is Associate Professor in the College of Education at the University of Maryland, College Park. Her research focuses on the experiences of high-achieving Black collegians and issues of race, equity and diversity in higher education. Prior to her academic appointment, she served for twelve years as an administrator in higher education. She has developed and implemented innovative programs in multicultural and racial relations for professional organizations in and outside of higher education.

Marybeth Gasman is Associate Professor of Higher Education in the Graduate School of Education at the University of Pennsylvania. She is the author of *Envisioning Black Colleges: A History of the United Negro College Fund* and lead editor of *Understanding Minority Serving Institutions*. Her research interests pertain to issues of race, class, and gender throughout the history of higher education, and she focuses specifically on Historically Black Colleges and Universities.

Wendell D. Hall is a doctoral candidate in the higher education program at the University of Maryland. He currently serves as an associate director for the Advisory Committee on Student Financial Assistance. His research interests include the influence of finances on college access, K-16 factors influencing student engagement, and diversity in higher education.

Frank Harris III is Assistant Professor of Postsecondary Educational Leadership and Student Affairs at San Diego State University. His Ed.D. in Higher Education is from the University of Southern California, Rossier School of Education. His research is broadly focused on student development in higher education and explores questions related to the social construction of gender and race on college campuses, college men and masculinities, and racial/ethnic disparities in college student outcomes.

Chance W. Lewis is the Houston Endowment Inc. Endowed Chair and Associate Professor of Urban Education in the Department of Teaching, Learning and Culture in the College of Education at Texas A&M University. His research interests focus on improving the educational attainment of African American students, particularly African American males in K-12 and postsecondary settings. Dr. Lewis is also the co-editor of *White Teachers/Diverse Classrooms: A Guide to Building Inclusive Schools: Promoting High Expectations and Eliminating Racism.*

Dave Louis is Associate Director of the Honors Program at Texas A&M University. He earned his doctoral degree in educational administration at Texas A&M University. Dr. Louis has also taught across undergraduate, masters and doctoral levels in the Department of Educational Administration & Human Development at Texas A & M. He is interested in issues of student achievement, persistence, and success.

Roland Mitchell is Assistant Professor of Higher Education in the Educational Theory, Policy and Practice Department at Louisiana State University. He teaches courses that focus on the history of higher education and college teaching. His current research interests include theorizing the impact of historical and communal knowledge on pedagogy and an exploration of the understandings that allow educators to provide service to students from different cultural, ethnic, and social backgrounds.

Samuel D. Museus is Assistant Professor in the Higher Education and Asian American Studies Programs at the University of Massachusetts, Boston. Dr. Museus also earned his Ph.D. in Higher Education Administration from Pennsylvania State University. His research primarily focuses on how culture, and race, and campus environments shape the experiences and outcomes of college students of color.

Robert T. Palmer is Assistant Professor of Student Affairs Administration at the State University of New York-Binghamton. He received his Ph.D. in Higher Education Administration from Morgan State University. His research examines the experiences of minority students primarily in the context of minority-serving institutions and racial/ethnic minority students in STEM.

Penny A. Pasque is Assistant Professor of Adult and Higher Education in the Department of Educational Leadership and Policy Studies and Women's and Gender Studies at the University of Oklahoma (OU). She received a Ph.D. from the Center for the Study of Higher and Postsecondary Education at the University of Michigan. Her research includes addressing in/equities in higher education and student affairs, exploring the connections between higher education and society, and exploring complexities in critical qualitative methodologies.

Rebecca Ropers-Huilman is Professor of Higher Education in the Department of Organizational Leadership, Policy, and Development and an Affiliate of the Department of Gender, Women, and Sexuality Studies at the University of Minnesota-Twin Cities. Her more than 40 publications include 4 books related to women's experiences in higher education, including *Reconstructing Policy in Higher Education: Feminist Poststructural Perspectives* (published in 2009 with Elizabeth Allan and Susan Iverson). She is the editor of *Feminist Formations* (formerly known as the *National Women's Studies Association Journal*).

Terrell L. Strayhorn is Associate Professor of Higher Education and Sociology, Special Assistant to the Provost, and Director of the Center for Higher Education Research and Policy (CHERP) at the University of Tennessee, Knoxville. His research program centers on issues of access and equity, diversity and student learning as well as student retention and post-BA outcomes. Author/editor of 4 books, over 70 refereed journal articles, book chapters, and reports, Strayhorn is PI of a 5-year NSF grant and Visiting Scholar at the Carter G. Woodson Institute for African-American Studies at the University of Virginia.

Toyia K. Younger is a doctoral candidate in the Higher Education program at the University of Maryland-College Park. Her research focuses on the degree completion of African American transfer students at large public four-year institutions. She currently serves as Director of Student Affairs for the Association of Public and Land-Grant Universities in Washington, DC.

M. Christopher Brown II, *General Editor*

The *Education Management: Contexts, Constituents, and Communities* (EM:c^3) series includes the best scholarship on the varied dynamics of educational leadership, management, and administration across the educational continuum. In order to disseminate ideas and strategies useful for schools, colleges, and the education community, each book investigates critical topics missing from the extant literature and engages one or more theoretical perspectives. This series bridges the gaps between the traditional management research, practical approaches to academic administration, and the fluid nature of organizational realities.

Additionally, the EM:c^3 series endeavors to provide meaningful guidance on continuing challenges to the effective and efficient management of educational contexts. Volumes in the series foreground important policy/praxis issues, developing professional trends, and the concerns of educational constituencies. The aim is to generate a corpus of scholarship that discusses the unique nature of education in the academic and social spaces of all school types (e.g., public, private, charter, parochial) and university types (e.g., public, private, historically black, tribal institutions, community colleges).

The EM:c^3 series offers thoughtful research presentations from leading experts in the fields of educational administration, higher education, organizational behavior, public administration, and related academic concentrations. Contributions represent research on the United States as well as other countries by comparison, address issues related to leadership at all levels of the educational system, and are written in a style accessible to scholars, educational practitioners and policymakers throughout the world.

For further information about the series and submitting manuscripts, please contact:

Dr. M. Christopher Brown II | *em_bookseries@yahoo.com*

To order other books in this series, please contact our Customer Service Department at:

(800) 770-LANG (within the U.S.)
(212) 647-7706 (outside the U.S.)
(212) 647-7707 FAX

Or browse online by series at www.peterlang.com